W9-AVR-959

Conversations with Raymond Carver

Conversations
with Raymond Carver

Edited by
Marshall Bruce Gentry and William L. Stull

University Press of Mississippi
Jackson and London

813
C 24

Library of Congress Cataloging-in-Publication Data
Conversations with Raymond Carver / edited by Marshall Bruce Gentry
  and William L. Stull.
    p. cm. — (Literary conversations series)
   Includes bibliographical references and index.
   ISBN 0-87805-448-0 (alk. paper). — ISBN 0-87805-449-9 (pbk. :
alk. paper)
   1. Carver, Raymond—Interviews.   2. Authors, American—20th
century—Interviews.   I. Carver, Raymond.   II. Gentry, Marshall
Bruce.   III. Stull, William L.   IV. Series.
PS3553.A7894Z6   1990
813'.54—dc20   90-12522
                                                                                 CIP

British Library Cataloging-in-Publication data available

Books by Raymond Carver

Near Klamath. Sacramento: English Club of Sacramento State College, 1968.
Winter Insomnia. Santa Cruz: Kayak, 1970.
Put Yourself in My Shoes. Santa Barbara: Capra, 1974.
At Night the Salmon Move. Santa Barbara: Capra, 1976.
Will You Please Be Quiet, Please? New York: McGraw-Hill, 1976.
Furious Seasons and Other Stories. Santa Barbara: Capra, 1977.
What We Talk About When We Talk About Love. New York: Knopf, 1981.
Two Poems ["The Baker" and "Louise"]. Salisbury, MD: Scarab, 1982.
The Pheasant. Worcester, MA: Metacom, 1982.
Fires. Santa Barbara: Capra, 1983; New York: Vintage, 1984; New York: Vintage
    Contemporaries, 1989.
Cathedral. New York: Knopf, 1983.
If It Please You. Northridge, CA: Lord John, 1984.
Where Water Comes Together with Other Water. New York: Random House, 1985.
The Stories of Raymond Carver. London: Picador, 1985.
Dostoevsky: A Screenplay. By Raymond Carver and Tess Gallagher. Santa Barbara:
    Capra, 1985.
The Best American Short Stories 1986. Edited by Raymond Carver with Shannon
    Ravenel. Boston: Houghton Mifflin, 1986.
My Father's Life. Derry, NH: Babcock & Koontz, 1986.
Ultramarine. New York: Random House, 1986.
Two Poems ["Reaching" and "Soda Crackers"]. Concord, NH: Ewert, 1986.
American Short Story Masterpieces. Edited by Raymond Carver and Tom Jenks.
    New York: Delacorte, 1987.
Those Days: Early Writings by Raymond Carver. Elmwood, CT: Raven, 1987.
In a Marine Light: Selected Poems. London: Collins Harvill, 1987.
Where I'm Calling From: New and Selected Stories. New York: Atlantic Monthly,
    1988; Franklin Center, PA: Franklin Library, 1988.
Elephant and Other Stories. London: Collins Harvill, 1988.
A New Path to the Waterfall. New York: Atlantic Monthly, 1989.

Contents

Introduction

When the Japanese interviewer Michiko Miyamoto asked Jay
McInerney to introduce her to Raymond Carver in the spring of 1983,
McInerney hesitated. "The thing is," the young writer said of his
famous teacher at Syracuse University, "he doesn't like interviews
very much."[1] Carver had recently won a Pulitzer Prize nomination
for *Cathedral*, his third major-press short-story collection, and he was
soon to receive one of the American Academy's first Strauss
"Livings," a coveted fellowship bringing him five years of tax-free
support. These and other honors notwithstanding, Carver's modesty
remained intact. To ease the journalist's puzzlement, McInerney put
the matter squarely: "He doesn't realize he's famous enough to be
interviewed."

Eventually, like some fifty other interviewers, Miyamoto got her
chance to meet the "legendary" Carver, and within minutes she
found McInerney's words confirmed. Although "of towering height"
(Carver was six feet two), the big-bodied man who opened his door
to her at the Hotel Carlyle in New York City was stoop-shouldered
and shambling. Carver's eyes were a penetrating blue, but thick
brows shadowed them. Dressed in a gray sweater, tan chinos, and
chukka boots, he eased himself into a fragile-looking armchair.
Before consenting to the interview, Carver had warned Miyamoto
that he had "ruined" his face. Now, fingering his chin, he explained,
"I cut myself shaving."

To a one, Raymond Carver's interviewers were struck by what
David Applefield called "the seeming contradiction between the
simplicity of the man and the crafted, stylized, and manipulated
stories" that had made him famous. The emblems of this dichotomy
were Carver's husky body and his barely audible voice. "Raymond
Carver is a big, weathered man," Nancy Connors wrote in 1986,
"with a voice so soft that he seems almost embarrassed to be

speaking at all."[2] Carver's hoarse whisper arose in part from the chain-smoking that was to bring about his death from lung cancer in 1988, at age fifty. ("I'm beginning to feel like a cigarette with a body attached to it," he told his very first interviewer in 1977.) But his soft-spoken manner was also constitutional. As the son of a saw-filer in the logging mills of Oregon and Washington, Carver had grown up among men and women whose few words covered unvoiced depths of feeling.

Carver's hushed voice compelled interviewers to lean toward him and listen. "The words rush out in a gust at times, haltingly at others," Roxanne Lawler noted, "as if Carver is choosing them as carefully as when he writes." Even after celebrity profiles of him had appeared in the *New York Times Magazine, People,* and *Vanity Fair,* his manner remained that of "an intensely interested friend," recalled William Stafford.[3] Carver's open, unassuming style put strangers at ease and turned formal meetings into two-way conversations. His deference, however, had its liabilities. For one thing, Carver's sibilant mumble defied electronic reproduction, leaving more than one reporter with no record but a hissing tape. For another, his genuine interest in his interlocutor's views (or his impatience with a line of leading questions) left several interviewers doing most of the talking themselves.

"For better or worse," Carver told Kasia Boddy, "I am an in-stinctual writer rather than a writer working out a program or finding stories to fit particular themes." Carver was skeptical of labels and abstractions, and his interest in analysis was slight. "I'm not that intellectual," he told Cassandra Phillips. "I work much closer to the bone." Only when pressed would he explicate a poem or story, and years as a college teacher had only confirmed his resistance to theory. "Do you know much about the deconstructionists?" John Alton asked him in 1986. "Enough to know that they're crazy," Carver answered. He had come up the hard way, investing fifteen years of work in his first story collection, *Will You Please Be Quiet, Please?* (1976). For this reason, no amount of urging could prompt him to malign a fellow writer, living or dead. Among the modern classics, his favorites were Hemingway, Flaubert, and Chekhov. Asked to comment on his contemporaries, he had a good word for everyone from A.R. Ammons to Tobias Wolff. As he wrote in one of his poems, "There's room on my boat / for just about everyone." Carver generously acknowledged the help he had received from teachers, editors, and friends, and with his own time he was generous to a fault.

"Writing is an act of discovery," Carver told Francesco Durante in 1987. At their best, his interviews are acts of discovery also. Conversation allowed him to test his convictions, answer his critics, and rehearse ideas that he would later develop in essays and reviews. More than once, the experience of being interviewed prompted him to write a poem. (Two poems that illustrate this process are "Interview" and "The Projectile.") If Carver said something once, he usually repeated it, each time with deepening conviction. Moreover, before the publication of some of his major craft interviews—those with Mona Simpson, David Applefield, and Michael Schumacher, for example—he received a transcription of his talk. These "draft" interviews he edited and supplemented, polishing his remarks nearly to the level of literature.

The twenty-five interviews selected and reprinted here come from small-town and big-city newspapers, popular magazines and intellectual quarterlies, foreign and domestic sources. They span the decade of Carver's post-alcoholic "second life," extending from his thirty-ninth year to his fiftieth birthday. The earliest interview dates from July 1977, a month after Carver took his last drink and a year before he and Tess Gallagher began their association. The latest ones, conducted almost simultaneously, come from the spring of 1988, a few weeks before Carver and Gallagher were married and not long before his death. Although Carver published his first story in 1960 and won a number of awards and fellowships during the 1970s, no formal interviews were conducted during what he came to call his "bad Raymond" days. Nonetheless, those bad days are much discussed in the interviews reprinted here, as are the "gravy" days that followed them.

Carver told the *Paris Review* that if he believed in signs, his sign would be the sign of the turtle. "I write in fits and starts," he said. This observation holds true as well of his literary conversations. Over months and years Carver's thinking follows a recursive spiral pattern of discovery, reassessment, and progression. Pursuing a slow, sometimes unsteady course, he breaks new ground, consolidates his position, and moves ahead, typically in a new direction. For example, many but not all his lasting "obsessions" (he disliked the word *theme*) are evident in his first interview: his devotion to craft and clarity, his gratitude to his teachers John Gardner and Richard C. Day, his fascination with secrecy and survival. At the same time, other "polestars" of his life and art remain as yet undisclosed, most notably his near-fatal alcoholism, a subject he did not openly discuss until 1983. Speaking to Kasia Boddy in 1987, Carver listed the topics that emerge as constants in his work: "the relationships between men and women, why we oftentimes lose the things we put the most value on, the mismanagement of our own inner resources. I'm also interested in survival, what people can do to raise themselves up when they've been laid low." Having survived a spirit-breaking succession of "crap jobs" as well as two bankruptcies, Carver rightly counted himself a "paid-in-full member" of the working poor. "They're my people," he told Stewart Kellerman. "I could never write down to them."[4]

Arranged, as here, in chronological order, Carver's interviews group themselves into five distinct but sometimes overlapping stages, with each phase demarcated by a turning point in his life and work. The two earliest interviews, dating from the summer of 1977 and the spring of 1978, reveal Carver at a personal and artistic crisis point. The "limitless waste" of his first life is behind him, but what lies ahead remains unclear. In assembling *Will You Please Be Quiet, Please?* (1976) and *Furious Seasons* (1977), he had all but exhausted his stock of fiction. ("My cupboard was bare," he later said.) Now, in conversations with Cassandra Phillips and David Koehne, he tentatively sets a new and different course. Guiding him is a talismanic quotation from Ezra Pound: "Fundamental accuracy of statement is the ONE sole morality of writing. . . . " This precisionist aesthetic was to shape Carver's fiction over the next three years as he wrote and rewrote the stories that would make up his "minimalist" masterpiece *What We Talk About When We Talk About Love* (1981). Indeed, he repeats Pound's dictum in "A Storyteller's Shoptalk," a seminal essay that he published shortly before *What We Talk About* appeared.[5]

At this point in Carver's odyssey, Pound was his true Penelope. But there were also siren voices luring him toward the rocks. The newly sober Carver told Cassandra Phillips that he was working on a novel, "an *African Queen* sort of thing" set in German East Africa after

World War I. Could a less likely subject for Raymond Carver be imagined? The outcome of this abortive effort at long fiction was *The Augustine Notebooks,* an excerpt from which eventually appeared in the *Iowa Review.*[6] Fortunately, by the time Carver reached Iowa City and spoke to David Koehne, he had abandoned the novel and gone back to writing poems and stories, the short forms where his genius lay.

No major interviews with Raymond Carver appear to have been conducted between 1979 and 1982, not even after *What We Talk About When We Talk About Love* received a glowing front-page notice in the *New York Times Book Review.*[7] A longstanding tradition of critical disdain for the short story partially explains this inattention. A second factor prolonging the silence was the exhausting effort Carver had invested in the book. As he explained to Mona Simpson two years later, *What We Talk About* was the most "self-conscious" book he had ever written. "I pushed and pulled and worked with those stories before they went into the book to an extent I'd never done with any other stories," he said. In fact, some of the stories in the collection had been previously published in as many as three different versions, each more compressed and less explicit than the last. Taking his cue from Hemingway's theory of omission (and urged on in this practice by his longtime editor, Gordon Lish), Carver cut his stories "to the marrow, not just to the bone" for *What We Talk About.* Donald Newlove's capsule review suggests the outcome: "Seventeen tales of Hopelessville, its marriages and alcoholic wreckage, told in a prose as sparingly clear as a fifth of iced Smirnoff."[8]

What We Talk About won Carver accolades from Frank Kermode and others as "a full-grown master" of the storyteller's art. In addition, the bare-boned collection proved immensely influential on a younger generation of short-story writers coming of age in the 1980s. Jayne Anne Phillips, for one, declared it "a book of fables for this decade."[9] But the radical excisions had taken a toll on Carver's strength. For six months after *What We Talk About* went to press, he felt unable to write anything. Moreover, in retrospect he found the pared-down story texts aesthetically unsatisfying, especially after reviewers began dubbing him a literary "minimalist." The connotations of the word troubled him. "There's something about 'minimalist' that smacks of smallness of vision and execution that I

don't like," he told Mona Simpson. Worse yet, the easy-to-apply
label stuck to him. Interviewers and critics found it irresistible, and it
was only years later, long after Carver had outgrown the "minimal"
style of *What We Talk About,* that he was released from it. ("No
minimalist he," chimed the *New York Times Book Review* editors
when *Where I'm Calling From,* Carver's new and selected stories,
appeared in 1988.[10])

Once again, Carver had reached a crisis point. As he explained to
Simpson, "Any farther in that direction and I'd be at a dead end." To
exit the blind alley, over the next two years he executed a stylistic
turnabout. Between 1981 and 1983 Carver restored and sometimes
expanded a number of the story texts he had reduced for *What We
Talk About.* (The fruits of these revisionary labors are gathered in
Fires [1983] and *If It Please You* [1984].) Moreover, during the same
period he wrote nearly a dozen new stories in a richer, fuller, and
more hopeful key. "My stories are going to have more affirmation
now than they did five years ago," he told a student interviewer at
the University of Akron in the spring of 1982. It is at this point in
Carver's development, during the widening phase of what Adam
Meyer has aptly termed an "hourglass pattern," that the second
group of interviews takes place.[11]

Among the conversations from this second stage, surely the high
point is Carver's long craft interview with Mona Simpson and Lewis
Buzbee, published in the summer 1983 issue of the *Paris Review.*
There and in an almost equally extensive interview with Kay Bonetti,
he speaks of his visceral resolve to leave his "minimal" style behind
and write "more generous" fiction. With Simpson he discusses for
the first time what had until then been a story "too tedious to talk
about": the tale of real-life alcoholic and marital wreckage that forms
the background of his fiction. Again and again during this period,
Carver speaks of his newly won self-confidence. This feeling gained
reinforcement in May 1983, when the American Academy awarded
him one of its first Mildred and Harold Strauss "Livings," a five-year
fellowship bringing him an annual tax-free income of $35,000. What
with *Cathedral* receiving nominations for the National Book Critics
Circle Award and the Pulitzer Prize, late 1983 was a high time for
Raymond Carver. It was also a time of upheaval, as a third group of
interviews, conducted between 1984 and mid-1986, reveals.

By 1984, Carver was a celebrity. Profiles of him appeared not only in the *New York Times Magazine* but also in London's *Sunday Times* and Amsterdam's *Haagse Post*. Resigning his professorship was a condition of his fellowship, but for the time being Carver remained in Syracuse, where Gallagher continued teaching. Instead of basking in the limelight, however, he found the East Coast publicity "hubbub" interfering with his work. "I would consider it a good day if I could take care of my correspondence," he told Larry McCaffery and Sinda Gregory.

In late January 1984, Carver fled west. Since 1982, he and Gallagher had summered in her home town of Port Angeles, a low-key mill town and fishing village on the north coast of Washington's Olympic Peninsula. In Port Angeles, Gallagher's newly built "Sky House" overlooking the Strait of Juan de Fuca was standing empty. Seeking peace and quiet, Carver moved into it alone. His intention was to write stories, perhaps even the long-deferred first novel. Instead, as he looked out the windows at the deep blue water, he found himself writing poems. "No one could have been more surprised than I was," he later told William L. Stull, "because I hadn't written any poetry in over two years. I would write myself out every day, then at night there was nothing left. The bowl was empty. I went to bed at night not knowing if there would be anything there the next morning, but there always was."

Once again, Carver's life and art had changed their course. At first, those who spoke with him during this third phase of interviewing could scarcely believe what they heard. The premier short-story writer of the 1980s had forsaken prose for poetry. (Bruce Weber, the first to note the change, treated the poems as a passing self-indulgence.) Over the next two years, however, Carver produced no new fiction. Instead, what he brought forth were two books of poems, *Where Water Comes Together with Other Water* (1985) and *Ultramarine* (1986). Carver's fiction, especially the pared-down texts in *What We Talk About,* had won him a reputation as a rootless chronicler of working-class despair. But when McCaffery and Gregory interviewed him in Port Angeles in the summer of 1984, what they found was a happy man. "I feel directly in touch with my surroundings now in a way I haven't felt in years," Carver said.

The "great gift" of the poems had arrived unexpectedly, and just as suddenly it seemed to depart. "I'd be hard put right now to sit down and write a poem," Carver said in November 1986, shortly after *Ultramarine* appeared. But his bowl had not remained empty. Late in 1985, he began writing fiction again. "Boxes," the first of seven new stories published over the next eighteen months, appeared in the *New Yorker* on 24 February 1986. As at earlier turning points, with the change of genres came a change in Carver's literary conversations. A fourth distinctive group of interviews extends from the fall of 1986 to the fall of 1987.

The recursive spiral pattern of Carver's thinking is clearly evident in his writings from the middle 1980s. In the poem "Woolworth's, 1954" (*Paris Review*, Fall 1984) and the story "Intimacy" (*Esquire*, August 1986), for example, a semi-autobiographical speaker steps back into his past, locates himself anew in the present, and tentatively moves forward, into the unknown. A similar process of self-regeneration emerges in the many biographical portraits of Carver written during this time. (Perhaps the most revealing of these is David Carpenter's "What We Talk About When We Talk About Carver."[12]) Interviewers noted the backward-then-forward pattern too. "Carver admits that his past and present are two different lives," wrote Michael Schumacher. "He is lucky to be alive, he says, adding that his stories and poems 'bear witness' to his past and, unfortunately, to all too many people's presents."

During these years, Carver was regularly cast as a "godfather" to younger American neorealists, a role he neither claimed nor wanted. (When the Italian interviewer Silvia Del Pozzo asked him whether he had "fathered" David Leavitt, Bret Easton Ellis, and Jay McInerney, Carver answered, "I'm only the father of my own kids."[13]) Journalistic hyperbole aside, by the late 1980s there could be little doubt that he was the foremost short-story writer of his generation. Carver's own self-assessment, although more modest, reflected the security he now felt in his "second life." As he told Nicholas O'Connell and others, "I'm just bearing witness to something I know something about."

If Carver's image of himself had changed, so too had his literary practice. Gone was the obsessive revising and republishing that had characterized his work in the early 1980s. "There was a period when I rewrote everything," he told Stull in 1986. "But I haven't done any of that in years." What's more, where formerly he felt bound to cut his stories to the minimum, he now felt confident enough to let them grow. The seven new stories were "longer, more detailed, and somehow more affirmative," he told David Applefield. And with this change in style came a change in subject matter. "Now they deal not just with husband and wife domestic relationships but with family relationships," he added: "son and mother, or father and children; and they go into these relationships more extensively." Perhaps most miraculous of all, Carver found himself writing poems and stories simultaneously, something he had never done before. The cumulative effect of these changes was a pressing sense of possibility. "I feel now like there's everything to do and little enough time to do it in," he told Michael Schumacher.

As a fifth and final group of interviews reveals, the time remaining to Raymond Carver proved tragically short. In September 1987 he experienced a series of pulmonary hemorrhages. The diagnosis was cancer, and in October surgeons removed two-thirds of his left lung. After a brief remission, the cancer reappeared in Carver's brain in March 1988, and a seven-week course of radiation treatments followed. *Where I'm Calling From,* a major collection of his new and selected fiction, was scheduled to appear in May. The publication of the book, coupled with a host of honors marking Carver's fiftieth birthday on 25 May, proved the occasion for a last round of interviews. Carver's final published story, "Errand" (*New Yorker,* 1 June 1987), had taken for its subject the last days of his lifelong inspiration, Anton Chekhov. Now, facing death himself, he spoke and acted with Chekhovian boldness. On the one hand, Carver told interviewers what he hoped might be his epitaph. "I can't think of anything else I'd rather be called than a writer," he said, "unless it's a poet." On the other, he insisted that his best work still lay ahead. "I'm going to make it," he told Kellerman. "I've got fish to catch and stories and poems to write."[14]

Time ran out before Carver could write the stories. But in the weeks following his marriage to Tess Gallagher on 17 June, he and his wife assembled his final book of poems, *A New Path to the Waterfall* (1989). In July, Carver and Gallagher made a fishing trip to Alaska. Raymond Carver died at home in Port Angeles early in the morning of 2 August. "In the last few years," he had remarked to Kellerman, "some light and radiance and, if you will, grace has come

into my life."[15] Carver's final conversations attest to these blessings,
as does "Late Fragment," the last poem in his final book:

And did you get what
you wanted from this life, even so?
I did.
And what did you want?
To call myself beloved, to feel myself
beloved on the earth.[16]

As in other volumes in the Literary Conversations series, the
interviews are reprinted uncut and largely unedited. Book titles have
been regularized into italics. Typographical errors and obvious factual
mistakes (including the wrong year commonly given for Carver's
birth) have been silently corrected. Titles and quotations from
Carver's works have been checked against his books and corrected.
The interviews are arranged in chronological order according to the
dates on which they were conducted. These dates are given in the
headnotes as precisely as could be determined.

The twenty-five interviews included in this book represent roughly
half the interviews the editors were able to locate. A number of these
conversations appear in expanded form. The *Paris Review* interview
follows the version collected in *Writers at Work,* Seventh Series. Kay
Bonetti's interview for *Saturday Review* is supplemented with dialogue from an audiotape that is available from the American Audio
Prose Library, P.O. Box 842, Columbia, Missouri 65205. The interview by Larry McCaffery and Sinda Gregory, first published in the
Mississippi Review (Winter 1985), appears in the revised form
included in *Alive and Writing* (1987). Gordon Burn supplied an
expanded text of his interview with Carver for the London *Times.*
Three published interviews—those by Roxanne Lawler, Hansmaarten
Tromp, and William L. Stull—are supplemented with additional
material transcribed from the interviewers' tapes. These transcriptions
have been edited slightly for the sake of intelligibility. Interviewers
asked Carver certain questions repeatedly, and there is inevitable
repetition in his answers.

Many people contributed to the making of this book. We are
deeply grateful to the writers and publishers who granted us permission to reprint materials. Several interviews are presented here in

English translation for the first time. We thank Michiko Miyamoto, Hansmaarten Tromp, and Riccardo Duranti for helping us obtain foreign-language publications. Our thanks go also to the translators who restored Carver's words into English: Naoko Takao, Stephen T. Moskey, and Susanna Peters Coy. Robert A. Tibbetts provided access to the Raymond Carver archive in the William Charvat Collection of American Fiction at The Ohio State University Library. For additional research assistance, we thank Christine Guyonneau and Shirley Bigna of the Krannert Memorial Library at the University of Indianapolis, along with Bonnie Anderson. Cheri Burton typed many of the interview texts, as well as a mountain of correspondence relating to this volume. Our wives, Alice Ruth Friman and Maureen Patricia Carroll, enhanced our efforts with insightful comments and valued encouragement. At every stage of this project we benefited from the editorial acumen of Seetha Srinivasan.

Throughout his richly productive "second life," Raymond Carver dedicated his books to a fellow writer who had been intimately involved in the making of his works. Because we owe a similar debt of gratitude, this book is for Tess Gallagher.

MBG
WLS
March 1990

1. Statements from interviews included in this volume are cited by interviewer, publication, and/or year. Quotations from other interviews, articles, and books are footnoted.

2. "Form's Master Sees a Revival," [Cleveland, Ohio] *Plain Dealer,* 30 November 1986, p. 1H.

3. "Suddenly Everything Became Clear to Him," *Washington,* November 1988, p. 104.

4. "'Grace Has Come into My Life,'" *The New York Times Book Review,* 15 May 1988, p. 40.

5. *The New York Times Book Review,* 15 February 1981, pp. 9, 18. Retitled "On Writing," this essay is reprinted in *Fires.*

6. "From *The Augustine Notebooks,*" *Iowa Review,* 10 (Summer 1979), 38-42.

7. Michael Wood, "Stories Full of Edges and Silences," *The New York Times Book Review,* 26 April 1981, pp. 1, 34. For a minor interview from this period, see Stephen Wigler, "Extraordinary Insights into Ordinary People," [Rochester, New York] *Sunday Democrat and Chronicle,* 21 June 1981, pp. 1-2C.

8. *Saturday Review,* April 1981, p. 77.

9. "The Secret Places of the Heart," *New York,* 20 April 1981, p. 77.

10. "And Bear in Mind," *The New York Times Book Review,* 22 May 1988, p. 36.

11. "Now You See Him, Now You Don't, Now You Do Again: The Evolution of Raymond Carver's Minimalism," *Critique,* 30 (Summer 1989), 239-51.

12. *Descant* [Toronto], No. 56/57 (Spring-Summer 1987), pp. 20-43.

13. "Sono quasi il loro papà," *Panorama* [Milan], 23 March 1986, p. 95.

14. "For Raymond Carver, A Lifetime of Storytelling," *The New York Times,* 31 May 1988, sec. C, p. 17.

15. " 'Grace Has Come into My Life,' " p. 40.

16. *A New Path to the Waterfall* (New York: Atlantic Monthly Press, 1989), p. 122.

Chronology

1938   Raymond Clevie Carver, Jr., was born in Clatskanie,
            Oregon, on 25 May, first child of Ella Beatrice Casey and
            Clevie Raymond Carver, a saw-filer in the Wauna Sawmill.
1941   Carvers move to Yakima, Washington.
1943   RC's only sibling, James Carver, was born in Yakima on 5
            August.
1956   RC graduates from Yakima High School in June. He and
            his mother then follow his father to Chester, California,
            where RC and his father both work in a sawmill. In
            November, RC returns alone to Yakima.
1957   On 7 June RC marries sixteen-year-old Maryann Burk in
            Yakima, where he works as a pharmacy deliveryman.
            Their daughter Christine LaRae born on 2 December.
1958   In August, RC moves his wife, daughter, and in-laws to
            Paradise, California, where he enters nearby Chico State
            College as a part-time student. His son, Vance Lindsay,
            born on 17 October. RC's first publication, a letter titled
            "Where Is Intellect?" appears in the Chico State *Wildcat*
            on 31 October.
1959   In June, the Carvers move to Chico, California. In the fall,
            RC takes Creative Writing 101, taught by John Gardner.
1960   During the spring semester, RC founds and edits the first
            issue of the Chico State literary magazine, *Selection*. In
            June, the Carvers move to Eureka, California, where RC
            works in the Georgia-Pacific sawmill. In the fall, he
            transfers to Humboldt State College in nearby Arcata and
            begins taking classes taught by Professor Richard C. Day.
1961   RC's first published story, "The Furious Seasons," ap-
            pears in *Selection*, No. 2 (Winter 1960-61). A second
            story, "The Father," appears in the spring issue of the

Humboldt State literary magazine, *Toyon.* In June, the
Carvers move to Arcata, California.

1962   RC's first play, *Carnations,* is performed at Humboldt
State College on 11 May. His first published poem, "The
Brass Ring," appears in the September issue of *Targets.*

1963   In February, RC receives his A.B. degree from Humboldt
State. During the spring, he edits *Toyon.* Under his own
name he includes the stories "Poseidon and Company"
and "The Hair." Under the pseudonym John Vale he
includes a Hemingway satire, "The Aficionados," and a
poem, "Spring, 480 B.C." RC receives a $500 fellowship
for a year's graduate study at the Iowa Writers' Workshop.
After spending the summer in Berkeley, where RC works
in the University of California library, the Carvers move to
Iowa City, Iowa. "The Furious Seasons," revised and
republished in the fall issue of *December,* is listed among
"Distinctive Short Stories in American and Canadian
Magazines, 1963" in *The Best American Short Stories 1964.*

1964–66   In June 1964, the Carvers return to California and settle
in Sacramento, where RC is hired as a day custodian at
Mercy Hospital. After one year, he transfers to the night
shift. In the fall of 1966, RC joins a poetry workshop led
by Dennis Schmitz at Sacramento State College.

1967   The Carvers file for bankruptcy in the spring. RC's father
dies on 17 June. On 31 July RC is hired as a textbook
editor at Science Research Associates (SRA). In August,
the Carvers move to Palo Alto, California, where RC
meets his future editor Gordon Lish. Martha Foley
includes RC's story "Will You Please Be Quiet, Please?"
in *The Best American Short Stories 1967.*

1968–69   In the spring of 1968, RC's first book, *Near Klamath*
(poems), is published by the English Club of Sacramento
State College. Maryann Carver receives a one-year
scholarship to Tel Aviv University, and RC takes a year's
leave of absence from SRA. The Carvers move to Israel in
June but return to California in October. From November
1968 until February 1969 they live with relatives in
Hollywood, where RC sells movie theater programs. In

February, he is rehired by SRA as "advertising director," and the Carvers move to San Jose, California.

1970   RC receives a National Endowment for the Arts Discovery Award for poetry. In June, the Carvers move to Sunnyvale, California. RC's story "Sixty Acres" is included in *The Best Little Magazine Fiction, 1970,* and his first regularly published book, *Winter Insomnia* (poems), is issued by Kayak Press. On 25 September, RC's job at SRA is terminated. Severance pay and unemployment benefits allow him to write full-time for nearly a year.

1971   In the spring, the San Francisco Foundation selects RC for "honorable mention/special commendation" in its annual Joseph Henry Jackson Award competition. Gordon Lish, now fiction editor at *Esquire,* publishes RC's story "Neighbors" in the magazine's June issue. RC is appointed visiting lecturer in creative writing at the University of California, Santa Cruz, for 1971-72, and in August the Carvers move to Ben Lomond, California. RC's story "Fat" appears in the September issue of *Harper's Bazaar,* and "A Night Out" is included in *The Best Little Magazine Fiction, 1971.* At Santa Cruz, RC serves as founding advisory editor of the magazine *Quarry* (now *Quarry West*).

1972   RC receives a Wallace E. Stegner Fellowship at Stanford University for 1972-73 and a concurrent appointment as visiting lecturer in fiction writing at UC Berkeley. In July, the Carvers buy a house in Cupertino, California.

1973   Appointed visiting lecturer at the Iowa Writers' Workshop for 1973-74, RC moves alone to Iowa City. At the Iowa House, a campus residence, he lives two floors below John Cheever. RC's story "What Is It?" is included in the O. Henry Awards annual, *Prize Stories 1973,* and five of his poems are reprinted in *New Voices in American Poetry.*

1974   RC is appointed visiting lecturer at UC Santa Barbara for 1974-75 and named advisory editor of the UCSB literary magazine *Spectrum.* Alcoholism and domestic problems force him to resign in December, and the Carvers subsequently file for their second bankruptcy. RC's story

"Put Yourself in My Shoes" is published as a Capra Press chapbook in August and included in *Prize Stories 1974*. Unemployed, RC returns to Cupertino, California. He remains there with his family for the next two years, during which he does little writing.

1975   "Are You a Doctor?" is included in *Prize Stories 1975*.

1976   *At Night the Salmon Move,* RC's third book of poetry, is published by Capra Press in February. In March, his first major-press book, the short-story collection *Will You Please Be Quiet, Please?* is published by McGraw-Hill under its Gordon Lish imprint. RC's story "So Much Water So Close to Home" is included in the first *Pushcart Prize* anthology. Between October 1976 and January 1977, RC undergoes four hospitalizations for acute alcoholism. The Carvers' house in Cupertino is sold in October, and RC and his wife begin living apart.

1977   *Will You Please Be Quiet, Please?* receives a National Book Award nomination. RC moves alone to McKinleyville, California, and on 2 June he stops drinking. Reunited with his wife, he continues living in McKinleyville through the year. In November, *Furious Seasons and Other Stories* is published by Capra Press. That month, at a writers conference in Dallas, Texas, RC meets the poet Tess Gallagher.

1978   In January, RC teaches a two-week M.F.A. course at Goddard College in Plainfield, Vermont. He receives a John Simon Guggenheim Fellowship, and from March through June, he and his wife live together on a trial basis in Iowa City. They separate in July, with RC leaving for the University of Texas, El Paso, where he has been appointed visiting distinguished writer-in-residence for 1978-79. In August, he meets Tess Gallagher for the second time, and the two writers begin their close association. RC's book reviews begin appearing in the *Chicago Tribune, Texas Monthly,* and the *San Francisco Review of Books*.

1979   On 1 January, RC and Tess Gallagher begin living together in El Paso. They spend the summer in Chimacum, Washington, on the Olympic Peninsula, near Gallagher's home town of Port Angeles. "From *The Augustine Notebooks*," a fragment of Carver's never-completed novel, appears in the summer issue of *Iowa Review*. In September, RC and Gallagher move to Tucson, where she teaches at the University of Arizona. RC is appointed Professor of English at Syracuse University in Syracuse, New York. He defers the appointment for one year in order to draw on his Guggenheim Fellowship and write.

1980   RC receives a National Endowment for the Arts Fellowship for fiction. Because of an unexpected retirement at Syracuse, he begins teaching in January, one semester earlier than planned. From May through August, RC and Gallagher live in a borrowed cabin in Port Angeles. In September, the two move to Syracuse, where Gallagher joins the University as Coordinator of the Creative Writing Program. RC and Gallagher jointly purchase a house in Syracuse.

1981   RC and Gallagher continue their routine of teaching in Syracuse from September to May and summering in Port Angeles. RC's essay "A Storyteller's Shoptalk" (later retitled "On Writing") appears in the *New York Times Book Review* on 15 February. His second major-press story collection, *What We Talk About When We Talk About Love,* edited by Gordon Lish, is published by Knopf on 20 April. "The Bath" wins *Columbia* magazine's Carlos Fuentes Fiction Award. RC makes his first appearance in *The New Yorker* with the story "Chef's House," published on 30 November. Thereafter, he becomes a frequent contributor to the magazine. "What We Talk About When We Talk About Love" is included in *The Pushcart Prize, VI.*

1982   During the summer, RC and Gallagher travel to Switzerland. In September, RC's story *The Pheasant* is published in limited edition by Metacom Press. Guest editor John Gardner includes "Cathedral" in *The Best American Short Stories 1982.* (Gardner dies in a motorcycle

accident on 14 September.) RC and his wife, separated
since July 1978, are legally divorced on 18 October. RC's
essay "Fires" appears in the autumn issue of *Antaeus*.
Film director Michael Cimino commissions RC and
Gallagher to rewrite a screenplay based on the life of
Dostoevsky. RC is elected a member of the Corporation
of Yaddo, an arts retreat in Saratoga Springs, New York.

1983   Capra Press publishes *Fires: Essays, Poems, Stories* on 14
April. "A Small, Good Thing," RC's revision/expansion of
"The Bath," is awarded first place in *Prize Stories 1983*. It
is also included in *The Pushcart Prize, VIII*. On 18 May,
the American Academy and Institute of Arts and Letters
awards RC and Cynthia Ozick its first Mildred and Harold
Strauss Livings: renewable five-year fellowships that carry
annual tax-free stipends of $35,000. As a condition of the
award, RC resigns his professorship at Syracuse. His
essay "John Gardner: Writer and Teacher" appears in the
summer issue of *The Georgia Review* and becomes the
foreword to Gardner's posthumous *On Becoming a
Novelist*. RC's third major book of stories, *Cathedral*, is
published by Knopf on 15 September. On 12 December,
it receives a National Book Critics Circle Award nomination. RC edits a Special Fiction Issue of *Ploughshares*,
and guest editor Anne Tyler includes "Where I'm Calling
From" in *The Best American Short Stories 1983*.

1984   In January, RC flees the publicity "hubbub" in Syracuse
and moves alone into Gallagher's newly built "Sky
House" in Port Angeles. RC writes poetry during the day
and occasional nonfiction during the evening. On 22
April, his review of Sherwood Anderson's *Selected Letters*
appears in the *New York Times Book Review*. RC con-
tributes a foreword to *We Are Not in This Together:
Stories by William Kittredge*. In the summer, he and
Gallagher make a reading tour of Brazil and Argentina for
the U.S. Information Service. In the fall, they return to
Syracuse, where Gallagher arranges to teach only one
semester each year. "Purple Lake," an unproduced
screenplay written by RC and Michael Cimino, is regis-

tered on 10 September. RC's essay "My Father's Life" appears in the September issue of *Esquire,* and his story *If It Please You* is published in September as a Lord John Press limited edition. Seven of RC's poems are reprinted in *The Generation of 2000,* and his story "Careful" is included in *The Pushcart Prize, IX. Cathedral* receives a Pulitzer Prize nomination.

1985   In January, RC buys a house in a working-class district of Port Angeles. He and Gallagher share their two residences in Port Angeles from January through August, and in September they return to Syracuse. Five of RC's poems appear in the February issue of *Poetry* (Chicago). Thereafter, he becomes a regular contributor. Random House publishes RC's poetry collection *Where Water Comes Together with Other Water* on 1 May. RC and Gallagher travel to England, where *Fires* and *The Stories of Raymond Carver* are published on 16 May. *Dostoevsky: A Screenplay,* co-authored by RC and Gallagher, is published in the fall by Capra Press. On 17 November, RC's review of two Hemingway biographies appears in the *New York Times Book Review.* That month, he also receives *Poetry* magazine's Levinson Prize.

1986   RC serves as guest editor of *The Best American Short Stories 1986.* Random House publishes his poetry collection *Ultramarine* on 7 November, the same day that RC and Gallagher are featured readers at the Modern Poetry Association's Poetry Day celebration in Chicago.

1987   On 3 April, Delacorte publishes *American Short Story Masterpieces,* edited by RC and Tom Jenks. In May, Raven Editions publishes *Those Days: Early Writings by Raymond Carver.* "Errand," RC's last published story, appears in *The New Yorker* on 1 June. From April to July, RC and Gallagher travel in Europe, visiting Paris, Wiesbaden, Zürich, Rome, and Milan. In London, Collins Harvill publishes *In a Marine Light,* a selection of Carver's recent poems, on 1 June. In September, RC experiences pulmonary hemorrhages, and on 1 October doctors in Syracuse remove two-thirds of his cancerous left lung. RC is inducted into the New York Public Library "Literary Lions" on 11 November. Guest editor Ann Beattie includes "Boxes" in *The Best American Short Stories 1987.*

1988   In January, RC buys a new house in Port Angeles. "Errand" is awarded first place in *Prize Stories 1988,* and guest editor Mark Helprin includes it in *The Best American Short Stories 1988.* RC serves as judge of *American Fiction 88.* In March, his cancer reappears, this time in the brain. During April and May, he undergoes a seven-week course of radiation treatments in Seattle. *Where I'm Calling From,* a major collection of his new and selected stories, is published in May by Atlantic Monthly Press. On 4 May, RC receives a Creative Arts Award Citation for Fiction from Brandeis University. On 15 May, he receives an honorary Doctor of Letters degree from the University of Hartford. On 18 May, he is inducted into the American Academy and Institute of Arts and Letters. In early June, cancer reappears in RC's lungs. He and Gallagher marry in Reno, Nevada, on 17 June. Working together, they assemble his last book of poetry, and in July they make a fishing trip to Alaska. After a brief stay in Virginia Mason Hospital in Seattle, RC dies at his new house in Port Angeles on 2 August at 6:20 a.m. He is buried in the Ocean View Cemetery in Port Angeles on 4 August, the same day that Collins Harvill publishes *Elephant and Other Stories* in London. RC's poem "Gravy" appears in *The New Yorker* on 29 August, and his essay "Friendship" is published in the autumn issue of *Granta.* A memorial service for him is held at Saint Peter's Church in New York City on 22 September.

1989   The Seattle Foundation awards its Maxine Cushing Gray Fellowship to Gallagher and, posthumously, to RC. Atlantic Monthly Press publishes RC's last book of poems, *A New Path to the Waterfall,* on 15 June. "Dreams Are What You Wake Up From," a BBC *Omnibus* documentary on RC's life and writing, is televised in England on 22 September. On 27 November, the English-Speaking Union confers its Ambassador Book Award on *Where I'm Calling From.*

Conversations with Raymond Carver

Accolade-Winning Author Returns to Humboldt

Cassandra Phillips/1977

From the *Times-Standard* [Eureka, CA], 24 July 1977, 1-2.
Reprinted by permission of the *Times-Standard.* Conducted July
1977.

"He came to Second Street, the part of town people called 'Two
Street.'"

And from there, Ralph Wyman, a Eureka school teacher who has
just learned of his wife's infidelity, loses his money in a card game,
gets mugged and stumbles back home.

The line is from a story by Raymond Carver. Its title, "Will You
Please Be Quiet, Please?" is also the name of Carver's first book of
fiction.

Along with four other books, *Will You Please Be Quiet, Please?*
was nominated this year for perhaps the most prestigious literary
prize in the United States—the National Book Award for fiction.

It lost, but Carver will tell you, without arrogance or hesitation, that
his book should have won.

"I read all the other nominees and I think that I won every foe," he
said, and laughed.

Besides its nomination for the National Book Award, *Will You
Please Be Quiet, Please?* received accolades in virtually every major
literary journal and has sold 4,500 copies in hardback, a respectable
number for a book of short stories.

(It will appear next February in paperback.)

Carver first came to Humboldt County in the early 1960s as a
Humboldt State University student, and stayed until graduating in
1963.

He picked HSU, very simply, "because there was work over here."
His father, then working in a Fortuna sawmill, wangled Carver a job
at Georgia-Pacific Corp.

After an absence of 13 years, Carver has returned. He is living in
McKinleyville in a nice but modest home which illustrates that critical
acclaim and fabulous wealth do not necessarily go hand in hand.

"I'm not recognized in the Safeway," he said wryly.

3

Carver, 39, is a very large man who looks like he would be more at home in a sawmill than at a publisher's party. He chain smokes ("I'm beginning to feel like a cigaret with a body attached to it") and speaks softly.

This is his first "formal" interview and he is "embarrassed."

"I was born in Oregon, Clatskanie, Ore., population of about 700. It's right on the Columbia River," he said.

His parents had emigrated from Arkansas during the Depression.

The Carver family moved to Yakima, Wash., when Ray was four. There he grew up, met his wife-to-be, Maryann, and became the first member of his family ever to graduate from high school.

As a boy, he said, "My favorite author was Edgar Rice Burroughs. I read all of his books, and most of them five, six and eight times."

Burroughs could be called Carver's first literary model. During his boyhood he wrote "little stories about monsters, ants, laboratories and mad doctors."

But it was not until Carver was a freshman at Chico State College that he started writing seriously.

"I met a very extraordinary fellow over there who has since gone on to become one of the best-known writers in the country. John Gardner. And we became pals."

(Gardner's first teaching job was at Chico State. At that time he had not published any of the books—*The Sunlight Dialogues, Nickel Mountain, October Light*—which have made him famous.)

"He used to go over my early manuscripts, word for word, line by line. And I really think that's the only way writing can be taught," Carver said.

Gardner also loaned Carver the key to his office so his talented student could write in privacy.

"In his office on the weekends I used to go through his manuscripts and steal titles from his stories," Carver confessed. "I mean take his titles, which struck me as awfully good, as I recall, and rephrase them, and put them on my own stories . . . .

"Then I began to show him my stories with his titles, and he had to give me a little lecture on the basic proprieties and the like," he said.

Further, "He (Gardner) had a lot of correspondence from other writers in his office, which I naturally read. Anyway, I learned a good deal about this and that from all my snooping."

Carver's interest in snooping is reflected in one of his best stories, "Neighbors," in which a couple, looking after their vacationing neighbors' apartment, wind up spending most of their time exploring it.

When Carver transferred to HSU, he came under the tutelage of Richard Day, still an English professor there.

"I enrolled for two classes with Day," Carver said, "and then followed him around campus for a week or two before I got up the nerve to even speak to him."

They became, and remain, good friends.

It was during his junior year at HSU that Carver, on one momentous day, received word that he had sold his first story and his first poem. Both sales were to "little magazines."

"I got a dollar for the poem, a check for a dollar, and contributors' copies for the story," he recalled, laughing.

After one year of graduate work in creative writing at the University of Iowa, Carver, with his wife and two children, moved to Sacramento where he wrote steadily and held "a succession of one shabby job after another."

The writer's first "white collar" job offer came almost out of the blue, from Science Research Associates (SRA), textbook publishers in Palo Alto.

"I had an office, a telephone and everything—all that stuff," he said.

After one year at SRA, Carver and family went abroad for a year. When they returned, he found himself advertising director for the firm.

"I had an expense account, and so forth, and I started abusing it, of course," he said, again laughing. "I got fired."

One would expect such an event to be catastrophic, but, as it turned out, losing the SRA job was the best thing that could have happened to Carver.

"I got a great deal of severance pay and I could draw unemployment. And, at the same time, I had just won a National Endowment for the Arts grant. And so for the first time in my life I had some dough."

By this time, Carver had published stories and poems in a number of little magazines and had attracted an agent. With money and time to write, he sold stories to *Esquire* and *Harper's Bazaar* magazines. Additionally, his first book of poems was published and his short stories were winning prizes and being anthologized.

After nine productive months of writing, Carver embarked on an academic career. He held one-year appointments at U.C. Santa Cruz, U.C. Berkeley, the University of Iowa and U.C. Santa Barbara.

"It was a terrifying prospect to be a teacher, but I wound up doing a good job," he said.

He was publishing stories and poems all the while, winning O. Henry short story prizes in 1973-74-75.

In 1975, Carver left academia for full-time writing. His wife, meanwhile, had gotten a job teaching high school in Los Altos. (She has taken a year's leave of absence to be with Carver in McKinleyville.)

In September, a new book of short stories, entitled *Furious Seasons* and published by Capra Press, will hit the bookstands. And, only two weeks ago, Carver sold a story to *Esquire*. It will appear in December.

And now, with the security of an advance from his publisher, McGraw-Hill, Carver is preparing to write his first novel.

(The first purchases made with the advance money, he said, were fishing rods and reels.)

The novel will be a radical departure from his short stories. The subject is German East Africa during World War I, involving not mill workers and door-to-door salesmen, but patrician German military officers.

"It'll be an *African Queen* sort of thing," he said.

And, he said he feels "confident" about the project. "I know my limitations, but I really don't know what I can't do," he said. "I've never had this chance that I have right now."

Yet Carver will readily admit, "I'm not that intellectual. I work much closer to the bone. I'm not excited by intellectualism in poetry or fiction . . . the pyrotechnics."

On writing, he said, "At least 70 percent of it comes down to energy. You can mentally and physically feel it begin to flag as you start closing on 40, after you've damaged yourself this way and that for whatever reasons, necessary or imagined."

Nevertheless, Carver said he writes a story quickly, then spends several days "polishing" it. He writes daily "when I'm really hot" and then may "drift along for a week or two and not do anything."

If he has an aesthetic credo, it is a quote from Ezra Pound that Carver has typed on an index card and keeps near his work desk:

"Fundamental accuracy of statement is the ONE sole morality of writing, as distinct from the morality of ideas in the writing."

"I can't very well imagine any other life than writing," he said. "If I had it to do over, however, I'd rather be a composer. But then I can't even read musical notation, so that's out.

"I just want to write as well and truly as I can," he said.

Echoes of Our Own Lives

David Koehne/1978

From the *Daily Iowan* [University of Iowa—Iowa City], 18 April 1978, 2. Reprinted by permission of the *Daily Iowan*. Conducted 15 April 1978.

It is late afternoon, a Saturday, and we are sitting in my apartment drinking coffee. Outside the living room window some neighborhood children are arguing. A station wagon moves slowly down the street. It could be the opening scene from one of his short stories, because it is seemingly ordinary. Raymond Carver lights his cigarette, gestures slightly with the match, leans forward.

"You are not your characters, but your characters are you," he says.

An interesting observation, considering the many roles that Carver has played in his lifetime. He has been a janitor, a sawmill hand, a deliveryman, a retail clerk, and an editor for a publishing firm. He taught fiction writing at several universities, including the Iowa Writers' Workshop in 1973-74.

For the next few months, however, Carver will simply be living in Iowa City, working on several writing projects before leaving the Midwest to join the faculty of Goddard College in Vermont.

"This is a new time in my life. My children are both grown, and I just received a Guggenheim Fellowship. I have large blocks of time to work with," he says.

"I've been working on a novel. I had already received an advance from the publisher, but they've agreed to accept a collection of short stories this fall, instead."

Carver has previously published two collections of his short stories: *Will You Please Be Quiet, Please?*, which was a National Book Award nominee for 1977, and *Furious Seasons,* which contains his Pushcart Prize-winning story, "So Much Water So Close to Home."

Carver thinks of himself primarily as a fiction writer, although he has published three excellent volumes of poetry and is assembling a fourth.

"A year ago I thought I'd never write another poem. I don't know

8

exactly what it is, but since I've been in Iowa City I've written an entire book. The past few weeks have been very good."

We talk for a while about the division that is sometimes evident between a writer's poetry and her/his prose. I suggest that Carver's poems often resemble his fiction. He lights another cigarette.

"I believe a plot line is very important. Whether I am writing a poem or writing prose I am still trying to tell a story. For a long time I wrote poems because I didn't have the time to write short stories. The nice thing about a poem is that there is instant gratification. And if something goes wrong, it's right there. It would be a hard thing for me to work for months on a novel and then have it be bad. It would be a tremendous investment for me, and I don't have a very long attention span."

If it is fair to say that Carver's poems resemble his short stories, it is equally true that his short stories have a poetic intensity. The language is very clear and deceptively simple. The reader is never certain where the action is going until she/he arrives.

Raymond Carver has tremendous skill with dialogue, and his characters remain tangible in the most bizarre situations.

In the story "What's in Alaska?" Mary and Carl spend an evening with Jack and Helen, trying out the water pipe Jack received for his birthday. Carver not only simulates the conversations of four stoned adults with amusing accuracy, he succeeds in subtly suggesting a series of conflicts that create a kind of subliminal tension in the reader, a tension that culminates in the disturbing last line of the story.

Carver's fiction quite often encourages a kind of empathic response in his readers. This is due to his keen eye for common, small details, details we imagine unique to our personal histories. Therefore we sometimes forget we are reading fictions, suspect that we are dealing with echoes of our own words, our own lives.

We refill our coffee cups and I ask him about process, the origins of his stories. He pauses for a moment.

"A lot of things come from experience, or sometimes from something I've heard, a line somewhere."

I mention that often his titles are taken from lines in his stories. He leans forward.

"You start writing. Sometimes you don't find what you are trying to say in the story until you turn a line, and then suddenly you know where the story is going. You just have to discover as you go. Then when you get that first draft, you go back.

"Everything is important in a story, every word, every punctuation mark. I believe very much in economy in fiction. Some of my stories, like 'Neighbors,' were three times as long in their first drafts. I really like the process of rewriting.

"Beginnings are very important. A story is either blessed or cursed with its opening lines. Editors have so many manuscripts to look through that often all they do is look at the first paragraph or two, unless it's an author they know."

Apparently Carver knows what he's doing, because his stories have been included in some of the most competitive collections in the country: *Best American Short Stories* and O. Henry *Prize Stories*.

The longest pause in our conversation follows my question, "What do you think about writing programs, such as the Iowa Writers' Workshop? I know you were a student here several years ago."

"I think writing programs can be a good thing, a place to learn craft. Of course, one problem is that a lot of people who are active in the writing program are never heard from again after they leave it. They move away from the school and they just stop writing.

"My time at Iowa wasn't very productive. I didn't put much work up. I was here for two semesters and I left before I could get my M.F.A.

"The important thing is to find someone you can work with. For me it was John Gardner. He was there at a very important time in my development."

Carver will read in the English lounge at 8 p.m. today; he will read, perhaps, the title story from his new collection of short fiction, *Why Don't You Dance?* [not published under this title].

"I might read another story, also," he says. "'Put Yourself in My Shoes.' I'll decide on Tuesday."

Carver stands up, looks at me, his cup in his hand. "Is there any more coffee?" he asks.

Raymond Carver Speaking

Robert Pope and Lisa McElhinny/1982

From *The Akros Review*, no. 8/9 (Spring 1984), 103-14. Reprinted by permission of *The Akros Review* and Robert Pope. Conducted Spring 1982.

Raymond Carver visited The University of Akron in the spring of 1982. These are selected comments from his question and answer discussion with a class in the American short story. Lisa McElhinny transcribed and edited this interview, and we cut out the questions to avoid unnecessary interruption to the text of Mr. Carver's talk.

Too often the short story has been regarded, certainly by most publishers over the last few years, as a kind of bastard stepchild of American literature. Short story writers, by and large, have not been taken all that seriously for some strange reason. Publishers are not interested in collections of short stories unless you're an established author. But even today a book of short stories by a reputable publisher will not sell more than 1,500 to 2,000 copies. In that regard short story writers are worse off than poets. I'm happy to say that the situation is changing, has begun to change in the last several years. Short story writers'—like Leonard Michaels, Ann Beattie, Barry Hannah, and myself—collections have been getting more critical attention, and I think there's a real renaissance in the short story going on these days.

I feel like I'm a part of a tradition. I feel very comfortable writing short stories. I feel more short stories that I want to write very badly, and I hope I will this summer—I have to—I'm under contract to deliver up a book manuscript of stories this fall. After that I may write a novel or I may not. I took money once to write a novel, and I didn't write it. I wrote short stories instead. I think I worked on the novel two weeks then stopped and went back to writing short stories.

For a good many years there was a sort of pressure put upon me, implicit and not so implicit, to write this novel. Everyone from my wife to my publisher said, "You have to write a novel." But I continued to write short stories and poems. But I may write a novel. I may write a novel next year. I don't know. I'm happy doing what I'm doing. I no longer have those pressures.

There are any number of good writers, in all of literature, who have never written novels. Chekhov, for instance, wrote some great long stories, some novellas, tried to write a novel and couldn't, said he didn't have an attention span that would enable him to write a novel. He got bored easily. He liked beginnings and endings. I really feel that's true in my case. I couldn't imagine spending three years on a novel and then having it turn out to be a bad novel. Although this is oftentimes what happens. Most often a writer's first novel is never published because usually it's bad, usually. There are exceptions— Thomas Mann's first novel, for example. I don't think writing short stories should necessarily be a stepping-stone to writing a novel, but it seems to me that it's a good place for prose writers to start because you have to learn to use language.

I think that too often people are in it for the big kill. They think if they write a novel they're going to get famous, get rich. Most working novelists don't make any money. I have a friend who's published three novels, all critically well received. He's earned a total of eight thousand dollars, and he worked on those books eight years. When you come right down to it, those aren't very good wages. That's why most serious writers have to do other things to earn a living—whether it's teaching, or being vice president of an insurance company, or working six months out of the year in logging camps and spending the rest of the time writing.

Teaching doesn't inspire me. I'm not getting ideas from my teaching or ideas from my students. But it pays the rent and provides me with a good living. For too many years I worried about how I was going to make the next month's rent, or what would happen if my kids got sick. I didn't have dental or health insurance. They needed bicycles. Come September they needed clothes for school. That kind of hand-to-mouth existence takes too much out of you. It's just no way to live at all. Now I'm not worrying about how to pay the rent, and I'm writing more. I have summers off. I have a month off at Christmas. I'm paid very well for what I do. I'm paid better for the hours that I put in than for anything else I've ever done, and I've done every crap job in the world. There's nothing ennobling about working fifty weeks a year, ten hours a day in a rubber plant, or in a sawmill, or anything else, and getting two weeks' vacation a year, and going off to a state park. Work those eight-to-five jobs, or those eleven-to-seven-in-the morning-jobs, and you come home so wiped out that you're too tired to do anything. I'm getting more work done now than I ever did then. In the ideal world, if this were just a peaceable kingdom, writers wouldn't have to work at all. They'd just get a check in the mail every month. But since this isn't the case, I have no complaints. The money could be worse. It has been worse. So I'm happy to be able to do what I'm doing.

I'm sent a lot of books from publishers, bound galleys, and things like this at the stage right before final publication, hoping that I'll review the book, or give the book a comment, or something like that. Often I'm sent a novel that will be in the bookstore in, say, a few months. It will be selling for fifteen, sixteen dollars, and this thing will be seven or eight hundred pages long. I'm really daunted when I pick that up. It weighs about three or four pounds. It's a—I'm sure it's a failure on my part. I'm glad I read *War and Peace* when I did. But I have read it—twice—and I hope to read it two more times before I die. I think that's a great book, a great book. And I'm not suggesting, by any means, that something has to be short to be good. John Cheever's new novel is very short, and it's very bad.

I certainly feel that there's more of a similarity between writing a short story and writing a poem than there is between writing a short story and writing a novel.

I think reading and writing poetry is, perhaps, the best training that a young writer can undergo. Poe called it the single effect.

I started writing short stories and poetry at the same time. I had a poem and a story accepted on the same day from two different magazines. That was a great day. It was truly a red letter day. About as good as anything that's ever happened to me. I got paid one dollar for the poem and a promise of contributor's copies for the story. Get rich quick, you see.

I don't think you should cast about looking for an idea for a story. I think the idea ought to take you over in some way, but everything in my stories is subject to change. I'm a great believer in rewriting. I like to rewrite. Most writers of my acquaintance, and most writers I know anything about, have been great rewriters. It's instructive and heartening to us all, all of those who want to be writers, to look at the early drafts of the great writers. I think that Tolstoy, Dostoevsky, and Hemingway were all great rewriters.

Hemingway was oftentimes given to exaggeration, but he said he wrote the ending to *A Farewell to Arms* forty times, the last half of the book. Now even if you divide that by two that's a lot of rewriting.

And I've seen photographs of the galleys for Tolstoy's *War and Peace*. He had written that book five times from stem to stern with pen and ink, and he was making corrections in the galley proofs right down to the time of publication. And he made such extensive corrections that the book had to be reset. The printers had to take it and set the type again because he had so many additions and so many corrections.

Frank O'Connor, a great Irish short story writer, probably the best short story writer in this century, would rewrite his stories twenty, thirty, forty times—those great long stories of his. And then he would oftentimes rewrite them after they were published. He said, you just put down any old rubbish on that first draft, and you put black on white, black on white—just let it go, that first draft, just get anything out.

I think Hemingway said that he wrote with his fingers. When he was in a car wreck in Montana and there was talk of him losing his right arm, he thought he might lose his ability to write.

Too often, students or young writers who are not settled get stuck on the second or third page of their story. They can't think it out, and so they stop. Their head gets in the way of the story. Then they keep making these abortive efforts, and they stop their stories. You've just got to rush through and get it out. And then you'll see what your story's about. Oftentimes a writer doesn't know what he's going to say until he sees what he said.

There's a book by Flannery O'Connor called *Mystery and Manners,* a book of occasional prose pieces that was put together and published after her death, that I understand is still doing very well, and I certainly recommend it. She said she scarcely ever knew where her stories were going when she began them. She would start with an idea in her head, or with an image in her head, with a few lines, and then this would develop into that and that would suggest something else. She said when she began "Good Country People," certainly a great and famous story for us, that she didn't know that there was going to be a woman in the story with a Ph.D. and an artificial leg. She didn't know there was going to be a Bible salesman calling. She didn't know the ending of the story until she was eight sentences from the end of it. It just came to her as she heard it. And I, oftentimes, work this way.

I know vaguely where I'm going. And then I write the first draft or rough draft so rapidly that I don't stop and take care of the niceties. There are certain scenes that I know I'll have to go back and tend to later. I just skip over them—x them, a note to myself and push on rapidly. I try to do the story once in maybe thirty-five or forty pages, in longhand, knowing I'll have to go back, and that the real work will begin later after I get it typed up. And then it's not at all uncommon to do ten or fifteen drafts, twenty drafts of that story. And then I find myself changing it, maybe even after it's been published in a magazine, by looking at it again in proof. Prior to or according to a book or something, I might change it. I think it's very common. I've known poets who work this way, eminent poets, some of the best poets we have—Robert Bly, Galway Kinnell, Donald Hall.

Donald Hall told me that he spent three years writing a poem through eighty drafts, eighty or one hundred drafts. Now he was doing other things in the meanwhile, but he would take the poem out of its drawer and look at the poem, send it to the typewriter again, do a little work to it, put it back in the drawer and go on to something else. By the time he was finished he'd done eighty or a hundred drafts, and it was only about sixteen lines long. All the poets I know are serious. All of the poets I know write and rewrite and rewrite.

John Gardner was a great rewriter. He spent twenty years on one novel. Meanwhile he was writing other things, other novels. But he'd write on this novel, then put it in a drawer. Then he'd work on something else, and then he'd go back and take this novel out of the drawer and send it to the typewriter again and do some more work on it. If it wasn't right, he'd put it back in the drawer and go back to

something else, work on that then go on to something else. But he
was working on other stuff, so that finally things began to get
finished. The first novel that Gardner published was not the first
novel that he wrote.

I'm a great admirer of Chekhov's short stories, and I will borrow from
Chekhov at the risk of parody. I'll borrow something that he said. He
divides works of literature into two classes—things he likes and things
he doesn't like. I really don't have any theories for writing stories. I
know what I like. I know what I don't like. I don't like dishonesty in
writing. I don't like tricks. I like an honest story, well told. No matter if
there's romance in the story or whatever.

Oftentimes if you read enough stories—especially if you're reading
stories in manuscript, whether students' stories, or stories sent to you
as the editor of a magazine—you can tell if the story's going to be
worth anything in the first two or three sentences. There's something
about the way the words are working, something about the way it
looks, the way it feels to you.

I've edited three literary magazines myself, and I know the man
who was fiction editor at *Esquire* for eight years. He was only reading
manuscripts from agents, or manuscripts that were submitted to him
and had *personal* marked across the envelope. He might have been
dealing with say thirty or forty stories in any given day. So if he
missed a day, the next day he'd have sixty stories to look at. But he
wouldn't read all those stories. He'd read the first few sentences, the
first paragraph, sometimes the first page. Then if he was invited into
the writer's story, if it was seductive enough, he'd keep going. So I'm
suggesting that if you're a writer yourself, you don't save your best
shot for last.

Then there are the O. Henry Awards, the annual collection of
American fiction that comes out every March. Roughly three thousand short stories are published in this country each year. All of those
stories, published in magazines from *The Akros Review* to *The New
Yorker,* are eligible for consideration for inclusion in this volume.
William Abrahams, the editor, has assistants who do some screening.
He might be presented with one hundred and fifty stories. He
doesn't have time to read one hundred and fifty stories. He can't. I'm
talking about published stories. Take twelve issues of *Redbook*, say,

and read the first paragraphs, maybe the second—if it doesn't work, you go on. There are too many other things clamoring for our attention these days. You've just got to have it up there, up front to a degree. Look at the beginning of any short story that you admire. Look at Chekhov's beginnings, the first sentence or two. You're right there in that room, and it's irresistible. Or look at Hemingway, or Frank O'Connor, or Flannery O'Connor. Look at those first few sentences. There's no way you can stop.

Going back to Hemingway, Hemingway is an author whose work I admire greatly. I still go back and read his work with pleasure. You're probably familiar with his comment comparing a literary work to an iceberg: nine-tenths of the iceberg is under water. But as long as the writer knows what he's leaving out, that's okay. If he's just writing and doesn't know that he's leaving out crucial things, then that's not so good. If you read Hemingway's stories, you get just enough and no more.

There's a story called "Cat in the Rain," which is one of my favorite stories by Ernest Hemingway. Nothing much happens in the story, but you know that the relationship between the husband and wife is going bad. She goes out to look for a cat that she sees from her hotel room window, and it's the rainy season, and I guess the story's set close to Spain, and her husband's not much interested, and there's a detail that sticks in my head—he's lying on a bed reading a book, but his head's at the foot of the bed, and his feet are at the headboard. It's a wonderful story. It's a very simply told story. It's marvelous.

The people that I don't like I generally don't read. I made the comment about John Cheever's new novel, *Oh What a Paradise It Seems,* which I didn't care for at all, but I think he's a great writer. I think he's just marvelous. His collected stories that came out some years ago, I think might be read fifty years from now. I think he's a great writer.

There's a group of writers who do a lot of work with Fiction Collective, and their work—there are exceptions, they publish some people whose work I do have regard for, like Jerry Bumpus. But too many of the books that they publish are nutty, and they're silly, and they're trivial. They're experimental in the worst sense. They're full of gimmicks, and they're ultimately boring. It's like a practical joke. A practical joke, you know, is not very funny after a while. I don't like jokes or tricks when I'm reading a piece of fiction.

There are stories of Donald Barthelme's that I don't care for, but then I think that he's written some very wonderful stories. He's done some very wonderful things in short story form. He's his own man. He's often imitated but never duplicated. It's people who, for instance, try to write like Barthelme but don't have Barthelme's particular genius and humor who bother me. You're always reading poor Barthelme imitations. You get characters that the author doesn't care anything about stuck in foolish or ridiculous situations, and you know somebody's been reading too much of certain experimental writers who write things like a father's babysitting, and the baby's crying is interrupting his TV show, and so he gets up and puts the baby into the furnace. What kind of stuff is this? Who needs that? Then he goes back to watching his TV show or makes a ham sandwich or something. That kind of stuff is cold, to say the least. But there are people writing stories like this, and sometimes they're getting them published. I don't want to get into talking about names or personalities, but there's a whole class or genre of writing like that. They seem to have lost their moorings. They don't have any bearings, moral bearings, either for the work of art or in their lives or something—I don't know.

As far as I'm concerned, the best art has its reference points in real life. Even Donald Barthelme's work, his best work, has some things that connect up.

I guess it is not a new idea, by any means, that art can exist for the sake of art itself. This goes back certainly to the 19th century when they began writing this way. I guess I get bored easily. I get bored with writers writing about writing. An author has one of his characters ask, "How much longer can this go on?" That's what I want to know. How much longer can this go on? I'm just not interested.

You know there were some anthologies that came out, anti-story anthologies, where the editor tells you at the beginning that nothing's going to happen to these people. These people are not people. Nothing's going to happen in these stories. Nothing's going to change. The editors don't care about, the writers don't care about what they're doing. Anything can happen. Anything goes. Read these stories at your own risk. I don't know.

I wrote "Neighbors" in about 1970, or '71. In 1968, through a curious set of circumstances, I found myself in Tel Aviv, Israel, with my wife and children, and we had some neighbors who were going to be away for a week. They asked us if we would look after their apartment and feed the cat. And I remember I said sure. I remember walking into their apartment and shutting the door behind me. There were a lot of plants and things like that, and it was really kind of spooky because, when I shut the door, I knew that it was possible to do anything in there that I wanted to do.

I didn't write the story for some years. I was too caught up in the business of living and trying to stay alive and stay afloat. I went back to California and went to work for a publishing company. Then when I saw myself able to do some writing, I found I'd never forgotten that experience of walking into that room, and shutting the door behind me, and being able to do whatever I wanted to do. So then I made the story around that. Oftentimes this is the way I've written stories, long after the sparking thing has happened, quite a long time after the incident that might have sparked the story has happened.

You need some sort of encouragement. You need the world out there to give you some sign that they know that you're alive, and that they're taking part. This kept me alive during the 1960's—getting an occasional poem accepted in a magazine, getting an occasional short story accepted. Not getting them accepted in any of the big magazines but in the small magazines like *Akros, Western Humanities,* and *Carolina Quarterly.* This kept me going.

At one time, I just didn't have the heart or the time to do any writing. The only light at the end of the tunnel was an oncoming train. It's been a continual series of starting-overs for me. And I start over any number of times. I'm better disciplined now than I used to be. Not better disciplined, but I have more time to work now. The writing has become a way of life, and that wasn't always the case. I think it has something to do with my getting older, something to do with the fact that I think I'm getting better at what I do. I can see some results. Some things have, many things have happened, many good lessons. I've been lucky. I've also worked hard, but you have to.

It's heartbreaking to see somebody work hard and be obsessive about their writing, their work, and nothing happens. This is often the case with plenty of writers. After a while, they give up. They stop sending out their stories or their novels, or they're just not getting published. Almost as bad, something gets published, and the writer is bitter because it didn't put him at the top of the bestseller list. And he doesn't think he's getting as much attention as he deserves from the editors. It's a very easy thing to start trashing everybody. This is something that happens too. And there's nothing worse than a poet or fiction writer who's gone bitter. Worse things can happen than to write a novel and not have it published—writing a novel and having it published and then turning bitter and sour and thinking that the world has passed you by. I don't know, it's a good question. We could talk about it forever. It's hard.

I got my collection published because an editor was willing to go to the wall for the stories. He saw the stories and the manuscript and said, "We have to publish these." And they were published against serious objections from a few superiors. But they let him publish the stories. When the collection began to make them money, I became their fair-haired boy. They couldn't say enough good things about the book and about the editor. We were treated like the plague at the beginning. It can get squalid out there. It really can.

Every good thing that happens just makes me that much more anxious to get on with the work. It makes me write all the more, write all my heart out. The success that this last book had in terms of the number of copies it sold, in terms of the critical recognition it got, in terms of the money I made from the book, all those things just made me want to write more. And deadlines don't bother me. It's like working in harness in a way, and that's good. But I think that the discipline ought to be there whether you know you have a deadline or not, because you can get a deadline extended. For instance, I can get my deadline extended from the end of November to the first of March. But that's not entering into my way of thinking. I like to write stories.

And too, it must be said that my stories are changing now. I couldn't write those same stories again, for better or for worse. I think that's only natural. You can't write the same stories, you can't paint the same paintings, or compose the same music all your life. Again, I don't feel the changes taking place in my writing right now are something that I sat down in the morning and decided on. I didn't think that, "Well, now I'm going to change the way I write. My stories are going to have more affirmation now than they did five years ago." It's just happening.

I can't read anyone's story, a student's or a writer friend's, without a pencil. I assume that when someone says to me, "read this," and it's in manuscript form, that they're asking me to make it better, to make some suggestions if I can. I worked as an editor for a textbook publishing company for a number of years out in Palo Alto, California— earned my living there. So when I'm reading a manuscript, I'm reading it with a pencil. And I tell my students to take what suggestions they can use. If it feels right to you, do it. Nine times out of ten, a suggestion is worthwhile. The other times, if it doesn't feel right, stay away from it. Don't do it. Stick to your guns.

I just had an essay accepted for a book called *Influences* that Harper & Row is going to bring out next November or December, and the editor there, Ted Solotaroff, made a xerox of the essay and sent it back, telling me how enthusiastic they were about it. He asked me to look at the suggestions he had made, and if I found them acceptable he would make the changes. He gave a number of things here and there, and he was dead on. He was absolutely right. He really was. And of course I didn't say to him, "I can't make any changes in my prose." That's stupid. All he did was make a suggestion, and, gee, it was dead right. So of course I made those changes. He was right. That's what editors are for, good editors. And good editors are pretty rare.

There are editors who work in publishing houses who really shouldn't be allowed in the door. They don't know grammar. They don't know syntax. They wouldn't know good diction if they saw it. They wouldn't know the first thing about working with an author.

And then there are editors like Maxwell Perkins, who was Hemingway's editor, Thomas Wolfe's editor, and James Jones' editor. He was something of a genius. He didn't do the writing for Wolfe as Wolfe's detractors claim, but he made suggestions of things for Wolfe

to cut and so forth. Wolfe would come in with a trunk of manuscripts—5,000, 16,000 pages. And Perkins was very patient. He read
enough of the stuff to know that, "Well, here's something." So the
thing to do was to get some coherent form. He sat down with Wolfe
and started suggesting cuts. "Cut this. You know we don't need all
this rubbish in here. Cut this."

F. Scott Fitzgerald did the same thing for Hemingway with *The Sun
Also Rises*. Hemingway started the novel thirty pages before it
actually starts as it's published today. Those pages that Fitzgerald cut
for Hemingway were published about two or three years ago in
Antaeus. They were the first chapter of *The Sun Also Rises*, the lost
first chapter. Fitzgerald saw the book in manuscript, and he said,
"Gee, you're wrong here. It doesn't start here. It starts with Cohn,
with the boxing champion rather than with Princeton." Fitzgerald was
right on the money with the stuff he cut out.

Ezra Pound did the same thing with T. S. Eliot's *The Waste Land*.
As it stands now, it's less than half the length it was when Pound took
pencil to it. Pound was a born editor. He took vast liberties when he
was working in Europe and was European editor for *Poetry*
magazine, which comes out of Chicago. He would send over poems
from European writers, symbolists for instance, and if there was a
passage or stanza in the poem that he didn't understand—it wasn't
clear to him, or he didn't like it—he'd just cut it out. In some cases
he'd rewrite a section and make it better. I don't think I've ever heard
of anyone complaining about Pound. He helped W. B. Yeats with his
poems. He just sat down with Yeats and took a pencil to Yeats'
poems, said, "Look, William, straighten up here."

Editors can be very helpful. It can make it a lot easier if you've got
a good writing instructor or a good editor. Most often they can't write.
Sometimes they can. But they have a good eye.

I've had some suggestions that have been helpful. But I haven't
had all that many because usually by the time I let something go I'm
just so sick of it I can't work on it anymore. I've gone through and
taken out commas and put commas back in and things like that. Of
course, if someone comes along with a notion that would improve a
story of mine, I'd be happy to entertain that notion.

I was reading Flaubert's letters this spring, and once a week—
when he was writing outside of Paris at this country house that he

had—once a week a dear pal of his would come and visit him. All the people in Paris were clamoring for him to come and live where all the action was. And he said, "I don't want to live where all the action is. I couldn't really work." So he stayed out at this country house, and lived with his mother, and worked on *Madame Bovary*, which he thought he was going to be able to write in a year and which took him five years to write. But he'd get his week's writing done. And sometimes he'd only write a paragraph after working all day long. And then maybe he'd have a good week, and he'd get twenty pages done. And this friend of his would come out, and read what he had written, and act as his editor. And he'd say, "This needs to come out. This needs to be changed. This needs to be fixed." And even right before *Madame Bovary* went to press, this friend of Flaubert's said, "These thirty pages at the end of the book have got to come out." And Flaubert looked at it, agreed, and took those thirty pages out.

So take advice, if it's someone you trust, take any advice you can get. Make use of it. This is a farfetched analogy, but it's in a way like building a fantastic cathedral. The main thing is to get the work of art together. You don't know who built those cathedrals, but they're there.

Ezra Pound said, "It's immensely important that great poems be written, but makes not a jot of difference who writes them."

That's it. That's it exactly.

Raymond Carver: No Shortcuts to a Good Story

Jim Spencer/1982

From *The Virginian-Pilot* [Norfolk, VA], 1 October 1982, sec. B, 1, 9. Reprinted by permission of *The Virginian-Pilot* and *The Ledger-Star.* Conducted 29 September 1982.

On the wall beside his desk, Raymond Carver, the king of American short story writers, keeps posted several 3-by-5 index cards. They are filled with the wisdom of other authors, but serve to remind him of his task at hand. Printed on one is a quote from Ezra Pound that has become Carver's First Commandment: "Fundamental accuracy of statement is the ONE sole morality of writing." Printed on another is a sentence fragment from Anton Chekhov that suggests the end to which his considerable literary means strive: ". . . and suddenly everything became clear to him."

Make no mistake. Carver, who will lecture and read Thursday at the Fifth Annual Old Dominion University Literary Festival, doesn't operate with crystalline understanding of his subject matter. Nor is he likely to make great pronouncements in the course of a story. He is a teacher by example; not his own, but those of the characters he has created for more than a decade. They struggle through the tense and, occasionally, internecine social warfare of modern life, exposed most often for the instant of a single event. After 5,000 or so words they disappear and are replaced by someone else.

To say that they leave matters unsettled belabors the obvious. It also misses the point and the genius of a short story writer like Carver. At 44, his name is not a household word like Allen Ginsberg or Ken Kesey, who also will appear at the ODU festival, nor is it ever likely to be. Celebrity goes to revolutionary poets and novelists who inspire hit movies. Short story writers carve out small niches in the halls of academe. Carver has taught at the University of Iowa, the University of California and, for the last three years, at Syracuse University.

"When I started out my expectations were very low," he admitted

in a telephone interview Wednesday. "Being a short story writer or a
poet in this country is to leave yourself open to live in obscurity."

By that standard, his career has been immensely successful. His
collection of stories *Will You Please Be Quiet, Please?* was nominated
for the 1977 National Book Award for Fiction, an honor rarely be-
stowed on short story writers. His stories appear regularly in
anthologies and magazines. He has won the Best American Short
Story Award, and one of his pieces was included among the
O. Henry Awards' *Prize Stories of the Seventies.*

Still, at the mention of his name, most people respond, "Raymond
who?"

Carver writes as man or woman, sometimes in first person ("I'd
never met Bud's wife, but once I'd heard her voice over the phone"),
sometimes in third person ("He felt a sudden pain in his side,
imagined his heart, imagined his legs folding under him, imagined a
loud fall to the bottom of the stairs"). For lack of a better term, his
style is familiar—terse sentences, words repeated in the manner of
speech, not literature. "I try to write in the language we speak," he
said. "The language of human discourse. I may write a story 15 or 20
times before it's done. If the first draft is 40 pages, the story will likely
be 20 pages when it's finished. Art is made to seem effortless, but it
takes some work."

Dialogue plays a vital role in Carver's writing, with scenes played
out rather than described. Among those who influenced him were
Gordon Lish, former fiction editor at *Esquire* magazine, and novelist
John Gardner, with whom he studied at Chico State University in
California. Gardner died recently in a motorcycle accident, and
Carver eulogized him in a memorial service.

Carver's two children are grown. He is divorced and lives in a quiet
neighborhood not far from the Syracuse campus. He is not reclusive,
but neither does he depend totally upon his own experiences as the
sources for his stories. "I don't think I've ever written a story set in a
classroom," he said.

Instead, he employs a creative process made all the more remarkable by the variety of his work. The spore of his inspiration is
sometimes nothing more than a single sentence.

"The stories don't come out of nowhere," he said. "They have
reference points in real life, like spoken lines I overheard. For

instance, I once overheard someone say (to someone else), 'That's the last Christmas you'll ever ruin for us.' The line rattled around in my head for a while."

Eventually, he built a short story around it.

Another time, this phrase kept running through Carver's mind: "He was running the vacuum cleaner when the telephone rang." For several days he walked around thinking about it. Finally, he wrote it down. Then he wrote another line. Then another. And another. By the end of the day he had the first draft of a short story. "It was," he said, "like writing a poem."

At one time in his life, this kind of spontaneity made Carver wary. It smacked of a disorganization that he didn't associate with great art. It was only after he read about a similar phenomenon in Flannery O'Connor's essay, "Writing Short Stories," that he found himself in good company.

O'Connor said that writing is discovery, and if Carver is doing nothing else, he is discovering things. However, his revelations are startling only in relation to his characters—a man decides that the surprisingly pleasant dinner he had a few years before with a friend was the undoing of his marriage, a reluctant husband begins to understand his wife's blind friend by drawing a picture with his eyes closed.

Little lessons, not pontifications.

"I don't want to preach to anybody or for anybody," Carver said. "There may be great thoughts, but I just don't know anything else but to write as much as I can and as accurately as I can."

Lately, he has been more prolific than ever. Peruse the table of contents of *The New Yorker, The Atlantic* or *Harper's* and, like as not, in one of them there will be a story by Raymond Carver. In 1981, he published his second collection of short stories, *What We Talk About When We Talk About Love.* A third is scheduled for release in 1983.

"My stories are coming faster," he said. "I'm writing with more assurance and confidence than I did before, maybe because I'm older."

Or maybe because he has come to grips with what he is. A few years ago, Carver took a publisher's advance on a novel. He began to write it. Two weeks later he quit. "I just lost interest in it," he said.

"I may write a novel someday, but I have no pressure on me, because I'm successful as a short story writer."

Perhaps, then, he should tack another 3-by-5 aphorism to the wall beside his desk, this one a pearl of his own. "One good story," said Raymond Carver, "is worth a dozen bad novels."

As Raymond Carver Muses, His Stature Grows

Jim Naughton/1982

From the *Post-Standard* [Syracuse, NY], 23 November 1982,
sec. A, 1, 4. Reprinted by permission of Jim Naughton. Conducted November 1982.

When Raymond Carver was a boy he was walking to school with a
friend who got hit by a car. The boy wasn't hurt, but years later,
Carver wondered what if?

Several years ago Carver's telephone rang late at night. When he
answered, the caller hung up. Carver was not disturbed by the call,
but he wondered what if the call had come when he was upset about
something else?

Two years ago Carver turned the fruits of his wonderings into a
short story called "The Bath," which was published in *What We Talk
About When We Talk About Love,* a critically acclaimed collection
that was featured on the front page of *The New York Times Book
Review.*

Still, when he thought about the story, Carver wondered what if he
had written it differently?

During his Christmas vacation last year in early January, he sat
down to answer the question. When he finished the new version,
Carver remembers feeling "a rush" because he had written something special.

The story that emerged, "A Small, Good Thing," was recently
awarded first prize by the editor of *Prize Stories 1983: The O. Henry
Awards,* which will be published in April by Doubleday. The prize-
winning story is generally recognized as the best short story published
in the country in the previous year.

"A Small, Good Thing," which was published in the literary
magazine *Ploughshares* in the summer of 1982, deals with parents'
anguish after their child is hit by a car and later, mysteriously, dies.

Carver went back to the story because it was "unfinished
business."

"I wrote the story and I didn't go far enough with it," he said in his
office at Syracuse University Monday.

"I saw a place to stop it and I stopped it . . . but the notion of what could have happened stayed with me."

William Abrahams, who edited the collection and made the choice, said he feels the story marks a new direction in Carver's career.

"I think it's a magnificent story, deeply moving. I think it's one of the most impressive he's ever written.

"The original can't compare to this," he said. "The original seemed like the bare bones of a story he could have done.

"In this new version which must be at least twice the length, he's able to develop the people as people. All this has a terrific intensity."

Carver too feels his writing has taken a new turn. "I feel it is [a departure]," he said. "All those stories I wrote last winter are different.

"There is definitely a change going on in my writing and I'm glad of it. It happened when I wrote the story 'Cathedral.' I date the change from that story."

"Cathedral" has won a distinction of its own. It is the first story in *The Best American Short Stories 1982*, which was edited by Carver's friend, the late John Gardner.

"These stories are fuller, more generous somehow," Carver said of his recent work. "I hope without losing any of the other virtues."

He said the change occurred because: "I went as far as I wanted to go with reducing the stories to bare bones minimums."

Reducing stories to bare bones mininums is how Carver made his name as a fiction writer. His collection of stories *Will You Please Be Quiet, Please?* was nominated for the National Book Award in 1977.

"That put him on the map in terms of the general public," said Tobias Wolff, Carver's colleague in Syracuse University's Creative Writing Program. Wolff has had two of his own stories included in previous editions of the O. Henry collection.

"He has for at least 10 years now been considered one of its best practitioners by anyone who is aware of the state of the short story," he said.

Carver did not come easily to this eminence. He grew up in a working-class family in Yakima, Wash., married young and worked as a laborer. He was 19 when he met Gardner, then an unpublished writer teaching at Chico State College in California. Carver was sweeping floors to feed his young wife and their two children and writing on the side. In the early '60s Gardner gave him encouragement and the key to his office so he would have a place to write.

Carver published books of poetry in 1968 and 1970, struggling to support his family all the while. His marriage broke up after a trip to the Middle East in the early '70s, but it was around that point that his stories began to be noticed. *Esquire* bought a story called "Neighbors" and several others. He published another book of poetry and the critically acclaimed *Will You Please Be Quiet, Please?* in 1976. In the six years since then his popularity has increased dramatically.

The style that made Carver famous is best characterized by some words of his own taken from "The Bath." "No pleasantries, just this small exchange, the barest information, nothing that was not necessary."

This sparsely eloquent style became so well known in literary circles that Abrahams says he reads 10 to 15 stories a year by people who are trying to write like Raymond Carver.

Some critics have charged that Carver's work is too bare, that it is minimalistic. Wolff disagrees. "There is a tremendous richness, a music to his work. His work has the kind of music that Hemingway's had."

Abrahams, who felt things were "deliberately flattened out" in some of Carver's early work, said his recent stories have "taken him to a higher level of art."

For his efforts Carver joins writers like Hemingway, Fitzgerald, Faulkner, Sherwood Anderson, Ring Lardner, Katherine Anne Porter, Flannery O'Connor, Isaac Bashevis Singer and Joyce Carol Oates, as first-prize winners.

Abrahams makes an even headier comparison. "It reminds me of Chekhov to tell you the truth," he said.

Success has changed Raymond Carver's life, but not fundamentally. He still lives quietly on Maryland Avenue and teaches his writing classes at the university. He is on the road a bit more often.

"I'm busier at every level," he said. "But it hasn't changed the way I feel about myself or my family or my loved ones.

"I feel comfortable with my life. Not comfortable like a fat lazy cat, but comfortable, you know what I mean, comfortable being in my own skin."

Raymond Carver
Mona Simpson and Lewis Buzbee/1983

From *Writers at Work: The Paris Review Interviews*, Seventh Series, ed. George Plimpton (New York: Viking Press, 1986), 299-327. Copyright © 1986 by The Paris Review, Inc. All rights reserved. Reprinted by permission of Viking Penguin, Inc. This interview is a revised and expanded version of "The Art of Fiction LXXVI," by Mona Simpson, which appeared in *The Paris Review*, no. 88 (Summer 1983), 192-221. Conducted Winter 1983.

Raymond Carver lives in a large, two-story, wood-shingled house on a quiet street in Syracuse, New York. The front lawn slopes down to the sidewalk. A new Mercedes sits in the driveway. An older VW, the other household car, gets parked on the street.

The entrance to the house is through a large, screened-in porch. Inside, the furnishings are almost without character. Everything matches—cream-colored couches, a glass coffee table. Tess Gallagher, the writer with whom Raymond Carver lives, collects peacock feathers and sets them in vases throughout the house—the most noticeable decorative attempt. Our suspicions were confirmed: Carver told us that all the furniture was purchased and delivered in one day.

Gallagher has painted a detachable wood "No Visitors" sign, the lettering surrounded by yellow and orange eyelashes, which hangs on the screen door. Sometimes the phone is unplugged and the sign stays up for days at a time.

Carver works in a large room on the top floor. The surface of the long oak desk is clear; his typewriter is set to the side, on an L-shaped wing. There are no knickknacks, charms, or toys of any kind on Carver's desk. He is not a collector or a man prone to mementos and nostalgia. Occasionally, one manila folder lies on the oak desk, containing the story currently in the process of revision. His files are well in order. He can extract a story and all its previous versions at a moment's notice. The walls of the study are painted white like the rest of the house, and, like the rest of the house, they are mostly bare. Through a high rectangular window above Carver's desk, light filters into the room in slanted beams, like light from high church windows.

Carver is a large man who wears simple clothes—flannel shirts, khakis or jeans. He seems to live and dress as the characters in his stories live and dress. For someone of his size, he has a remarkably low and indistinct voice; we found ourselves bending closer every few minutes to catch his words and asking the irritating "What, what?"

Portions of the interview were conducted through the mail, during 1981-82. When we met Carver, the "No Visitors" sign was not up and several Syracuse students dropped by to visit during the course of the interview, including Carver's son, a senior. For lunch, Carver made us sandwiches with salmon he had caught off the coast of Washington. Both he and Gallagher are from Washington State and at the time of the interview, they were having a house built in Port Angeles, where they plan to live part of each year. We asked Carver if that house would feel more like a home to him. He replied, "No, wherever I am is fine. This is fine."

Interviewer: What was your early life like, and what made you want to write?

Carver: I grew up in a small town in eastern Washington, a place called Yakima. My dad worked at the sawmill there. He was a saw-filer and helped take care of the saws that were used to cut and plane the logs. My mother worked as a retail clerk or a waitress or else stayed at home, but she didn't keep any job for very long. I remember talk concerning her "nerves." In the cabinet under the kitchen sink, she kept a bottle of patent "nerve medicine," and she'd take a couple of tablespoons of this every morning. My dad's nerve medicine was whiskey. Most often he kept a bottle of it under that same sink, or else outside in the woodshed. I remember sneaking a taste of it once and hating it, and wondering how anybody could drink the stuff. Home was a little two-bedroom house. We moved a lot when I was a kid, but it was always into another little two-bedroom house. The first house I can remember living in, near the fairgrounds in Yakima, had an outdoor toilet. This was in the late 1940s. I was eight or ten years old then. I used to wait at the bus stop for my dad to come home from work. Usually he was as regular as clockwork. But every two weeks or so, he wouldn't be on the bus. I'd stick around then and wait for the next bus, but I already knew he wasn't going to be on that one, either. When this happened, it meant he'd gone drinking with friends of his from the sawmill. I still remember the sense of doom and hopelessness that hung over the supper table when my mother and I and my kid brother sat down to eat.

Interviewer: But what made you want to write?

Carver: The only explanation I can give you is that my dad told me lots of stories about himself when he was a kid, and about his dad and his grandfather. His grandfather had fought in the Civil War. He fought for both sides! He was a turncoat. When the South began losing the war, he crossed over to the North and began fighting for the Union forces. My dad laughed when he told this story. He didn't see anything wrong with it, and I guess I didn't either. Anyway, my dad would tell me stories, anecdotes really, no moral to them, about tramping around in the woods, or else riding the rails and having to look out for railroad bulls. I loved his company and loved to listen to him tell me these stories. Once in a while he'd read something to me from what he was reading. Zane Grey westerns. These were the first real hardback books, outside of grade-school texts, and the Bible, that I'd ever seen. It wouldn't happen very often, but now and again I'd see him lying on the bed of an evening and reading from Zane Grey. It seemed a very private act in a house and family that were not given to privacy. I realized that he had this private side to him, something I didn't understand or know anything about, but something that found expression through this occasional reading. I was interested in that side of him and interested in the act itself. I'd ask him to read me what he was reading, and he'd oblige by just reading from wherever he happened to be in the book. After a while he'd say, "Junior, go do something else now." Well, there were plenty of things to do. In those days, I went fishing in this creek that was not too far from our house. A little later, I started hunting ducks and geese and upland game. That's what excited me in those days, hunting and fishing. That's what made a dent in my emotional life, and that's what I wanted to write about. My reading fare in those days, aside from an occasional historical novel or Mickey Spillane mystery, consisted of *Sports Afield* and *Outdoor Life,* and *Field & Stream.* I wrote a longish thing about the fish that got away, or the fish I caught, one or the other, and asked my mother if she would type it up for me. She couldn't type, but she did go rent a typewriter, bless her heart, and between the two of us, we typed it up in some terrible fashion and sent it out. I remember there were two addresses on the masthead of the outdoors magazine; so we sent it to the office closest to us, to Boulder, Colorado, the circulation department. The piece came back, finally, but that was fine. It had gone out in the world, that manuscript—it had been places. Somebody had read it besides my mother, or so I hoped anyway. Then I saw an ad in *Writer's Digest*. It was a photograph of a man, a successful author, obviously, testifying to something called the Palmer Institute of Authorship. That seemed like just the thing for me. There was a monthly payment plan involved. Twenty dollars down, ten or fifteen dollars a month for three years or thirty years, one of those things. There were weekly assignments with personal responses to the assignments. I stayed with it for a few months. Then, maybe I got bored; I stopped doing the work. My folks stopped making the payments. Pretty soon a letter arrived from the Palmer Institute telling me that if I paid them up in full, I could still get the certificate of completion. This seemed more than fair. Somehow I talked my folks into paying the rest of the money, and in due time I got the certificate and hung it up on my bedroom wall. But all through high school it was assumed that I'd graduate and go to work at the sawmill. For a long time I wanted to do the kind of work my dad did. He was going to ask his foreman at the mill to put me on after I graduated. So I worked at the mill for about six months. But I hated the work and knew from the first day I didn't want to do that for the rest of my life. I worked long enough to save the money for a car, buy some clothes, and so I could move out and get married.

Interviewer: Somehow, for whatever reasons, you went to college. Was it your wife who wanted you to go on to college? Did she encourage you in this respect? Did she want to go to college and that made you want to go? How old were you at this point? She must have been pretty young, too.

Carver: I was eighteen. She was sixteen and pregnant and had just graduated from an Episcopalian private school for girls in Walla Walla, Washington. At school she'd learned the right way to hold a teacup; she'd had religious instruction and gym and such, but she also learned about physics and literature and foreign languages. I was terrifically impressed that she knew Latin. Latin! She tried off and on to go to college during those first years, but it was too hard to do that; it was impossible to do that and raise a family and be broke all the time, too. I mean broke. Her family didn't have any money. She was going to that school on a scholarship. Her mother hated me and still does. My wife was supposed to graduate and go on to the University of Washington to study law on a fellowship. Instead, I made her pregnant, and we got married and began our life together. She was seventeen when the first child was born, eighteen when the second was born. What shall I say at this point? We didn't have any youth. We found ourselves in roles we didn't know how to play. But we did the best we could. Better than that, I want to think. She did finish college finally. She got her B.A. degree at San Jose State twelve or fourteen years after we married.

Interviewer: Were you writing during these early, difficult years?

Carver: I worked nights and went to school days. We were always working. She was working and trying to raise the kids and manage a household. She worked for the telephone company. The kids were with a babysitter during the day. Finally, I graduated with the B.A. degree from Humboldt State College and we put everything into the car and in one of those carryalls that fits on top of your car, and we went to Iowa City. A teacher named Dick Day at Humboldt State had told me about the Iowa Writers' Workshop. Day had sent along a story of mine and three or four poems to Don Justice, who was responsible for getting me a five-hundred-dollar grant at Iowa.

Interviewer: Five hundred dollars?

Carver: That's all they had, they said. It seemed like a lot at the time. But I didn't finish at Iowa. They offered me more money to stay on the second year, but we just couldn't do it. I was working in the library for a dollar or two an hour, and my wife was working as a waitress. It was going to take me another year to get a degree, and we just couldn't stick it out. So we moved back to California. This time it was Sacramento. I found work as a night janitor at Mercy Hospital. I kept the job for three years. It was a pretty good job. I only had to work two or three hours a night, but I was paid for eight hours. There was a certain amount of work that had to get done, but once it was done, that was it—I could go home or do anything I wanted. The first year or two I went home every night and would be in bed at a reasonable hour and be able to get up in the morning and write. The kids would be off at the babysitter's and my wife would have gone to her job—a door-to-door sales job. I'd have all day in front of me. This was fine for a while. Then I began getting off work at night and going drinking instead of going home. By this time it was 1967 or 1968.

Interviewer: When did you first get published?

Carver: When I was an undergraduate at Humboldt State in Arcata, California. One day, I had a short story taken at one magazine and a poem taken at another. It was a terrific day! Maybe one of the best days ever. My wife and I drove around town and showed the letters of acceptance to all of our friends. It gave some much-needed validation to our lives.

Interviewer: What was the first story you ever published? And the first poem?

Carver: It was a story called "Pastoral" and it was published in the *Western Humanities Review.* It's a good literary magazine and it's still being published by the University of Utah. They didn't pay me anything for the story, but that didn't matter. The poem was called "The Brass Ring," and it was published by a magazine in Arizona, now defunct, called *Targets.* Charles Bukowski had a poem in the same issue, and I was pleased to be in the same magazine with him. He was a kind of hero to me then.

Interviewer: Is it true—a friend of yours told me this—that you celebrated your first publication by taking the magazine to bed with you?

Carver: That's partly true. Actually, it was a book, the *Best American Short Stories* annual. My story "Will You Please Be Quiet, Please?" had just appeared in the collection. That was back in the late sixties, when it was edited every year by Martha Foley and people used to call it that—simply, "The Foley Collection." The story had been published in an obscure little magazine out of Chicago called *December.* The day the anthology came in the mail I took it to bed to read and just to look at, you know, and hold it, but I did more looking and holding than actual reading. I fell asleep and woke up the next morning with the book there in bed beside me, along with my wife.

Interviewer: In an article you did for *The New York Times Book*

Review you mentioned a story "too tedious to talk about here"—
about why you choose to write short stories over novels. Do you
want to go into that story now?

Carver: The story that was "too tedious to talk about" has to do
with a number of things that aren't very pleasant to talk about. I did
finally talk about some of these things in the essay "Fires," which was
published in *Antaeus*. In it I said that finally, a writer is judged by
what he writes, and that's the way it should be. The circumstances
surrounding the writing are something else, something extraliterary.
Nobody ever asked me to be a writer. But it *was* tough to stay alive
and pay bills and put food on the table and at the same time to think
of myself as a writer and to *learn* to write. After years of working crap
jobs and raising kids and trying to write, I realized I needed to write
things I could finish and be done with in a hurry. There was no way I
could undertake a novel, a two- or three-year stretch of work on a
single project. I needed to write something I could get some kind of a
payoff from immediately, not next year, or three years from now.
Hence, poems and stories. I was beginning to see that my life was
not—let's say it was not what I wanted it to be. There was always a
wagonload of frustration to deal with—wanting to write and not being
able to find the time or the place for it. I used to go out and sit in the
car and try to write something on a pad on my knee. This was when
the kids were in their adolescence. I was in my late twenties or early
thirties. We were still in a state of penury, we had one bankruptcy
behind us, and years of hard work with nothing to show for it except
an old car, a rented house, and new creditors on our backs. It was
depressing, and I felt spiritually obliterated. Alcohol became a
problem. I more or less gave up, threw in the towel, and took to full-
time drinking as a serious pursuit. That's part of what I was talking
about when I was talking about things "too tedious to talk about."

Interviewer: Could you talk a little more about the drinking? So
many writers, even if they're not alcoholics, drink so much.

Carver: Probably not a whole lot more than any other group of
professionals. You'd be surprised. Of course there's a mythology that
goes along with the drinking, but I was never into that. I was into the
drinking itself. I suppose I began to drink heavily after I'd realized that
the things I'd wanted most in life for myself and my writing, and my
wife and children, were simply not going to happen. It's strange. You

never start out in life with the intention of becoming a bankrupt or an alcoholic or a cheat and a thief. Or a liar.

Interviewer: And you were all those things?

Carver: I was. I'm not any longer. Oh, I lie a little from time to time, like everyone else.

Interviewer: How long since you quit drinking?

Carver: June second, 1977. If you want the truth, I'm prouder of that, that I've quit drinking, than I am of anything in my life. I'm a recovered alcoholic. I'll always be an alcoholic, but I'm no longer a practicing alcoholic.

Interviewer: How bad did the drinking get?

Carver: It's very painful to think about some of the things that happened back then. I made a wasteland out of everything I touched. But I might add that towards the end of the drinking there wasn't much left anyway. But specific things? Let's just say, on occasion, the police were involved and emergency rooms and courtrooms.

Interviewer: How did you stop? What made you able to stop?

Carver: The last year of my drinking, 1977, I was in a recovery center twice, as well as one hospital; and I spent a few days in a place called DeWitt near San Jose, California. DeWitt used to be, appropriately enough, a hospital for the criminally insane. Toward the end of my drinking career I was completely out of control and in a very grave place. Blackouts, the whole business—points where you can't remember anything you say or do during a certain period of time. You might drive a car, give a reading, teach a class, set a broken leg, go to bed with someone, and not have any memory of it later. You're on some kind of automatic pilot. I have an image of myself sitting in my living room with a glass of whiskey in my hand and my head bandaged from a fall caused by an alcoholic seizure. Crazy! Two weeks later I was back in a recovery center, this time at a place called Duffy's, in Calistoga, California, up in the wine country. I was at Duffy's on two different occasions; in the place called DeWitt, in San Jose; and in a hospital in San Francisco—all in the space of twelve months. I guess that's pretty bad. I was dying from it, plain and simple, and I'm not exaggerating.

Interviewer: What brought you to the point where you could stop drinking for good?

Carver: It was late May 1977. I was living by myself in a house in a little town in northern California, and I'd been sober for about three weeks. I drove to San Francisco, where they were having this publishers' convention. Fred Hills, at that time editor-in-chief at McGraw-Hill, wanted to take me to lunch and offer me money to write a novel. But a couple of nights before the lunch, one of my friends had a party. Midway through, I picked up a glass of wine and drank it, and that's the last thing I remember. Blackout time. The next morning when the stores opened, I was waiting to buy a bottle. The dinner that night was a disaster; it was terrible, people quarreling and disappearing from the table. And the next morning I had to get up and go have this lunch with Fred Hills. I was so hung over when I woke up I could hardly hold my head up. But I drank a half pint of vodka before I picked up Hills and that helped, for the short run. And then he wanted to drive over to Sausalito for lunch! That took us at least an hour in heavy traffic, and I was drunk and hung over both, you understand. But for some reason he went ahead and offered me this money to write a novel.

Interviewer: Did you ever write the novel?

Carver: Not yet! Anyway, I managed to get out of San Francisco back up to where I lived. I stayed drunk for a couple more days. And then I woke up, feeling terrible, but I didn't drink anything that morning. Nothing alcoholic, I mean. I felt terrible physically—mentally, too, of course—but I didn't drink anything. I didn't drink for three days, and when the third day had passed, I began to feel some better. Then I just kept not drinking. Gradually I began to put a little distance between myself and the booze. A week. Two weeks. Suddenly it was a month. I'd been sober for a month, and I was slowly starting to get well.

Interviewer: Did AA help?

Carver: It helped a lot. I went to at least one and sometimes two meetings a day for the first month.

Interviewer: Did you ever feel that alcohol was in any way an inspiration? I'm thinking of your poem "Cheers," published in *Esquire.*

Carver: My God, no! I hope I've made that clear. Cheever remarked that he could always recognize "an alcoholic line" in a writer's work. I'm not exactly sure what he meant by this but I think I know. When we were teaching in the Iowa Writers' Workshop in the fall semester of 1973, he and I did nothing *but* drink. I mean we met our classes, in a manner of speaking. But the entire time we were there—we were living in this hotel they have on campus, the Iowa House—I don't think either of us ever took the covers off our typewriters. We made trips to a liquor store twice a week in my car.

Interviewer: To stock up?

Carver: Yes, stock up. But the store didn't open until ten A.M. Once we planned an early morning run, a ten o'clock run, and we were going to meet in the lobby of the hotel. I came down early to get some cigarettes and John was pacing up and down in the lobby. He was wearing loafers, but he didn't have any socks on. Anyway, we headed out a little early. By the time we got to the liquor store the clerk was just unlocking the front door. On this particular morning, John got out of the car before I could get it properly parked. By the time I got inside the store he was already at the checkout stand with a half gallon of Scotch. He lived on the fourth floor of the hotel and I lived on the second. Our rooms were identical, right down to the same reproduction of the same painting hanging on the wall. But when we drank together, we always drank in his room. He said he was afraid to come down to drink on the second floor. He said there was always a chance of him getting mugged in the hallway! But you know, of course, that fortunately, not too long after Cheever left Iowa City, he went to a treatment center and got sober and stayed sober until he died.

Interviewer: Do you feel the spoken confessions at Alcoholics Anonymous meetings have influenced your writing?

Carver: There are different kinds of meetings—speaker meetings where just one speaker will get up and talk for fifty minutes or so about what it was like then, and maybe what it's like now. And there are meetings where everyone in the room has a chance to say something. But I can't honestly say I've ever consciously or otherwise patterned any of my stories on things I've heard at the meetings.

Interviewer: Where do your stories come from, then? I'm especially asking about the stories that have something to do with drinking.

Carver: The fiction I'm most interested in has lines of reference to the real world. None of my stories really *happened,* of course. But there's always something, some element, something said to me or that I witnessed, that may be the starting place. Here's an example: "That's the last Christmas you'll ever ruin for us!" I was drunk when I heard that, but I remembered it. And later, much later, when I was sober, using only that one line and other things I imagined, imagined so accurately that they *could* have happened, I made a story—"A Serious Talk." But the fiction I'm most interested in, whether it's Tolstoy's fiction, Chekhov, Barry Hannah, Richard Ford, Hemingway, Isaac Babel, Ann Beattie, or Anne Tyler, strikes me as autobiographical to some extent. At the very least it's referential. Stories long or short don't just come out of thin air. I'm reminded of a conversation involving John Cheever. We were sitting around a table in Iowa City with some people and he happened to remark that after a family fracas at his home one night, he got up the next morning and went into the bathroom to find something his daughter had written in lipstick on the bathroom mirror: "D-e-r-e daddy, don't leave us." Someone at the table spoke up and said, "I recognize that from one of your stories." Cheever said, "Probably so. Everything I write is autobiographical." Now of course that's not literally true. But everything we write is, in some way, autobiographical. I'm not in the least bothered by "autobiographical" fiction. To the contrary. *On the Road.* Céline. Roth. Lawrence Durrell in *The Alexandria Quartet.* So much of Hemingway in the Nick Adams stories. Updike, too, you bet. Jim McConkey. Clark Blaise is a contemporary writer whose fiction is out-and-out autobiography. Of course, you have to know what you're doing when you turn your life's stories into fiction. You have to be immensely daring, very skilled and imaginative and willing to tell everything on yourself. You're told time and again when you're young to write about what you know, and what do you know better than your own secrets? But unless you're a special kind of writer, and a very talented one, it's dangerous to try and write volume after volume on The Story of My Life. A great danger, or at least a great temptation, for many writers is to become too autobiographical in their approach to their fiction. A little autobiography and a lot of imagination are best.

Interviewer: Are your characters trying to do what matters?

Carver: I think they are trying. But trying and succeeding are two different matters. In some lives, people always succeed; and I think it's grand when that happens. In other lives, people don't succeed at what they try to do, at the things they want most to do, the large or small things that support the life. These lives are, of course, valid to write about, the lives of the people who don't succeed. Most of my own experience, direct or indirect, has to do with the latter situation. I think most of my characters would like their actions to count for something. But at the same time they've reached the point—as so many people do—that they know it isn't so. It doesn't add up any longer. The things you once thought important or even worth dying for aren't worth a nickel now. It's their lives they've become uncomfortable with, lives they see breaking down. They'd like to set things right, but they can't. And usually they do know it, I think, and after that they just do the best they can.

Interviewer: Could you say something about one of my favorite stories in your most recent collection? Where did the idea for "Why Don't You Dance?" originate?

Carver: I was visiting some writer friends in Missoula back in the mid-1970s. We were all sitting around drinking and someone told a story about a barmaid named Linda who got drunk with her boyfriend one night and decided to move all of her bedroom furnishings into the backyard. They did it, too, right down to the carpet and the bedroom lamp, the bed, the nightstand, everything. There were about four or five writers in the room, and after the guy finished telling the story, someone said, "Well, who's going to write it?" I don't know who else might have written it, but I wrote it. Not then, but later. About four or five years later, I think. I changed and added things to it, of course. Actually, it was the first story I wrote after I finally stopped drinking.

Interviewer: What are your writing habits like? Are you always working on a story?

Carver: When I'm writing, I write every day. It's lovely when that's happening. One day dovetailing into the next. Sometimes I don't even know what day of the week it is. The "paddle-wheel of days," John Ashbery has called it. When I'm not writing, like now, when I'm tied up with teaching duties as I have been the last while, it's as if I've never written a word or had any desire to write. I fall into bad habits. I stay up too late and sleep in too long. But it's okay. I've learned to be patient and to bide my time. I had to learn that a long time ago.

Patience. If I believed in signs, I suppose my sign would be the sign of the turtle. I write in fits and starts. But when I'm writing, I put in a lot of hours at the desk, ten or twelve or fifteen hours at a stretch, day after day. I love that, when that's happening. Much of this work time, understand, is given over to revising and rewriting. There's not much that I like better than to take a story that I've had around the house for a while and work it over again. It's the same with the poems I write. I'm in no hurry to send something off just after I write it, and I sometimes keep it around the house for months doing this or that to it, taking this out and putting that in. It doesn't take that long to do the first draft of the story, that usually happens in one sitting, but it does take a while to do the various versions of the story. I've done as many as twenty or thirty drafts of a story. Never less than ten or twelve drafts. It's instructive, and heartening both, to look at the early drafts of great writers. I'm thinking of the photographs of galleys belonging to Tolstoy, to name one writer who loved to revise. I mean, I don't know if he loved it or not, but he did a great deal of it. He was always revising, right down to the time of page proofs. He went through and rewrote *War and Peace* eight times and was still making corrections in the galleys. Things like this should hearten every writer whose first drafts are dreadful, like mine are.

Interviewer: Describe what happens when you write a story.

Carver: I write the first draft quickly, as I said. This is most often done in longhand. I simply fill up the pages as rapidly as I can. In some cases, there's a kind of personal shorthand, notes to myself for what I will do later when I come back to it. Some scenes I have to leave unfinished, unwritten in some cases; the scenes that will require meticulous care later. I mean all of it requires meticulous care—but some scenes I save until the second or third draft, because to do them and do them right would take too much time on the first draft. With the first draft it's a question of getting down the outline, the scaffolding of the story. Then on subsequent revisions I'll see to the rest of it. When I've finished the longhand draft I'll type a version of the story and go from there. It always looks different to me, better, of course, after it's typed up. When I'm typing the first draft, I'll begin to rewrite and add and delete a little then. The real work comes later, after I've done three or four drafts of the story. It's the same with the poems, only the poems may go through forty or fifty drafts. Donald

Hall told me he sometimes writes a hundred or so drafts of his
poems. Can you imagine?

Interviewer: Has your way of working changed?

Carver: The stories in *What We Talk About* are different to an
extent. For one thing, it's a much more self-conscious book in the
sense of how intentional every move was, how calculated. I pushed
and pulled and worked with those stories before they went into the
book to an extent I'd never done with any other stories. When the
book was put together and in the hands of my publisher, I didn't
write anything at all for six months. And then the first story I wrote
was "Cathedral," which I feel is totally different in conception and
execution from any stories that have come before. I suppose it
reflects a change in my life as much as it does in my way of writing.
When I wrote "Cathedral" I experienced this rush and I felt, "This is
what it's all about, this is the reason we do this." It was different than
the stories that had come before. There was an opening up when I
wrote the story. I knew I'd gone as far the other way as I could or
wanted to go, cutting everything down to the marrow, not just to the
bone. Any farther in that direction and I'd be at a dead end—writing
stuff and publishing stuff I wouldn't want to read myself, and that's
the truth. In a review of the last book, somebody called me a
"minimalist" writer. The reviewer meant it as a compliment. But I
didn't like it. There's something about "minimalist" that smacks of
smallness of vision and execution that I don't like. But all of the
stories in the new book, the one called *Cathedral,* were written within
an eighteen-month period; and in every one of them I feel this
difference.

Interviewer: Do you have any sense of an audience? Updike
described his ideal reader as a young boy in a small midwestern town
finding one of his books on a library shelf.

Carver: It's nice to think of Updike's idealized reader. But except
for the early stories, I don't think it's a young boy in a small midwestern town who's reading Updike. What would this young boy
make of *The Centaur* or *Couples* or *Rabbit Redux* or *The Coup?* I
think Updike is writing for the audience that John Cheever said he
was writing for, "intelligent, adult men and women," wherever they
live. Any writer worth his salt writes as well and as truly as he can and
hopes for as large and perceptive a readership as possible. So you

write as well as you can and hope for good readers. But I think you're also writing for other writers to an extent—the dead writers whose work you admire, as well as the living writers you like to read. If they like it, the other writers, there's a good chance other "intelligent, adult men and women" may like it, too. But I don't have that boy you mentioned in mind, or anyone else for that matter, when I'm doing the writing itself.

Interviewer: How much of what you write do you finally throw away?

Carver: Lots. If the first draft of the story is forty pages long, it'll usually be half that by the time I'm finished with it. And it's not just a question of taking out or bringing it down. I take out a lot, but I also add things and then add some more and take out some more. It's something I love to do, putting words in and taking words out.

Interviewer: Has the process of revision changed now that the stories seem to be longer and more generous?

Carver: Generous, yes, that's a good word for them. Yes, and I'll tell you why. Up at school there's a typist who has one of those space-age typewriters, a word processor, and I can give her a story to type and once she has it typed and I get back the fair copy, I can mark it up to my heart's content and give it back to her; and the next day I can have my story back, all fair copy once more. Then I can mark it up again as much as I want, and the next day I'll have back a fair copy once more. I love it. It may seem like a small thing, really, but it's changed my life, that woman and her word processor.

Interviewer: Did you ever have any time off from having to earn a living?

Carver: I had a year once. It was a very important year for me, too. I wrote most of the stories in *Will You Please Be Quiet, Please?* in that year. It was back in 1970 or 1971. I was working for this textbook publishing firm in Palo Alto. It was my first white-collar job, right after the period when I'd been a janitor at the hospital in Sacramento. I'd been working away there quietly as an editor when the company, it was called SRA, decided to do a major reorganization. I planned to quit, I was writing my letter of resignation, but then suddenly—I was fired. It was just wonderful the way it turned out. We invited all of our friends that weekend and had a firing party! For a year I didn't have to work. I drew unemployment and had my severance pay to live on. And that's the period when my wife finished her college degree. That was a turning point, that time. It was a good period.

Interviewer: Are you religious?

Carver: No, but I have to believe in miracles and the possibility of resurrection. No question about that. Every day that I wake up, I'm glad to wake up. That's why I like to wake up early. In my drinking days I would sleep until noon or whatever and I would usually wake up with the shakes.

Interviewer: Do you regret a lot of things that happened back then when things were so bad?

Carver: I can't change anything now. I can't afford to regret. That life is simply gone now, and I can't regret its passing. I have to live in the present. The life back then is gone just as surely—it's as remote to me as if it had happened to somebody I read about in a nineteenth-century novel. I don't spend more than five minutes a month in the past. The past really *is* a foreign country, and they do do things differently there. Things happen. I really do feel I've had two different lives.

Interviewer: Can you talk a little about literary influences, or at least name some writers whose work you greatly admire?

Carver: Ernest Hemingway is one. The early stories. "Big Two-Hearted River," "Cat in the Rain," "The Three-Day Blow," "Soldier's Home," lots more. Chekhov. I suppose he's the writer whose work I most admire. But who doesn't like Chekhov? I'm talking about his stories now, not the plays. His plays move too slowly for me. Tolstoy. Any of his short stories, novellas, and *Anna Karenina*. Not *War and Peace*. Too slow. But *The Death of Ivan Ilyich, Master and Man*, "How Much Land Does a Man Need?" Tolstoy is the best there is. Isaac Babel, Flannery O'Connor, Frank O'Connor. James Joyce's *Dubliners*. John Cheever. *Madame Bovary*. Last year I reread that book, along with a new translation of Flaubert's letters written while he was composing—no other word for it—*Madame Bovary*. Conrad. Updike's *Too Far to Go*. And there are wonderful writers I've come across in the last year or two like Tobias Wolff. His book of stories *In the Garden of the North American Martyrs* is just wonderful. Max Schott. Bobbie Ann Mason. Did I mention her? Well, she's good and worth mentioning twice. Harold Pinter. V. S. Pritchett. Years ago I read something in a letter by Chekhov that impressed me. It was a piece of advice to one of his many correspondents, and it went something like this: Friend, you don't have to write about extraordinary people who accomplish extraordinary and memorable deeds. (Understand I was in college at the time and reading plays about princes and dukes and the overthrow of kingdoms. Quests and the like, large undertakings to establish heroes in their rightful places. Novels with larger-than-life heroes.) But reading what Chekhov had to say in that letter, and in other letters of his as well, and reading his stories, made me see things differently than I had before. Not long afterwards I read a play and a number of stories by Maxim Gorky, and he simply reinforced in his work what Chekhov had to say. Richard Ford is another fine writer. He's primarily a novelist, but he's also written stories and essays. He's a friend. I have a lot of friends who are good friends, and some of them are good writers. Some not so good.

Interviewer: What do you do in that case? I mean, how do you handle that—if one of your friends publishes something you don't like?

Carver: I don't say anything unless the friend asks me, and I hope he doesn't. But if you're asked you have to say it in a way that it doesn't wreck the friendship. You want your friends to do well and write the best they can. But sometimes their work is a disappointment. You want everything to go well for them, but you have this dread that maybe it won't and there's not much you can do.

Interviewer: What do you think of moral fiction? I guess this has to lead into talk about John Gardner and his influence on you. I know you were his student many years ago at Chico State College.

Carver: That's true. I've written about our relationship in the *Antaeus* piece and elaborated on it more in my introduction to a posthumous book of his called *On Becoming a Novelist.* I think *On Moral Fiction* is a wonderfully smart book. I don't agree with all of it, by any means, but generally he's right. Not so much in his assessments of living writers as in the aims, the aspirations of the book. It's a book that wants to affirm life rather than trash it. Gardner's definition of morality is life-affirming. And in that regard he believes good fiction is moral fiction. It's a book to argue with, if you like to argue. It's brilliant, in any case. I think he may argue his case even better in *On Becoming a Novelist*. And he doesn't go after other writers as he did in *On Moral Fiction*. We had been out of touch with each other for years when he published *On Moral Fiction,* but his influence, the things he stood for in my life when I was his student, were still so strong that for a long while I didn't want to read the book. I was afraid to find out that what I'd been writing all these years was immoral! You understand that we'd not seen each other for nearly twenty years and had only renewed our friendship after I'd moved to Syracuse and he was down there at Binghamton, seventy miles away. There was a lot of anger directed toward Gardner and the book when it was published. He touched nerves. I happen to think it's a remarkable piece of work.

Interviewer: But after you read the book, what did you think then about your own work? Were you writing "moral" or "immoral" stories?

Carver: I'm still not sure! But I heard from other people, and then he told me himself, that he liked my work. Especially the new work. That pleases me a great deal. Read *On Becoming a Novelist*.

Interviewer: Do you still write poetry?

Carver: Some, but not enough. I want to write more. If too long a period of time goes by, six months or so, I get nervous if I haven't written any poems. I find myself wondering if I've stopped being a poet or stopped being able to write poetry. It's usually then that I sit down and try to write some poems. This book of mine that's coming in the spring, *Fires*—that's got all of the poems of mine I want to keep.

Interviewer: How do they influence each other? The writing of fiction and the writing of poetry?

Carver: They don't any longer. For a long time I was equally interested in the writing of poetry and the writing of fiction. In magazines I always turned to the poems first before I read the stories. Finally, I had to make a choice, and I came down on the side of the fiction. It was the right choice for me. I'm not a "born" poet. I don't know if I'm a "born" anything except a white American male. Maybe I'll become an occasional poet. But I'll settle for that. That's better than not being any kind of poet at all.

Interviewer: How has fame changed you?

Carver: I feel uncomfortable with that word. You see, I started out with such low expectations in the first place—I mean, how far are you going to get in this life writing short stories? And I didn't have much self-esteem as a result of this drinking thing. So it's a continual amazement to me, this attention that's come along. But I can tell you that after the reception for *What We Talk About,* I felt a confidence that I've never felt before. Every good thing that's happened since has conjoined to make me want to do even more and better work. It's been a good spur. And all this is coming at a time in my life when I have more strength than I've ever had before. Do you know what I'm saying? I feel stronger and more certain of my direction now than ever before. So "fame"—or let's say this newfound attention and interest—has been a good thing. It bolstered my confidence, when my confidence needed bolstering.

Interviewer: Who reads your writing first?

Carver: Tess Gallagher. As you know, she's a poet and short-story writer herself. I show her everything I write except for letters, and I've even shown her a few of those. But she has a wonderful eye and a way of feeling herself into what I write. I don't show her anything until I've marked it up and taken it as far as I can. That's usually the fourth or fifth draft, and then she reads every subsequent draft thereafter. So far I've dedicated three books to her and those dedications are not just a token of love and affection; they also indicate the high esteem in which I hold her and an acknowledgment of the help and inspiration she's given me.

Interviewer: Where does Gordon Lish enter into this? I know he's your editor at Knopf.

Carver: Just as he was the editor who began publishing my stories at *Esquire* back in the early 1970s. But we had a friendship that went back before that time, back to 1967 or 1968, in Palo Alto. He was working for a textbook publishing firm right across the street from the firm where I worked. The one that fired me. He didn't keep any regular office hours. He did most of his work for the company at home. At least once a week he'd ask me over to his place for lunch. He wouldn't eat anything himself, he'd just cook something for me and then hover around the table watching me eat. It made me nervous, as you might imagine. I'd always wind up leaving something on my plate, and he'd always wind up eating it. Said it had to do with the way he was brought up. This is not an isolated example. He still does things like that. He'll take me to lunch now and won't order anything for himself except a drink and then he'll eat up whatever I leave in my plate! I saw him do it once in the Russian Tea Room. There were four of us for dinner, and after the food came he watched us eat. When he saw we were going to leave food on our plates, he cleaned it right up. Aside from this craziness, which is more funny than anything, he's remarkably smart and sensitive to the needs of a manuscript. He's a good editor. Maybe he's a great editor. All I know for sure is that he's my editor and my friend, and I'm glad on both counts.

Interviewer: Would you consider doing more movie script work?

Carver: If the subject could be as interesting as this one I just finished with Michael Cimino on the life of Dostoevsky, yes, of course. Otherwise, no. But Dostoevsky! You bet I would.

Interviewer: And there was real money involved.

Carver: Yes.

Interviewer: That accounts for the Mercedes.

Carver: That's it.

Interviewer: What about *The New Yorker?* Did you ever send your stories to *The New Yorker* when you were first starting out?

Carver: No, I didn't. I didn't read *The New Yorker.* I sent my stories and poems to the little magazines and once in a while something was accepted, and I was made happy by the acceptance. I had some kind of audience, you see, even though I never met any of my audience.

Interviewer: Do you get letters from people who've read your work?

Carver: Letters, tapes, sometimes photographs. Somebody just sent me a cassette—songs that had been made out of some of the stories.

Interviewer: Do you write better on the West Coast—out in Washington—or here in the East? I guess I'm asking how important a sense of place is to your work.

Carver: Once, it was important to see myself as a writer from a particular place. It was important for me to be a writer from the West. But that's not true any longer, for better or worse. I think I've moved around too much, lived in too many places, felt dislocated and displaced, to now have any firmly rooted sense of "place." If I've ever gone about consciously locating a story in a particular place and period, and I guess I have, especially in the first book, I suppose that place would be the Pacific Northwest. I admire the sense of place in such writers as Jim Welch, Wallace Stegner, John Keeble, William Eastlake, and William Kittredge. There are plenty of good writers with this sense of place you're talking about. But the majority of my stories are not set in any specific locale. I mean, they could take place in just about any city or urban area; here in Syracuse, but also Tucson, Sacramento, San Jose, San Francisco, Seattle, or Port Angeles, Washington. In any case, most of my stories are set indoors!

Interviewer: Do you work in a particular place in your house?

Carver: Yes, upstairs in my study. It's important to me to have my own place. Lots of days go by when we just unplug the telephone and put out our "No Visitors" sign. For many years I worked at the kitchen table, or in a library carrel, or else out in my car. This room of my own is a luxury *and* a necessity now.

Interviewer: Do you still hunt and fish?

Carver: Not so much anymore. I still fish a little, fish for salmon in the summer, if I'm out in Washington. But I don't hunt, I'm sorry to say. I don't know where to go! I guess I could find someone who'd take me, but I just haven't gotten around to it. But my friend Richard Ford is a hunter. When he was up here in the spring of 1981 to give a reading from his work, he took the proceeds from his reading and bought me a shotgun. Imagine that! And he had it inscribed, "For Raymond from Richard, April 1981." Richard is a hunter, you see, and I think he was trying to encourage me.

Interviewer: How do you hope your stories will affect people? Do you think your writing will change anybody?

Carver: I really don't know. I doubt it. Not change in any profound sense. Maybe not any change at all. After all, art is a form of enter-tainment, yes? For both the maker and the consumer. I mean in a way it's like shooting billiards or playing cards, or bowling—it's just a different, and I would say higher, form of amusement. I'm not saying there isn't spiritual nourishment involved, too. There is, of course. Listening to a Beethoven concerto or spending time in front of a van Gogh painting or reading a poem by Blake can be a profound experience on a scale that playing bridge or bowling a 220 game can never be. Art is all the things art is supposed to be. But art is also a superior amusement. Am I wrong in thinking this? I don't know. But I remember in my twenties reading plays by Strindberg, a novel by Max Frisch, Rilke's poetry, listening all night to music by Bartók, watching a TV special on the Sistine Chapel and Michelangelo and feeling in each case that my life *had* to change after these experiences, it couldn't help but be affected by these experiences and *changed*. There was simply no way I would not become a different person. But then I found out soon enough my life was not going to change after all. Not in any way that I could see, perceptible or otherwise. I understood then that art was something I could pursue when I had the time for it, when I could afford to do so, and that's all. Art was a luxury and it wasn't going to change me or my life. I guess I came to the hard realization that art doesn't make anything happen. No. I don't believe for a minute in that absurd Shelleyan nonsense having to do with poets as the "unacknowledged legislators" of this world. What an idea! Isak Dinesen said that she wrote a little every day, without hope and without despair. I like that. The days are gone, if they were ever with us, when a novel or a play or a book of poems could change people's ideas about the world they live in or even about themselves. Maybe writing fiction about particular kinds of people living particular kinds of lives will allow certain areas of life to be understood a little better than they were understood before. But I'm afraid that's it, at least as far as I'm concerned. Perhaps it's different in poetry. Tess has had letters from people who have read her poems and say the poems saved them from jumping off a cliff or drowning themselves, etc. But that's something else. Good fiction is partly a bringing of the news from one world to another. That end is good in and of itself, I think. But changing things through fiction, changing somebody's political affiliation or the political system itself, or saving the whales or the redwood trees, no. Not if these are the kinds of changes you mean. And I don't think it should have to do any of these things, either. It doesn't *have* to do anything. It just has to be there for the fierce pleasure we take in doing it, and the different kind of pleasure that's taken in reading something that's durable and made to last, as well as beautiful in and of itself. Something that throws off these sparks—a persistent and steady glow, however dim.

Ray Carver: Keeping It Short

Kay Bonetti/1983

From *Saturday Review,* 9 (September/October 1983), 21-23. Supplemented by transcribed and edited excerpts from the sixty-minute audiotape that was the source of the interview: Kay Bonetti, "Raymond Carver," American Audio Prose Library, LC 83-740106 (CV III 1083). All material copyright © American Audio Prose Library, 1983. All rights reserved. Reprinted by permission of Kay Bonetti and the American Audio Prose Library, Inc. Conducted May 1983.

Raymond Carver has acquired a large audience and a distinguished reputation on the basis of two volumes of short stories: *Will You Please Be Quiet, Please?* (McGraw-Hill, 1976; nominated for the 1977 National Book Award) and *What We Talk About When We Talk About Love* (Alfred A. Knopf, 1981). A third collection, *Cathedral,* comes out this fall and includes Carver's story "A Small, Good Thing," which received first place in the 1983 O. Henry prize stories collection. He is also the author of several volumes of poetry.

Carver's stories reflect his upbringing as the child of a small-town sawmill laborer in the Pacific Northwest. They are peopled with blue-collar families, Indians, unemployed (often alcoholic) aerospace engineers—generally persons without the spiritual, emotional, or intellectual tools to express their plight. The force of Carver's two earlier works lies in what is implied; the stories in *Cathedral* are fuller and more reflective.

The following is an interview conducted in New York City during the annual meeting of the American Academy and Institute of Arts and Letters. There Carver received the Mildred and Harold Strauss Livings Award, which grants him a substantial, tax-free annual income for five years.

KB: This has been a big year for you, hasn't it?

Carver: It has indeed. Many things have happened—both good and bad—and there are many blessings to count, and I certainly do count them. Especially if you're referring to the attention that's been paid of late to my work. This most recent award is certainly very significant. Cynthia Ozick and I were the first recipients. The closest thing around might be the MacArthur Foundation Fellowship Awards. This might be better in the sense that this is renewable after five years. It's just a great, wonderful opportunity. My favorite TV show in the 1950s was *The Millionaire,* where once a week somebody would come around and deliver a check. This, to a degree, is what has happened in my case. I'm very happy with the award and I'm mindful of the great responsibility.

KB: What are the conditions of this award?

Carver: The only condition is that I not have another form of employment, like teaching for instance. On the day that I received notification of the award I was on leave of absence from my teaching duties at Syracuse University. And I called up my chairman, who's a very kind, decent, intelligent, and thoughtful man, and told him that I would not be coming back after the end of the semester. They were very happy for me, of course. And sorry to see me go because the writing program had just gotten into place up there.

KB: You mentioned that some very sad things have happened this last year. Is there anything you can talk about?

Carver: I lost my friend John Gardner. I lost another friend, Dick Hugo, who died in October. I just had news, when we were at Syracuse, right before I came to New York, that a friend and colleague up there is gravely ill and doesn't have much longer to live. My daughter was in an auto accident last fall with her baby. She and the baby are fine now, I'm happy to say, but it was a difficult situation for a time. So it's been a strange period here, these last twelve or fifteen months.

KB: Do you think it has anything to do with being in your forties?

Carver: No, I don't [chuckling]. My thirties were a difficult time for me. My thirties almost killed me, and I was very glad to celebrate my fortieth birthday. No, I think it's just that when we get into our forties, we're going to have to expect to bury some of our friends. There's only one alternative to that, of course—friends will bury us.

KB: But you're finally reaping the rewards of all that hard work of previous years.

Carver: Oh, it would seem that way. I never looked on my writing, frankly, as a career pursuit. I just set out to write stories and poems. I feel healthier and stronger and better suited for whatever I have to do

than I ever have before. All of this certainly has to do with the fact
that for many years, most of my thirties, until my thirty-ninth year, I
was a practicing alcoholic, and that took a lot of time and energy. I
laid waste a good many things in those years. Since I stopped
drinking six years ago it seems to have gotten immeasurably better—
there's no question of that.

KB: There have been books written about the subject of writers
and alcohol. Do you think there was any relationship between what
you do and the fact that you drank too much?

Carver: No, I think alcoholism is probably no higher amongst
writers or artists of any sort than it is amongst people of any other
professional group, be they lawyers or doctors or ophthalmologists.
There's a myth that goes along with writing and alcohol. But purely
and simply, drinking is *not* conducive to artistic production. Quite the
contrary, I think it's a disaster and a terrible hindrance. Writers are
more visible than the other people, that's all. We hear about John
Berryman's problems with alcohol or F. Scott Fitzgerald or William
Faulkner or Ernest Hemingway or Malcolm Lowry. But in *any* group
of professional people you find a lot of trouble with alcohol.

KB: Was there anything in particular that made you make that
decision to stop drinking?

Carver: Well, in a way it was made for me. In 1976, the last year
of my drinking, two of my books were published: *Will You Please Be
Quiet, Please?* and a book of poems, *At Night the Salmon Move.* But
my life seemed to have gotten completely away from me. It was out
of control, and I was hospitalized twice in a space of about twelve
months, which is some indication of how serious the problem was.
Finally, after the fourth hospitalization, it occurred to me that I was
not going to be able to drink socially any longer. So I stopped. I just
didn't drink one morning. And I didn't drink the next morning, and
the next morning. Fortunately I was able to get a week of sobriety
and a second week, and then, lo and behold, I'd been sober a
month, and I just took things very carefully. As they say in AA, "One
day at a time."

KB: Tell me about *Cathedral.*

Carver: There's an opening-up in this book that there's not been
in any of the other books. There was a period of several months
when I didn't write anything. And then the first story that I wrote was

"Cathedral," which is unlike anything I have ever done before. All the stories in this book are fuller and more interesting, somehow. They are more generous. They're not quite so pared down. I went as far in the other direction as I wanted to go. My life's changed to a degree since I started giving my work to a woman in Syracuse who has a word processor. She is able to type up the story and give me the fair copy, and I can mark it up and change it to my heart's content and give it back to her, and a few hours later I can have fair copy back again. I've never been able to work that way before, and I'm sure that that accounts to a degree for the fact that I was able to do, for me, so many stories in a fairly short period of time. But the rewriting and revising is something very dear to my heart and something close to the hearts of many writers of my acquaintance. Looking at the first drafts of great writers is very heartening and very instructive because there are so many changes. Tolstoy made so many changes in his proof that quite often the entire material would have to be set again, because he was revising right down to the time of publication. John Gardner worked that way. Any number of writers. I'm never quite finished with the work.

KB: Do most of your stories have a discernible germination point?

Carver: Most often they come from a spoken line. I have not written the story for it yet, but I heard someone say not too long ago, "He was so sick before he died." And that set up a whole conjuring of feeling in me because I have known people that this would fit. I haven't written that story, but I will. And there's the story "A Serious Talk." That story had its genesis in a single line: "That's the last holiday you'll ever ruin for us." That line is in the story, somewhere. We all have had or seen holidays ruined in some way or another, through a family altercation or something. Once I was riding on a plane and I saw, as we were coming down, the man sitting next to me take the wedding ring off his finger and put it into his pocket. All I had to do was to imagine what might be happening there, what might be going through his mind, or what he was up to, to give me the idea for a story. I don't go around with stories in my head all the time. But when I sit down to work, something's on my mind and I usually don't waste much time. I go right to it. There's that sense of excitement when you're working on something and you know that you've got a keeper. You know that this is something different, something special. It happened when I wrote the story called "Where I'm Calling From" that was in *The New Yorker* last summer. I was informed it's going to be in *The Best American Short Stories 1983*, coming out this fall. Somewhere in the midst of writing that story, at about the fifth or the sixth draft, I had this same rush, this same feeling of excitement, that this is different, this is good, this is what makes us come back and do this work over and over again.

KB: Is it a coming-together of form and content?

Carver: I think it is. It's that and it's a coming-together of everything. You're asking me now to describe the sensation of the creative process, and I'm not sure I'm up to that. I can just tell you that it is an aesthetic and intellectual and emotional feeling of fitness, of "everything is right here." I'm sure that musicians must feel this when they're writing music or maybe when they're performing. And certainly writers have to feel it, but not always. I wish it *were* there always, but it's there just enough that it keeps us coming back.

KB: You have said that a writer has to have more than talent: that he has to be able to render a world according to himself. You mentioned Cheever, Updike, Salinger, Singer, Elkin, Beattie, Ozick, and Barthelme.

Carver: Yes, and many more besides. Their stories are *their* stories and no one else's. They have their signature on them. I could pick up a story by John Cheever or by Stanley Elkin or by Mary Robison, and, having never read the story before, I would know who had written it. It's just like looking at a landscape by Cézanne or Renoir. We may never have seen that painting before, but looking at it we'd know whose work it is. And I like that.

KB: What's talent?

Carver: Well, talent is something that any writer has. Every aspirant writer, musician, painter—I would say nearly every one of them has talent. But talent is simply not enough.

KB: Are there any writers you could name who are, say, safely dead, who had talent but that just never quite got there?

Carver: No, at the moment I can't. But most of the dead writers are writers who had it together, or we wouldn't be talking about them. Like Joyce in *Dubliners* and Frank O'Connor and Flannery O'Connor and Isaac Babel, and Chekhov of course. Chekhov comes first to my mind. I've never met a writer who didn't love Chekhov.

KB: You have also said that you'd like to write on a three-by-five card, which would hang over your desk, what Geoffrey Wolff once said: "No Cheap Tricks." What's an example of trickery in writing?

Carver: Oh, I suppose I'm thinking of characters whom the author finds contemptible or has no interest in whatsoever—sticking these characters into ridiculous situations. I read a story in manuscript not so long ago in which the central figure wakes up one morning and decides he wants to change his life. So he takes his baby out of the cradle and puts the baby into the furnace downstairs, and then he proceeds to go down the street and flirt with a neighbor and so forth. It's a story that doesn't make any sense, it has no reason for being. Is the author trying to make a point? It's a story in which the author has no investment whatsoever. There's no value system at work, no moral grounding, if you will. Some stories start at a point and they don't go anywhere. The author is telling you to take it or leave it. It's self-expression run rampant. I mean, in my view art is a linking between people, the creator and the consumer. Art is *not* self-expression, it is communication, and I am interested in communication. But I'm not trying to make a case against experimental fiction. Donald Barthelme's fiction is experimental and he's quite a wonderful writer. He writes like nobody else.

KB: But your point would be that there are other writers who then set out to write like that—

Carver: And try to write like Donald Barthelme, and they don't have Donald Barthelme's particular and peculiar genius. They take the surfacy things in Barthelme and they make a mess of them. It's not *their* vision that they're working with, it's Donald Barthelme's.

KB: Nobody talks about the humor in your stories.

Carver: I'm glad you brought it up, because I feel that there is plenty of humor in them. There was a good long review of *Will You Please Be Quiet, Please?* in *Newsweek* when the book first appeared. And the reviewer did talk about the humor in the stories, and I was very glad to see that, because I think that there *is* humor in the stories—a little black humor maybe, but humor.

KB: Do you have a working routine, a way you work?

Carver: When I'm working on a story I work on it night and day. Sometimes I don't even know what day of the week it is. And when

I'm not working, I fall into bad habits: stay up late, watch TV, sleep-in too late in the mornings. I suppose I work in fits and starts.

KB: What is the relationship in your mind between your poems and your stories?

Carver: It's certainly a good question. I don't know if I have an appropriate response for it. I feel close to my poems. I'm *always* flattered when somebody comes up to me and tells me that they read a poem of mine and liked it. But I made a conscious decision some years ago that I was going to have to give my real attention and my most serious energy to my fiction, and that's what I've done.

KB: I notice that in your poems you tend to write about experiences, people that you have known. The speaker in the poems appears to be you.

Carver: Yes, I suppose so. In that regard, I suppose the poetry can be much more personal than the fiction.

KB: Were you going to learn to be a writer in school?

Carver: Oh, indeed. I met John Gardner early on at Chico State College when I was 19 or 20, and he was someone I admired a great deal. He was a graduate of the University of Iowa's Writers' Workshop. When I left Chico State and went to Humboldt State over in northern California, I met Dick Day, and he was a graduate of the Iowa Writers' Workshop. He said, "If you want to be a writer, hang out with other writers and learn to write. Go to Iowa." He was instrumental in helping me go to Iowa.

KB: What was your first real "break"?

Carver: I suppose a real turning point in my life happened in 1967, when one of my short stories was picked up from an obscure literary magazine and reprinted in *The Best American Short Stories,* edited by Martha Foley.

KB: And that was?

Carver: And that was "Will You Please Be Quiet, Please?"—the title story of the collection. It was the most momentous thing in regard to my writing that had ever happened to me.

KB: You've made it in a business where it's very difficult to do that with the short form. You have gained a huge reputation on the basis of two collections of short stories. When people speak of Raymond Carver they almost always speak of *Will You Please Be Quiet,*

Please? and *What We Talk About When We Talk About Love.* Are you conscious of that being very fortunate for you?

Carver: It doesn't happen very often with any writer who writes two novels, or certainly two books of short stories. I've become aware of that fact. I'm happy that it's happened, sure.

KB: Have you had a relationship with an agent or publisher that brought these things together?

Carver: Though I say there was a turning point in 1967, there was another turning point in the early 1970s when an editor at *Esquire* began publishing my stories in *Esquire* magazine. That's when the stories first began attracting some attention.

KB: Gordon Lish?

Carver: Yes. There's no question but that he's been an important individual in my life. I still have Gordon as my editor at Knopf, and I'm happy about that. And I happen to have a very good agent whom I'm very happy with. She's somebody I feel very close to and compatible with. I don't know what else to say except that everything is coming together now, at the right time in my life. All of these things would not have been right perhaps six or eight years ago, but everything now is right, and I thank my lucky stars for that.

KB: Do you remember what started the story "Nobody Said Anything"?

Carver: Yes. I think I could tell you something about that story. That story is not autobiographical. None of my stories have ever really happened, but stories don't just come out of thin air. They have to come from somewhere, at least the stories of the people I most admire. They have some reference points in the real world. And that story did. On one fishing trip when I was a kid I did catch a trout that was pretty green. I had never seen a trout quite like it, and it was eight or ten inches long. On a separate fishing trip I did see a fish that we called a summer steelhead, a steelhead trout that had gone to the ocean and come back up into fresh water and had gotten into a small creek and gotten stranded up there. But I didn't do anything. I didn't catch that fish. On yet another occasion I did halve a fish with another kid. It wasn't a steelhead trout. It was a sturgeon, about a ten-pound sturgeon, that had inexplicably gotten up into this creek. We yanked him up and we divided that fish. The rest of the story was put together as stories are put together, like a snowball rolling downhill. You know, things get added in the process of the rolling. That was when I was a kid and somehow there are these deeply rooted things that you don't forget and that go way back with you. Those circumstances, that particular time in my life, made a very large claim on my attention when I was in my early thirties. When I wrote that story I knew I had written something that was very special. That doesn't happen with all the stories I write. But with that particular story I felt like I had tapped into something. I knew what it was all about.

KB: I was curious about "Put Yourself in My Shoes."

Carver: I can tell you a little bit about that story. My former wife and I *did* rent a house from some people who were going to be away in Europe. And we never *did* meet these people. We rented it through a middleman, as it were. But the things that happened in that story, the story within the story, did *not* happen. When I wrote the story, as I recall, right around Christmas, there *were* Christmas carolers outside and things like this. And something else happened, let's see, that got into that story. When we were abroad, in the late 1960s, there was a woman who through a strange set of circumstances wound up at our house. She got sick in the house and we had to wait on her hand and foot for two or three days. Bring her soup. And she was beginning to order us around, you know, like the soup was too cold. So that was a strange piece of business in itself, and certainly worthy of another story. That got into my head. Like, what would have happened if this woman had died at our house? You know, she was an elderly woman. So all those things got into the story. I didn't know this guy was going to be a writer. I began that story with only one line in my head: "He was running the vacuum cleaner when the telephone rang." I think *every* young writer is cautioned against writing a story about a writer. We're told to write about other things and other people. If you want to write a story about a writer, make him a painter or something. But then *every* writer goes ahead and writes at least one story about a writer, and that's *my* story about a writer. He's home. His wife or girlfriend is working. He's home *trying* to write, but he's not writing. By the end of the story he's ready to write, because he *has* a story, he's heard all kinds of stories.

Raymond Carver

Michiko Miyamoto/1983

From *My New York Friends* (Tokyo: Shuei-sha, 1987), 218-31.
Reprinted by permission of Michiko Miyamoto and Shuei-sha,
Inc. Conducted 20 May 1983. Translated by Naoko Takao.

"What? You're going to see Raymond Carver? That's great! It's hard to find a nice guy like him nowadays, you know. Once there was a time when he was an alcoholic, but now he's healthy and working like crazy," said Robert Ward. Robert had been singing country music to his guitar in a nasal voice with a southern accent. I recalled that he used to be a country-music singer.

After talking enthusiastically about his new book, *Red Baker,* Robert started to play his guitar again, saying that he needed some rest. And he said that if he were to pick one person he wants to read his book, it would be Norman Mailer.

Mailer is better known for his face and conduct than for his work, and he is disliked by many people, especially feminists. As for me, I've always respected his personality as well as his books, and I've often wanted to criticize the prejudice against him. So I was pleased to hear Robert's feeling about Mailer.

It's understandable that Mailer has so many enemies, given his strong character and tendency to write in an overly avant-garde style. The short-story writer Raymond Carver, although he has a completely different style, is like Mailer in that his books are better appreciated by connoisseurs than by the general public. Because a friend of mine, Jay McInerney, studied with Carver, I tried several times to make contact with Carver through Jay at Syracuse University. But the reply I got was always a bit opaque.

"Well . . . I tried," Jay said. "But he doesn't like interviews very much." I tried every way possible to persuade Jay to help me meet Carver. But even though Jay must have been convinced of my eagerness and sincerity, his answer was always the same. "The thing is, you know, he says he feels embarrassed. He doesn't realize he's famous enough to be interviewed." After a while, Jay suggested a telephone interview, an idea that Carver himself had brought up. But this time I was the one to refuse. I'm uncomfortable talking to strangers over the phone. Twice I tried to reach Carver by mail, but there was no reply.

By this time, it was impossible for me to resist creating my own "legend of Raymond Carver." He isn't so famous a celebrity as to refuse publicity, I thought. So it could be that he really dislikes meeting people.

"Is he eccentric or peevish?" I asked.

"Oh, no!" Jay said. "He's a nice guy!"

Everyone who knows Carver personally praises his character. And anyone who calls himself a writer takes his hat off to Carver's books. But the more I heard about this "nice guy," the more the image of him as someone peevish took hold of me. As happens to anyone whose interview request is turned down snappishly, the object becomes even more attractive, despite the bad feelings. And I have a tendency to get even more stimulated if the object is a difficult one. Having heard all the talk about "the legend of Carver" from my friends and having read all his books, I was more than eager to see the truth for myself. At the same time, I was well aware of the difficulties involved in meeting someone from another state in this big country.

I started out by calling an editor in New York who was in charge of Carver's books. I asked him to contact me if Carver came to the city.

One day, a short column in the *Times* caught my attention. An association called the American Academy and Institute of Arts and Letters had chosen Carver as one of the winners of its literary awards. Immediately I called Gary Fisketjon, the editor at Random House. As I expected, Carver was coming to New York from Washington State to receive the award the following week. "I'll talk to him about it when he arrives," Gary said.

At Gary's suggestion, Carver finally telephoned me.

"This is Ray calling. . . ." After this offhand introduction, when I talked about Carver's books, he chimed in the same words over and over, either speaking fast or stammering. It was, surprisingly, a very simple way of talking. And he said something that no New Yorker would ever say: "Thank you very much for your interest. . . ."

When setting up an interview does not go smoothly, the cause is usually the "celebrity complex" peculiar to New Yorkers. But in

Carver's case, things seemed different. Jay was probably right: this guy is really shy. He must feel bashful about meeting people, even under the pretext of "an interview," because he's country-bred.

"Then I'll come to your hotel at four tomorrow," I said. "May I have two hours, if possible? And . . . can I bring along someone for picture-taking?"

"Yes, sure, yes, yes . . . ," he said. "I'm looking forward to meeting you."

After hanging up the phone I couldn't help but start giggling. I was happy that I could finally talk to Carver face to face. But more than that, it was refreshing to see my willful "image of Carver" breaking down.

While I was sitting there giggling, the phone rang again. It was Carver.

"Well . . . about the photographs. . . . I ruined my face a little bit just now . . . so. . . ."

"Oh, that's OK. It doesn't have to be photographs. How about sketches?"

"Yes. Fine. Sketches are good. If you need to have photographs, I'll have my agent send them along later."

When Carver mentioned his injury, he used the word *ruin.* At that moment, different images of his face flashed through my mind. Maybe half his face has radiation burns or some kind of deep, dark red stain. . . . At the same time, I recalled one of my favorite Carver stories, "Cathedral." (Translated into Japanese by Haruki Murakami, it is included in *Where I'm Calling From,* published by Chuokoron-sha in 1983.) In the story one of the characters is a blind man. Somehow, I associated the "ruin" on Carver's face with blindness or some such handicap. (Could it be that Raymond Carver has a permanent scar on his face?) Then I recalled that in the photograph on the back of his newly published book *Fires* his face is shadowed on one side. But wait, he said "just now," meaning it's nothing permanent. . . . Thinking these things over, I was excited in anticipation of the next day's meeting.

Carver was staying at a classy hotel, the Carlyle, on Madison Avenue. Many European art dealers and collectors favor it for its location. When I knocked on the gold and white door of his room, a man of towering height appeared almost sluggishly.

"Hello, I'm Ray. Come in, come in, . . . come in. . . ."

For the past six years Carver has been living with a poet, Tess Gallagher. After joining Carver in welcoming us warmly, Tess went out, saying, "I'll leave you people alone."

Wearing a gray sweater, tan cotton trousers, and suede chukka boots, Carver turned out to be a middle-aged man with short gray hair and deep-set eyes. Because of his hefty shoulders, he looks a little stooped.

"I cut myself shaving . . ." he said, touching a little cut to the right of his lower lip. He sat down on an antique French chair in the corner of the room, facing me. The "ruin" he had mentioned was a nick from a razor blade. Recalling his excuse on the telephone, I thought, "What an exaggeration! He must really be self-conscious." But soon enough I realized it was my willful imagination that had created the ridiculous image.

Carver was born in Oregon and raised in Washington State. For him, a boy who was married at eighteen to a sixteen-year-old girl and soon became the father of two, life was a constant struggle. In his Foreword to *On Becoming a Novelist* by John Gardner, the writer he respects as his first master, Carver tells how he and his family moved from Washington State to a little town in California in 1958. Eager to enter college, he rented an old house for twenty-five dollars a month. All he had when he left Washington was a hundred and twenty-five dollars that he had borrowed from the owner of the drugstore where he worked part-time. His wife, who became a mother while still a teenager, helped support the family by working as a waitress. Carver worked as a mill hand, a truck driver, a deliveryman, an apartment manager, a janitor, even a tulip-picker. He and his wife had grown up in poor families, and there were no relatives to help them out.

"But. . . I always wanted to write," he said. His parents had little education, but the stories his father told young Carver fascinated him. Soon he found himself dreaming about becoming a storyteller too.

Carver's struggle to write during his college years while raising his children is mentioned in his new book, *Fires*. Today, he talked about it repeatedly. "The most influential factor was my two children. I had to write on a kitchen table while feeding my kids. And I had to wash their clothes. . . . It was no time to write any major works."

The turning point for Carver came when his story "Neighbors" appeared in *Esquire* in 1971. Gordon Lish, then the magazine's fiction editor, returned the first story Carver sent him with a note saying, "I don't care for this, but do send on some more." Lish turned down Carver's next submission too, but the third one appeared in the magazine. From then on, Carver published fiction every year in major magazines and anthologies.

Shortly before I met Carver, Gordon Lish had published a novel, *Dear Mr. Capote.* Carver has a fierce sense of loyalty, and he mentioned Lish's name at every opportunity, repeating that he was grateful to him from the bottom of his heart. It didn't take long for me to remember Lish's name.

This loyalty arises in part from Carver's humble and thoughtful nature, but it is also true that he has the character of an "orthodox" writer. For example, the tenacity and effort he puts into revision is worth mentioning. He has taught writing at several colleges, and I think he must be a splendid teacher. To the question "Is it possible to teach writing?" he answered as I expected, "Of course it is," full of confidence. "Everyone has talent. All the students in my classes at Syracuse have talent."

"But how about drive?" I said.

"Right," he said. "Not everyone has drive. A person with talent but without drive won't go far in this world. Everyone has talent, but only those with drive keep writing. So the teacher's role is to bring out the best each student has. But a teacher can't do anything for a genius or someone without drive."

Carver has been traveling around the country like a gypsy since 1971, teaching in local colleges. This fall, for the first time, he has decided to become a full-time writer. "Finally, I don't have to teach anymore," he said, smiling. He went to fetch the program from the awards ceremony at the American Academy and Institute of Arts and Letters. "You see, here's my name," he said. "They're giving me $35,000 a year, tax free! Isn't that terrific?"

I started talking about a Japanese writer, Haruki Murakami, because I thought his translation of Carver's *Where I'm Calling From* was excellent. Again and again, Carver said it was an honor to have a writer for a translator. I remembered agreeing with Murakami's observation, "It's hard to imagine Raymond Carver's personality from his books," and I mentioned this to Carver. "In your work, you always keep a low profile, don't you?" I said. "Murakami said the same thing."

"Good, good, good . . ." Carver said. He has a habit of repeating the same short word, especially when he wants to agree or is impressed. "That's a nice comment. For me to hear that . . . you know. I take it as a compliment."

"Is it dangerous to write about oneself in fiction?" I asked.

"Yes, yes, 'es, 'es, very much so. Flaubert put it this way, 'Writers should be everywhere *present* and nowhere *visible.*'"

For a while, we talked about the time when Carver was an alcoholic. His children are now in their mid-twenties, and he gets along with them well. But at one point, drinking nearly ruined everything. Talking about that time, Carver's face darkened. "I guess drinking and writing don't mix too well."

"Yes," I said. "It's easier to drink than to write."

At that, Carver burst out laughing. He must have really known the feeling.

A Voice from the Wasteland
Patricia Morrisroe/1984

From *The Sunday Times Magazine* [London], 29 January 1984, 53-54. Copyright © Times Newspapers Limited 1984. Reprinted by permission of Times Newspapers Limited. Conducted Winter 1983/84.

The temperature is 10 below zero. But inside the local restaurant in Syracuse, New York, the air conditioner is running and the silverware is ice cold. Raymond Carver shivers and asks the waitress to warm his coffee. "Sure thing, honey," she says, dumping the contents of the old cup on to his half-eaten lunch. He looks down at his pastrami sandwich. It is submerged in black coffee. "Gee," he says, "I've never seen anyone do that before."

And Raymond Carver has seen a lot of things. Like the aimless drifters in his books, Carver, who is 45, has lived in dozens of places and worked at countless menial jobs. He can't remember the dates or many of the details. When he talks about the past, it tends to sound disjointed. "When I was in a laundromat in Iowa City. . . . When I was in a hospital in Calistoga. . . . When I was visiting some friends in Missoula."

If the hallmark of Carver's writing style is close attention to detail, he is extremely vague about the circumstances of his own life. Much of the problem can be attributed to his 10-year battle with alcohol. He started drinking heavily in his early thirties and suffered from periodic blackouts. "My life was a wasteland," he says. "I destroyed everything I touched. . . . There are certain things I don't want to remember."

Happily, those days are over. Since his first collection of stories was published in 1976, he has gained a reputation as one of the finest writers of short fiction in the United States. Last year was a particularly good one: the American Academy and Institute of Arts and Letters awarded him a $35,000 annual stipend for the next five years. For the first time in his life, Carver has the time and the money to do nothing but write. He quit his teaching job and completed two film scripts. He built a house and bought a brand new Mercedes.

Then last autumn, *Cathedral,* his latest collection of stories (published in Britain tomorrow) appeared in the U.S. to almost unanimous praise.

"I'm very pleased," Carver says, in his low, tentative voice. He smiles briefly and his eyes sparkle. A large man with bushy eyebrows and a jowly face, he projects a gentle, almost haunting sadness. "But it hasn't really affected me one way or another. Life had pretty much come to an end in 1977. My drinking had backed me into a corner. I was out of control, almost as good as dead. I stopped drinking in June that year and I consider that my greatest achievement."

Much has been written about the bleakness of Carver's vision of America. His stories are populated by ordinary people—waitresses, hairdressers, factory workers—who can't cope with daily life. Instead of seeking solace in friends or family, they turn to alcohol or television. They have dreams, but they don't have the words or the imagination to express them. When asked why he writes about such characters, Carver says it is because he knows them so well: "They are where I come from."

Carver was born in a small logging town in Washington State. His father, who was also an alcoholic, worked in a sawmill. As a child, Carver loved to read Zane Grey westerns and listen to his father tell stories. "I remember my dad talking about my grandfather who fought in the Civil War," he says. "When the South began losing, he joined forces with the North. He was a turncoat and I found that pretty exciting."

Carver says he doesn't know why he decided to become a writer. "Perhaps it was my father's stories," he says. "But ever since I can remember I wanted to write." After high school, he joined his father in the sawmill. By the time Carver was 20, he had two children and no marketable skills. Moving his family to Chico, California, he enrolled in a state university and paid his tuition doing odd jobs. From Chico, he travelled to Iowa to attend a writers' workshop but dropped out for lack of money. Back in California, he found work as a night janitor at a hospital. It was like this for the next 10 years.

Still, Carver kept writing. In the beginning, he worked on poems, simply because they were short and could often be finished in one sitting. With a full-time job and two children, he didn't have much spare time. Weighed down by financial pressures, and increasingly frustrated by his inability to gain control over his life, Carver turned to alcohol. It was a painful period, and Carver still winces when he talks about it.

Everything went bust, he says, on what he describes as a "whacky trip to Israel." It was 1968 and his wife, who was studying for her college degree, won some scholarship money. "They promised us a villa on the Mediterranean," Carver says. "I could just see myself, sitting at the typewriter with a magnificent view of the water. Instead the house was awful, the kids were miserable and we ran out of money. After a few months we packed up and headed to Holly-wood. I got a job selling theatre programmes. But something inside me said, 'It's over.' I had wanted that villa in the Mediterranean all my life, and at that point I knew I was never going to get it. My writing had done nothing but bring me grief. My wife and I split up. . . ." His voice disintegrates into a mumble, and he reaches for another cigarette.

Today, Carver has found his villa on the Mediterranean. It is a large, two-storey house in Syracuse with a sign outside that reads "No Visitors." He lives there with Tess Gallagher, a poet and short story writer. When he speaks her name, it's in a soft and tender voice that conjures up images of a warm kitchen and freshly baked bread. Not surprisingly, Carver conveys the same feeling in several of the stories in *Cathedral*. While many are still bleak and a touch despair-ing, there is also something hopeful and more compassionate. The title story about a blind man who comes to visit a married couple is perfect evidence of what Carver calls his "new opening up." Initially callous to the sightless man, the husband turns on the television and watches a show about cathedrals. When asked what they look like, the husband can't find the right words. Instead he pulls out a pencil and a grocery bag and, taking the blind man's hand, he closes his eyes and they draw one together.

"There is something different about the book," Carver says. "The stories are more generous, more interesting. 'Cathedral' was the first one I did and halfway through it I got this tremendous rush. It felt wonderful and I had the strong sense I was doing something right."

Recently, Carver completed a second screenplay with writer/ director Michael Cimino. It is an odd collaboration. Cimino, of *Heaven's Gate* fame, was virtually ostracised by American critics for being excessive in everything from the movie's length to its astronomical budget. Carver, on the other hand, has gained a reputation for his simple, minimalist prose. How did the two get along? "I never saw *Heaven's Gate*," he says, "and I think Cimino is a nice man. Last spring he commissioned me to write a screenplay on Dostoevsky. I think Carlo Ponti was involved but I haven't heard anything else about it." He shrugs.

The waitress interrupts the conversation. "Excuse me," she says, "but I'm going on my break. So maybe you could pay the bill?" The coffee stain is gone, and her blue-black hair has been sprayed into a 1950s bouffant. "Gee thanks," she says, picking up the tip with her long tangerine-coloured nails. "Now you have a Happy New Year, OK?"

Carver pauses for a second and then smiles. "Yeah," he says. "Happy New Year."

Any Good Writer Uses His Imagination to Convince the Reader

Hansmaarten Tromp/1984

From *Haagse Post* [Amsterdam], 4 August 1984, 40-43. Additional dialogue transcribed and edited from the audiotape that was the source of the interview. Printed by permission of Hansmaarten Tromp. Conducted 31 January 1984. Translated by Stephen T. Moskey.

The cross-eyed taxi driver stops the car, turns to me, and points to a large wooden sign in the front yard. *No Visitors.* Whimsical yellow and orange squiggles of paint fill the space beneath the black lettering, perhaps to avoid scaring away those with legitimate business here—doctors, for example, or deliverymen. Do foreign reporters fall into this category?

I smile uncomfortably at the driver and pay him an enormous fare for the half-hour ride from the airport to this quiet street in Syracuse, a dull college town near the Canadian border in Upstate New York.

After getting out of the taxi, I open the fence gate carefully, expecting the onslaught of a pair of attack dogs trained to tear trespassers to bits in minutes. Nothing happens.

The taxi drives slowly away. There is no sign of life anywhere in or around the two-story house. There's an old Volkswagen in front of the garage to the side of the house. Once the taxi is out of sight, I feel as though I'm the only living soul in the neighborhood.

I approach the front door and push the doorbell a few times. No answer. So I walk around the house and tap softly at each window I pass. When I reach the Volkswagen, having come full circle around the house, I notice that the side vent of the car is open, so I reach in and blow the horn.

A window above my head is pushed open and a man with a puffy face asks me what I think I'm doing here.

A little later, the two of us are sitting on the cream-colored sofa facing each other. Books are piled on the glass-topped coffee table in front of us, along with a vase filled with peacock feathers—the only decorative touch in the room. My host lights up a low-tar cigarette and asks me to forgive the fact that he's hard of hearing. When he's up in his study, he tells me, he can't hear a thing. Nor does he want to because he doesn't want to break his concentration. Ergo the sign on the front lawn. Ergo the disconnected doorbell. Ergo his reaction to my blowing the car horn—normally a signal from his companion that she's home.

And so now Raymond Carver and I are sitting side-by-side on a gigantic sofa, with enough room between us for an entire class of schoolchildren.

Raymond Carver has only recently been able to immerse himself in his writing, and can finally devote all his time to thinking, writing, and endlessly revising the stories which are receiving more and more attention at home and abroad.

He's also writing poetry these days and has taken a stab at writing a first novel, but what really counts is making the most of the time that's available to him. It's as if he wants to remain the master of his time and use it in such a way that he won't be reminded of the days when his writing had to be fit in around all sorts of part-time jobs, when he had to make the best of a few precious hours of writing sitting at the kitchen table or in an unheated garage. So he doesn't dare waste the freedom he now has to do nothing but write. "I feel very happy about all this," he says, "just, oh, . . . plain happy."

Raymond Carver has certainly felt less happy. Better put: until a few years ago, he was deeply unhappy. Life was passing him by in the same way it was passing by the characters in his stories: hopeless, aimless, and struggling with how to pay the monthly bills.

From the time of his marriage at an early age until just a few years ago, Carver's life was a mixture of the good and bad qualities which he would ascribe to the characters in such collections of short stories as *Will You Please Be Quiet, Please?* (1976) and *What We Talk About When We Talk About Love* (1981).

He was eighteen and she was two years younger. She was a student at a girls' school in Walla Walla, Washington, and not only knew something about literature, but also knew the correct way to hold a teacup and saucer. Carver was terribly taken with her; she even spoke Latin. He got her pregnant, and then they had to get married.

"I didn't have a single cent," he says, "nor did she. She came from

a poor family. Her mother had decided that her daughter would
pursue her education, but instead, she got pregnant. She was
seventeen when our first child was born and eighteen when the
second came along. We were teenagers with family responsibilities.
We were being forced to play roles which we, at our age, were
entirely unprepared to play. But we did the best we could. And
twelve years after we got married she finally got her bachelor's
degree.

"In those days, I worked days and wrote at night. I can't remember
a time when I wasn't working. My wife worked and had to take care
of the children, and the housework, too. Within a few years, I had
earned my bachelor's at Humboldt State College in California and
we left shortly thereafter for Iowa City with all our worldly goods on
the roof-rack of our station wagon. I'd heard that the University of
Iowa offered a highly respected writers' workshop. I'd heard that from
an instructor at my college in California. At that time I was already
writing a lot of short stories and poems, and that instructor had sent a
few of them to Iowa. I was admitted to the workshop and got a $500
scholarship so I could attend.

"That wasn't much money for a year's worth of study and taking
care of a family, even with the $2 an hour I earned working in the
university library and the money my wife earned working in a
restaurant. There was no way we could make it through a second
year in Iowa, so we went back to California. To Sacramento, where I
got a job as a night janitor in a hospital. I was paid pretty well for this
job, which gave me a lot of time during the nights on the job to write.
The first two years went by without a hitch; I arrived home early in
the morning, slept a few hours, and when I woke up, my wife had
already left for her job and the kids were at the babysitter's. The
whole day lay wide open before me. Just for writing.

"But then I stopped going straight home when I got off work,
stopping instead at a local bar. Alcohol got to be a problem. That was
because I had too damned many problems with the way my life was
turning out. I was just too young to be a father with much too much
responsibility to keep the family going. Those needs kept me doing
odd jobs which didn't fit my personality at all. When all I really
wanted to do was write. So that's why drinking took hold at a certain
point in my life. If I couldn't find a goal in life anyway, it just might as

well have been the bottle. Full-time drinking became my life's
ambition.

"People say that all writers drink a lot. That's a myth. It's closer to
the truth to say that writers don't drink any more than anyone else
with heavy or demanding professions. I never spent much time
thinking about the psychology of drinking. I got myself started on
drinking. And I began to drink heavily once I realized that the things
which I wanted most in my life, writing and having a wife and kids,
were not lined up neatly waiting to be had. I immediately became a
heavy drinker. It wasn't anything I wanted, it just happened. From
that point, until that memorable day in the spring of 1977, that was
my profession: alcoholic."

By the time I had come along honking the Volkswagen's horn,
Carver had already been at his writing for five hours and had gone
through countless cigarettes and caffeine-free colas. He doesn't have
to do odd jobs on the side anymore. Last year he received a Mildred
and Harold Strauss Livings stipend, a five-year, $35,000 annual
award that allows him to devote himself full-time to his writing. This
stipend allowed him to resign from his professorship at Syracuse
University, where he led a writers' workshop last year.

He was working on a poem for the past few hours, seemingly a
strange endeavor for someone who's made his reputation as a writer
of short stories. But Carver has also published two collections of
poetry, *Winter Insomnia* (1970) and *At Night the Salmon Move*
(1976). But his instant fame in America is based solely on his stories,
which are now being imitated by new writers. A recent article in *The
New York Times* by Tom Jenks, the literary editor of *Esquire*
magazine, points this out: "The manuscripts that I'm getting here
from young writers are written in a style characterized by short, to-
the-point sentences. Raymond Carver's style. Even the themes of
many of the stories reflect those of Carver, themes I'd say were
directly representative of neo-realism."

Carver's first two collections of short stories, as well as his 1983
collection, *Cathedral*, got enormous attention in the American press.
Irving Howe, writing in *The New York Times* about the latter
collection, said that some of Carver's short stories "can now be
counted among the classics of American literature." The *Times* itself

called *Cathedral* one of the thirteen best books of 1983, and the
book was nominated for a National Book Critics Circle prize,
awarded to the best of American prose.

Carver's stories reflect the human condition of contemporary American society and are populated by people who are wasting their lives at
the edge of the welfare society. They are usually surrounded by worn-
out consumer goods, like broken refrigerators, threadbare living room
furniture, and banged-up cars, and have attitudes which dictate that they
act in conventional ways and adapt themselves to their surroundings.

"They're stories about nameless people, in nameless places, doing
nameless things," wrote Jan Donkers two weeks ago in the *Haagse
Post* (Issue No. 29). "Stifled misery, dysfunctional marriages and
relationships, alcohol, a lot of alcohol, and most of all that feeling of
astonishment and resignation that comes when one recognizes that
invariably life is going to disappoint you, and there's no way to avoid
that disappointment." Or, as someone in one of Carver's stories says,
"How did this all happen to us? We started out good people."

What did happen to Carver on that spring day in 1977 when he
suddenly decided to give up drinking? He's just poured us a cup of
coffee, offered me a slice of strawberry pie, and lit up another one of
his countless cigarettes. "I'd spent most of the previous year in a
drying-out tank. I'd gotten to the point that I didn't have any control
over myself anymore. Blackouts. You know how that is: you get in
your car, drive to the university to teach a class, go to a party where
you pick up someone, end up in that someone's bed, and the
following morning don't remember any of it. You go through life on
automatic pilot. I reached the end of the line. I started getting myself
used to longer and longer 'dry spells.'

"I was living in California far from my children and my wife, from
whom I was separated, and hadn't had a drink in three weeks. There
was a publishers' conference in San Francisco and one of the editors
from the house which published my first collection of short stories
invited me to lunch, and was planning to offer me an advance on a
novel. Unfortunately, the night before the lunch date, one of my
friends gave a little party. After three weeks of being sober, and
halfway into the party, I poured myself a glass of wine. And that's the
last thing I remember. Blacked out, for the n-th time. The next
morning, I was up and out early waiting at the door of the package

store to buy a bottle of vodka. I finished off the bottle, and that saved
the lunch date. But afterwards I went home and went on a three-day
drinking binge.

"One morning I woke up sick as a dog. 'This has got to stop,
Carver,' I screamed at myself. I decided to stay off the bottle, even
though that made me sicker. But it turned out all right. First a week of
sobriety, then two. Then all of a sudden it was a month. Alcoholics
Anonymous helped me.

"I had my last drink on June 2, 1977. I'm more proud of that than
of any other accomplishment in my life. I'm a recovering alcoholic. I'll
always be an alcoholic, but never a practicing one. I don't touch a
drop of the stuff anymore. Only cola and Perrier."

The writer John Gardner, killed in an automobile accident in 1982,
had the greatest influence on Carver's writing. In the early 1960s
Carver enrolled at Chico State College to study writing under Gardner, who had at that time not yet published a single piece. "I was
intrigued by the possibility of studying under a real writer," says
Carver. "I'd written stories as a kid, but I wasn't yet a real writer.
Nonetheless, I was disappointed that he hadn't published anything
yet. People said that publishers thought his stories and novels were
too difficult, and that he carried around boxes of manuscripts with
him wherever he went.

"Gardner guessed that I didn't have a quiet place to do my writing;
he knew I had a family. One day, he offered me the key to his office.
This friendly gesture was a turning point in my life. He just gave me
the key. I understood that he expected me to work hard to keep it.
And I did.

"I sat in his office every weekend, with boxes full of his manuscripts
piled around me. *Nickel Mountain* was on top of one of them; I
remember it was published many years later. It was in that office, in
the presence of all those manuscripts, that I made my first serious
attempts at being a writer.

"Gardner was a noncomformist who looked like an FBI agent, like
a Presbyterian minister. He always wore a black suit, a white shirt,
and a tie. He was also a chain-smoker, one cigarette after another,
even in the classroom. He crushed out his butts in the metal
wastepaper basket next to the lectern. Back in those days, smoking in
the classroom was strictly forbidden, and there weren't even any

ashtrays. On the day of our first class, a member of the university administration who happened to be passing by pointed out to Gardner that smoking wasn't allowed during classes. He walked over to the window, opened it, threw out his cigarette, and made some comment about the closed-mindedness of certain people. Then he lit up another cigarette.

"Gardner's concept of a good story was that it should have a beginning, a middle, and an end. He often went to the blackboard to sketch out the structure of his ideas. He drew peaks and valleys and plateaus to illustrate a story line. I didn't understand much of what he was talking about. What I did learn from, however, was the oral commentary he gave on stories that he had us read aloud during class. Then he would ask himself, aloud, why the author would have written about, say, a handicapped person whose handicap was only revealed in the very last sentence of the story. 'So you think it's a good idea to wait until the end of the story to tell your reader that your main character doesn't have any legs?' he would ask the writer somewhat sarcastically. Any storytelling device that kept important information from the reader was, in Gardner's mind, cheating; you had to be as honest as possible in your writing.

"Honesty in writing is one of the things that has remained with me. And when I was myself teaching writers' workshops, I always hammered away at that point. Lack of it is one of the most common faults of beginning writers. Inexperienced writers often feel compelled to use words which they've picked up here or there, and which 'look good' on paper. Or which don't exactly express what the writer intended. Or which express false sentimentality.

"If I were to write a story about the lady next door, say, who's over there starving to death and I don't really care about her dying, then the reader feels my non-involvement on the very first page of the story; my feeling and my apathy are expressed by my choice of words.

"In one of my stories, 'A Small, Good Thing,' a small boy dies; his parents had ordered a big birthday cake from the bakery for him. I've never lost a son, but I have been in situations where I was afraid I would lose one of my children. Then I imagined the most gruesome conditions under which they could die. My imagination brought me to the point where I could write that story, not an actual occurrence. But by expressing my imagination as accurately as possible, I made the story believable. Because I write with the conviction of my imagination. Any good writer uses his imagination to convince the reader."

Even in his youth, Carver, now 46 years old, used his powers of fantasy to transform what he calls the "deathly boring" reality that surrounded him. He grew up in a small town of carpenters and lumbermen in Washington State, in a house where the Bible was the only book his alcoholic father owned. "He did tell me stories about my grandfather, who'd fought in the Civil War," Carver says, "but apart from that, I had to rely on my own imagination. When I got to be older, I did some reading on my own, mainly Zane Grey westerns. Maybe it was my father's exciting stories that got me started on writing. And the fact that I found my own life so meaningless and empty. Everything I read seemed so much more interesting than my own life! I'm a dreamer, and I've always lived my imaginings. That's why I started writing. Because otherwise everything was so awfully boring.

"Most of what I write is about myself, even though I never write anything autobiographical. But I'm not a narcissistic writer, or no more so than any other writer. A writer writes about what he knows, and in most cases that's himself. That's why the stories I write have connections to the world I know, the world in which I live or have lived. They create a link between me and a world that is part real, part imagination. My imagination.

"Some reviewers have criticized me because my characters are so powerless and seem to reconcile themselves to the bad luck or misfortune that crosses their path. And one story in particular, it's called 'Preservation,' has received a lot of criticism because it's about people who'd rather complain about their broken refrigerator than call in a mechanic to fix it. 'Why don't they just get that thing fixed?' asked one reviewer. 'Then they won't have to put up with it any-more.'

"But of course that's not how things work out for people who have barely enough money for busfare, or to fill up their gas tanks. As far as money is concerned, they don't have a penny to spare. If some-thing breaks, there's no money to fix it or replace it. *That's* the kind of life I describe. But before the press drew my attention to it, I didn't think my characters were that bad off. Know what I mean? This country is bursting at the seams with waitresses and taxi drivers and gas station attendants and hotel clerks. But are those people unhappier than people who've 'made it'? No, they're just regular people who want to make the best of it. Just like I wanted to make the best of it when I had the kind of jobs that were a dime a dozen. I won't deny the fact that you sometimes get desperate by being forced into certain kinds of jobs just to survive. But my own experience is that you try to make the best of it. That's not to say that in this kind of situation you don't hope for some sort of salvation, for a moment of insight, for a revelation that gives your life a new turn.

"At times like that, your whole life changes. It's happened to me twice: when I started drinking, and when I decided to stop.

"Almost all the characters in my stories come to the point where they realize that compromise, giving in, plays a major role in their lives. Then one single moment of revelation disrupts the pattern of their daily lives. It's a fleeting moment during which they don't want to compromise anymore. And afterwards they realize that nothing ever really changes."

Carver's characters know a lot less about their own motives and thoughts than Carver does. They aren't in therapy and they don't speculate about the existence of God. They commit acts and don't fully appreciate their consequences. The writer and readers are surely aware of this, and this is reflected in an extremely condensed writing style without curlicues and excessive details.

Carver's style has earned him the label of "minimalist" in some American literary circles, a term which makes him less than happy. "That word brings up associations with narrow vision and limited ability," he says. "It's true that I try to eliminate every unnecessary detail in my stories and try to cut my words to the bone. But that doesn't make me a minimalist. If I were, I'd really cut them to the bone. But I don't do that; I leave a few slivers of meat on them.

"I write the first draft of a story as quickly as possible, preferably at one sitting. Then I revise it, and revise it yet again.

"So, I throw a lot of material away. A first draft could be forty pages long, and only ten may be left by the time I'm satisfied with it. But it's not only a case of cutting words; I also add a lot of material. What I really like to do is play with words.

"I think that a well-written short story has as much value as any

number of mediocre novels. And too many mediocre novels are
being published. Writing a novel is a lot different from thinking out
and creating a short story. I've just gotten started on a novel, a totally
different discipline for me. The stress of writing a novel has an entirely
different twist to it, and that's why I started out on it as if I were
starting to write a short story. I'm on the right path, but I'm not just
sure where it's taking me. And Tess Gallagher, my companion, and I
just collaborated on a script for Michael Cimino, who directed *The
Deer Hunter.* After I finished rewriting a script for him last year about
the life of Dostoevsky, he asked me to write a story about juvenile
delinquents who return to society after serving time in prison.

"The care and attention I can give to my work, thanks to the
fellowship, without having to worry about picking up jobs here and
there, is tremendously liberating. It suits my nature. Look, being
gifted isn't enough. Everyone is gifted. Some writers, for example,
have the gift of being able to write a story at one sitting. I wasn't born
with that one. That's why I'm so conscientiously involved with my
writing: I compensate for the talent I don't have through hard work.
And that teaches me a lot about myself."

The cross-eyed taxi driver who'd given me his telephone number
earlier in the day arrives late in the evening to take me back to the
airport. On the way, he talks a mile a minute about his family. He
shows me a photograph of his eighteen-year-old daughter taken
before she was in a car accident and had to have her leg amputated.
He tells me about all the conveniences he and his wife had installed
in the house after the accident; she needed a wheelchair for quite a
while afterwards. "I'm a pretty happy guy, sir," he says, carefully
maneuvering his taxi through the traffic. "But sometimes I wonder
what I did to deserve my daughter's accident. I mean, why did it
happen?"

He drops me off at the terminal and toots his horn cheerfully as he
drives away. I wave goodbye to him. We started out good people.

Q: Are you writing a novel?
A: After I published my first book of short stories there was a
suggestion from all quarters that it was desirable for me to write a
novel. This came from my publisher, from my wife, from a number of

sources. I was interested, but I wasn't able to do it at the time. I
wasn't thinking in terms of a novel. I didn't have the concentration
three or four years ago. There were some specific reasons that had to
do with raising my children and the life I was leading then. But I
continued to write short stories, and after my next book of stories was
published, the publisher was happy that I had continued to write
short stories. So I never had the pressure applied to me again after
the first time. But I am now interested in writing a novel, more
interested in that than in anything else. I sat down to write a novel a
few weeks ago, and then I wrote the essay on my father for *Esquire*.
I've started to write a story now that has no end in sight, so that's a
good sign. I'm driving, you could say, but I don't know what road I'm
on. That makes me a little uneasy, but excited as well.

Q: Have publishers changed their attitude about short-story
collections?

A: It's a curious attitude, for they say the short story was born in
this country. But up until ten years ago short stories were not taken
very seriously here. Short-story collections were seen as inferior to
novels. They were not reviewed very well, and not many copies were
sold. With some writers, it was different, of course: Fitzgerald, Carson
McCullers, and Flannery O'Connor. But they had established
reputations for writing novels as well. Only recently has there been
anything like a renaissance of the short story. More magazines are
now publishing stories, and short-story writers are taken seriously.
They get serious attention on the front page of *The New York Times
Book Review*. That never happened before.

Q: Young writers seem particularly drawn to the short story form.
What do you think accounts for this?

A: It has to do with the fact that so many good writers teach at
universities. Donald Barthelme is teaching, as are Stanley Elkin and
William Gass. John Gardner was. For better or worse, it is hard to
mention almost any good writer who is *not* teaching. Joyce Carol
Oates is teaching at Princeton, and Elizabeth Hardwick is teaching at
Columbia. And of course there are any number of writers, such as
Italo Calvino, who guest-lecture at universities. I've taught. In the first
course, I asked for a show of hands to establish which students were
writing stories and which ones were writing novels. The short-story
writers far outnumbered the novel writers.

Q: How do you teach short-story writing?

A: Partly, I teach by example, the example of my own work. My way is not the only way to write short stories, but I think young students can learn certain things from me and my work. Word-economy, for instance. Writers can be taught not to make certain mistakes. One big mistake that almost all writers make when they start out writing is not being honest in the way they use words. They use words that they've heard but that don't fit the story material. I teach the same way I was taught to write. John Gardner was my teacher, and he would sit down with me and go over the work I'd done.

Q: You've written screenplays. Have you ever tried writing for the stage?

A: I wrote some plays many years ago, and one of them was produced at a college. It had such a terrible reception that I never wanted to write another play. The audience had the chance to meet the author after the play, but what happened was more like a public hanging. They attacked me, and there was no escape. It was a terrible experience. But I have an idea for a play now, and I like to read plays. I like some of Albee's plays and Chekhov's. When I read my own prose, I read with my ears as well as my eyes. I have a good inner ear for how the narrative passages sound as well as the dialogue. Talking about that inner ear brings something else to mind. When I was in my twenties I read some of Hemingway's early stories and the prose hit me. I would read and reread those stories and feel a physical excitement. The way his words felt on the page, their sound, was exciting.

Raymond Carver: A Chronicler of Blue-Collar Despair

Bruce Weber/1984

From *The New York Times Magazine*, 24 June 1984, 36-38, 42-46, 48-50. Reprinted by permission of Bruce Weber. Conducted Spring 1984.

Raymond Carver is indulging himself of late, using time that is available to him, finally, for writing and for not much else. He's working on poems these days, another indulgence, instead of the short stories he's become known for, but the key thing is all the available time. He's hoarding time for writing as if he were afraid things might change again and he'd have to go back to snatching an hour here and there, to working on a scratch pad in the car or in the garage, or else to not writing at all. He is just getting used to this liberty, the element in his life that has always been most elusive, a life that is, at long last, serene, prosperous and productive. "I feel good about things," he says, though he colors his words with cautiousness. The exuberant impulse is there, but it comes out in stammers. "I feel, I feel, uh . . . happy."

Today Carver has been at his desk since just before dawn. At 46, Carver is a large man, with hair in the throes of going gray, a pudding face, the beginnings of jowls. He's wearing a patterned polyester shirt, with an oversized, way-out-of-style collar, blue jeans and slippers that are coming apart. More than anything, he looks kind.

Now, in the early afternoon, after seven or eight hours, he has cut his workday short, and he is sitting—slouching, really, his customary posture—on the sofa of his new home on the outskirts of Port Angeles, a fishing and logging town on the northern shelf of the state of Washington's Olympic Peninsula. For several weeks, he has been living in the house by himself, with the phone mostly unplugged and few social distractions because he knows almost no one out here. Some of the best salmon fishing in the world is within walking distance of the house, and Carver is a lifelong fisherman, but, he says, he's been out with his waders only once, the afternoon he

84

arrived. This is a brilliant, early spring day, and the landscape, all precipitous terrain and deep colors, is beckoning through the windows, but Carver is loath to go outdoors. His mind is still tethered to his morning's work.

"Two in the bank today," he says, referring to the poems he's been revising. He's smoking relentlessly and drinking glasses of caffeine-free cola.

Last year, Carver was the recipient of a Mildred and Harold Strauss Livings stipend, a five-year annual sum of $35,000 granted by the American Academy and Institute of Arts and Letters, that freed him from his post as a teacher of creative writing on the faculty of Syracuse University. "It's always been a luxury for me to write," he says. And then he adds, protectively, "It's a luxury now that I don't want to forgo."

It's odd, perhaps, that Carver is working so hard on poems right now. For he has published two slim collections, *Winter Insomnia* and *At Night the Salmon Move,* but his career as a poet has so far been undistinguished. On the other hand, Carver's three books of short stories have made him, arguably, suddenly, America's pre-eminent writer in that genre.

The influence of Carver's skillful, quiet voice is being felt by a generation of still unpublished writers. According to Tom Jenks, who edits fiction at *Esquire,* "The style most often attempted by young writers is one marked by short, hard-edged sentences, like those of Ray Carver, and the subject matter often brushes up against Carver's as well—representative of what I would call a downside neo-realism."

Both of Carver's last two collections, *What We Talk About When We Talk About Love,* published in 1981, and *Cathedral,* which appeared last fall, garnered front-page attention in *The New York Times Book Review,* the latter collection prompting the critic Irving Howe to declare in his review, "A few of Carver's stories . . . can already be counted among the masterpieces of American fiction." Generally, opinion about *What We Talk About* conformed to that of the distinguished British critic Frank Kermode, who deemed it "the work of a full-grown master." *Cathedral* was chosen by *The Times* as one of the 13 best books of 1983, and was a fiction nominee of the National Book Critics Circle.

Such recognition is anomalous, on the whole, for a fiction writer who is not a novelist, but it comes at a time when short stories are creating a stir in the publishing industry. Since 1979, a period virtually coinciding with that of Raymond Carver's success, many publishers and critics have noted that the short story seems to be undergoing a renaissance. Recent years have seen the publication and critical welcoming of story collections by such new writers as Mary Robison, Mark Helprin, Tobias Wolff, Bette Pesetsky, the late Breece D'J Pancake, Jayne Anne Phillips, Janet Kauffman and Bobbie Ann Mason.

There has always been an appreciative market for the stories of established masters. *The Stories of John Cheever,* for example, published in 1978, has sold almost 200,000 copies in hard-cover and more than 500,000 in paperback and was one of the few story collections ever to land on *The Times's* best-seller list. But now publishers are saying that collections by previously unknown writers are, if not enormously profitable, then at least worth a risk. "Not long ago," says Robert Gottlieb, editor in chief of Alfred A. Knopf, Carver's publisher, "it would have been all too easy to publish a collection of stories by a talented writer and sell 2,000 copies at best. There's still the chance of disaster, of course, but now these writers can sell 5,000 and more copies, and get a lot of attention."

However, there remain skeptics. "There is no renaissance," says Ted Solotaroff, founder of the defunct *New American Review* and now an editor at Harper & Row. "There's just Ray Carver and Jayne Anne Phillips and Bobbie Ann Mason. For a brief period, the success of one or two books overturns the conventional wisdom that short stories don't sell. So writers have a little more incentive to write stories, and publishers are a little less cynical about publishing short-story collections." Frank Conroy, who is director of the literature program for the National Endowment for the Arts, and who is completing a book of stories of his own, adds: "You have to be careful how you use the term 'renaissance.' There are more competent story writers turning out work now than there were a few years ago. Whether there are more great ones, probably no."

Whatever the precise dimensions of the short-story surge, Raymond Carver is indisputably at the center of it. *Cathedral* has sold nearly 20,000 hard-cover copies, an extraordinary number for a book of serious stories by a writer whose reputation has not long been established. And this spring, Vintage Books published *Fires,* a paperback reprint of a limited edition of stories, poems and essays, plus a lengthy interview with Carver that originally appeared in *The Paris Review.* It's a curious smattering of Carver's work, what amounts to a Raymond Carver reader, and an industry testament to the interest his work has spawned that may well be unprecedented for a writer of such limited output.

Carver's stories are populated by characters who live in America's shoddy enclaves of convenience products and conventionality—people who shop at Kwik-Mart and who live in saltbox houses or quickly built apartment complexes. They don't seem to want much: ordinarily divided lives of work and home, food on the table, love and solace when they need them. They yearn for serenity rather than achievement.

Still, there is vast unhappiness in them; they don't get the little they want. Carver's people end up being deserted by common satisfactions, and the stories are moral tales, really, explaining why decent men and women, dealt crummy circumstances in a plentiful world, behave badly in their intimate battles with selfishness. Written in an accessible vernacular, resonant with cryptic petulance and loud silences, the stories speak the language of everyday profundity.

"He's an important writer from any number of standpoints," says Gordon Lish, Carver's editor at Alfred A. Knopf for both of the last two books. "Carver's way of staging a story, staging its revelations, is, I think, unique. Carver's sentence is unique. But what has most powerfully persuaded me of Carver's value is his sense of a peculiar bleakness," a comment that rightly places Carver in the peculiarly bleak tradition of Sherwood Anderson and Carson McCullers. "It's not that his people are impoverished," Lish continues, "except that they might be impoverished in spirit. It's not that they aren't educated, because in some cases they are. They just seem squalid. In every manifestation of human activity, they seem squalid. They're like hillbillies, but hillbillies of the shopping mall. And Carver celebrates that squalor, reveals that squalor, makes poetic that squalor in a way nobody else has tried to do."

In the 1960's and the early 1970's, some of our more ingenious fiction writers—Donald Barthelme and John Barth, Stanley Elkin and Thomas Pynchon, Joseph Heller and John Hawkes—translated the clamor of those years into fictional worlds spinning weirdly out of control, showing us the whimsy and contradictions in our lives with the artifice of narrative form and the farcical nature of characters trying to make a go of it in a behaviorally unbound society. Who can understand the world? they asked. Life is lunacy.

The stories of Raymond Carver tell us that we don't live that way any longer. And if the positive critical judgment of Carver and reader interest in his work prove anything, it is that we believe his vision. In the small struggles of individual lives, Carver touches a large human note: When hope flies and impervious helplessness descends, where will we get our next boost from? What do we do now? Life in Carver's America isn't incomprehensible. It's merely very difficult, and like the claims staked by every fine writer, his territory is not really so localized. "He has done what many of the most gifted writers fail to do," the critic Michael Wood wrote in *The New York Times Book Review*. "He has invented a country of his own." Carver country is a place we all recognize. It's a place that Carver himself comes from, the country of arduous life.

Seven years ago, Raymond Carver had hit bottom, having been virtually defeated by recurrent domestic and financial troubles during the previous 20 years, and having, over a prolonged period of alcoholism, nearly drunk himself dead. "My life had just sunk to a vastly low state," he says now. "I was a goner."

In the spring of 1977, Carver had separated for the last time from the woman who had been his wife since he was 18 and she was 16. He was living alone, on money he had borrowed from his wife, in a rented house in McKinleyville, Calif. He was estranged from his two children; he was broke and unemployed. His first collection of stories, *Will You Please Be Quiet, Please?*, had been published a year earlier, and had even been nominated for a National Book Award, but sales and royalties were insignificant. Moreover, he hadn't written a word since.

"In the last 15 months before I quit drinking," he recalls, "I was hospitalized once and I was in a detox center, a drying-out clinic, three times. I was in pretty serious shape. For all intents and purposes, I was finished as a writer and as a viable, functioning adult male. It was over for me. That's why I can speak of two lives, that life and this life."

Much of Carver's fiction sounds like that life, the first one, life as he no longer lives it. His characters, more often than not, are hapless, in the sense that their lives are without luck. They are married or not, employed or not, sober or not, solvent or not—but whatever the situation, things are in a state of undoneness. Hearing Carver speak about the demise of his first life, you know where the stories come from. His speaking voice sounds suddenly like his writing voice, deadpan, sparse, short on exposition and long on resignation.

Carver quit drinking on June 2, 1977, a day he calls "the line of demarcation" in his life. As he recounts the six months before that date, he is forthright, but the recollections come out softly and slowly and between deep breaths:

"The last of the dryings-out took place between Christmas and New Year's Eve of 1976. When I got out, I started drinking again. And then I went away, up to northern California, to live by myself. I went up there in February 1977. I tried to get sober. I stayed sober for a while, about three weeks. Then I got drunk again, and then I was sober for about another three weeks. And then I thought, 'Well, maybe I can go to San Francisco.' This was at the end of May. I was going to meet Fred Hills, from McGraw-Hill, about a novel he wanted me to write. And Noel Young, at Capra Press, I had some business with him. So I went down there and I had not had a drink for three weeks, and I spent the day in the company of Fred. And we went to several bars in the North Beach area, and he drank and I drank Cokes.

"I remember there was a party that night and a number of writers and editors were there. And wine was the house drink. I remember picking up a glass of wine early on in the party, drinking that glass of wine, and that's it. I do have another recollection, that somewhere in this party I was going around trying to find another glass that had some wine in it. But that's all I remember.

"When I woke up the next morning, I was hideously hung over, and I drank half a pint of vodka, and I drank all that day. I drank all through that weekend, and I don't think I went back up north until Tuesday. Then on Tuesday morning, somehow, I got to the plane back to Arcata. I asked the cabbie to stop for a bottle on the way to the plane. I got back to my house, and I was drunk when I got there, and then I was sick for four days. The fourth day, I was feeling a little better. And I didn't drink, didn't drink, didn't drink. No great long-range plans. It was just a day at a time."

Why this proved to be, as Carver calls it, "the last waltz," isn't clear even to him. The wine party was not the first occasion of his blacking out, the weekend wasn't the worst of his drunken episodes. Asked in his *Paris Review* interview to recall the worst, Carver responded: "Let's just say, on occasion, the police were involved and emergency rooms and courtrooms." Of the source of his ultimate resolve, he says, "It finally sank in on me after that that I was not going to be able to drink like a normal person. I guess I wanted to live."

Carver was born in Clatskanie, Ore., in 1938. He grew up in Yakima, a logging town in the central part of Washington, where his father worked in a mill as a saw-filer, and his mother held odd jobs, clerking and waitressing. After graduating from high school, Carver worked for six months in the mill, long enough to buy a car and some clothes. Then he moved out of his parents' house and married Maryann Burk, the girl he had gotten pregnant. Two children were born before Carver was out of his teens.

"I really don't feel that anything happened in my life until I was 20 and married and had the kids," he has written. And though many of his stories draw on his memories of Yakima and are set in the isolated, working-class environs of the Northwest, the spirit of his fiction derives from the years following, after he and his wife moved the family south, to Paradise, a small town in California.

In the fall of 1958, Carver enrolled as a part-time student at Chico State College. He wanted to be a writer, a desire somehow spawned by his early reading of pulp novels and magazines about fishing and hunting. At Chico State, he found a fan for that flame, his first teacher, the late John Gardner, then an unpublished novelist. Carver credits Gardner with being a seminal influence on his writing life, names him as the man who taught him about the integrity and honesty of fiction, about getting everything right, down to the commas, about the agony and difficulty of that, "a writer's values and craft."

Gardner's inspiration notwithstanding, for the Carvers, the 1960s

were a decade of hardship and drain, of living in rented houses or
apartments in unfamiliar places, of part-time schooling and dispiriting
full-time employment. Before he landed his first white-collar job, as
an editor at a textbook firm in Palo Alto, Carver picked tulips,
pumped gas, swept hospital corridors, swabbed toilets, managed an
apartment complex. His wife worked for the phone company, waited
tables, sold a series of book digests door-to-door. The kids kept them
brutally busy. There was a bankruptcy. Carver remembers baby-
sitters, laundromats, broken appliances, lines of creditors: bad times.

"I learned a long time ago," he says, "when my kids were little,
and we had no money, and we were working our hearts out and
weren't getting anywhere, even though we were giving it our best,
my wife and I, that there were more important things than writing a
poem or a story. That was a very hard realization for me to come to.
But it came to me, and I had to accept it or die. Getting milk and
food on the table, getting the rent paid, if a choice had to be made,
then I had to forgo writing."

After Paradise, they lived in other places: the San Francisco Bay
area, and other California towns like Arcata, Eureka, Sunnyvale,
Cupertino, Santa Cruz, Ben Lomond and Sacramento. There was a
brief stint in Iowa City, Iowa, in 1963-64, which Carver spent in the
writers' program at the University of Iowa. And in the late 1960s,
there was a trip to Israel, when Maryann Carver enrolled in a state-
sponsored program for students abroad, a planned year's sojourn
aborted after a few months because they ran out of money. Carver
recalls the trip as a low point, a final straw, and it was not long after
the return from Israel that his drinking began in earnest. Carver had
left his editing post to accompany his family, and the dashed hopes of
that journey (among other disappointments, they'd been promised a
villa on the Mediterranean, which Carver envisioned as an idyllic
writing space, and ended up living in a crammed suburb of Tel Aviv)
took on a significance for him that was revelatory.

"To make a long story short," he says, "we bagged it and came
home. I didn't write the entire time I was over there, and we came
back and lived in Hollywood for a while. We finally came back up
north, and I got my job back. But my life had changed by then and I
knew the world wasn't my oyster."

The transience Carver experienced in those years has found its expression in his fiction. It isn't that Carver's characters move around so much; for the most part, their lives stand still. Events swirl around them that they are powerless either to stop or take part in, and they feel stuck. The claims their lives have staked seem worthless; the future becomes cruelly shapeless. Carver's characters sense their limits, and their vaguely wandering minds are left deluged with tiny, immediate concerns and unspecific longing.

Carver's people (those who are working) are mailmen, janitors, housewives, teachers; others sell things or wait tables. Some have offices to go to. They feed the children, visit friends and drink or get stoned, enjoy fishing. They have possessions that they're always having fixed or trying to sell. They want to be unperturbed, want the time to pass easily. Contentment lies in the perpetuation of immediately gratifying experience. There is a lot of eating in Carver's stories, a lot of booze and cigarettes, and a lot of fast sex. Reviewers have often portrayed Carver's characters as destitute, whipped by life. But they aren't as tragic as that. Their lives are shabby, not empty, and excruciatingly ordinary.

"Until I started reading these reviews of my work, praising me, I never felt the people I was writing about were so bad off," Carver says. "You know what I mean? The waitress, the bus driver, the mechanic, the hotel keeper. God, the country is filled with these people. They're good people. People doing the best they could."

There is a pivotal, revelatory moment in virtually all the lives he describes. Whether it occurs during the story or has taken place before it begins, that moment upsets the patterns, however banal, in which his characters are accustomed to living. It is the moment at which complacency disappears. Carver focuses on his characters just when they realize that things will be the same forever, a realization that insures that they will never be the same again.

In "So Much Water So Close to Home," a man returns from a weekend fishing trip and goes to bed with his wife. The next morning, he confesses that on the first evening of the trip, he and his companions had found the body of a young girl floating in the river near their campsite, but that they'd decided to remain and fish for the weekend before leaving the woods to report it. The wife, who narrates the story, is hugely unsettled by her husband's having made love to her

still possessing such an ugly secret, and her revulsion catalyzes a
genuine despair.

In one version of the story (Carver, an incorrigible and persnickety
reviser, has written several and published two), she makes her lament
explicit: "Look at what has happened. Yet nothing will change for
Stuart and me. Really change, I mean. We will grow older, both of us,
you can see it in our faces already, in the bathroom mirror, for
instance, mornings when we use the bathroom at the same time. And
certain things around us will change, become easier or harder, one
thing or the other, but nothing will ever be really different. I believe
that."

In "Vitamins," a hospital janitor seeks relief from the uneventful
routine of his life. ("It was a nothing job. I did some work, signed the
card for eight hours, went drinking with the nurses.") He initiates
what promises to be a squalid affair with a friend of his wife's. Their
first date is obscenely intruded upon by a huge black man, a recently
returned Vietnam veteran. His sudden presence ruins the tryst and
turns the couple's thoughts toward bitter self-examination. "Maybe I
could go up to Portland," the woman says, leaving. "There must be
something in Portland. Portland's on everybody's mind these days.
Portland's a drawing card. Portland this, Portland that. Portland's as
good a place as any. It's all the same."

The story ends when the man returns home and finds his wife
stalking through the house in the middle of an unruly nightmare. The
final paragraph is a particularly Carveresque moment of quiet,
personal horror:

"I couldn't take any more tonight. 'Go back to sleep, honey. I'm
looking for something,' I said. I knocked some stuff out of the
medicine chest. Things rolled into the sink. 'Where's the aspirin?' I
said. I knocked down some more things. I didn't care. Things kept
falling."

Carver's is not a particularly lyrical prose. A typical sentence is
blunt and uncomplicated, eschewing the ornaments of descriptive
adverbs and parenthetical phrases. His rhythms are often repetitive or
brusque, as if to suggest the strain of people learning to express
newly felt things, fresh emotions. Time passes in agonizingly linear
fashion, the chronology of a given scene marked by one fraught and

simple gesture after another. Dialogue is usually clipped, and it is
studded with commonplace observations of the concrete objects on
the table or on the wall—rather than the elusive, important issues in
the air. The title of Carver's second story collection, *What We Talk
About When We Talk About Love,* is suggestive of both his subject
matter and technique, his interest in how we obliquely address the
grand concerns in our lives.

To illustrate, here is a passage from "A Serious Talk," in which a
man pays a post-Christmas visit to the family from which he's been
achingly separated. He gives his children their gifts, and then chats
with his fed-up, bitter wife:

"Vera?"
She looked at him.
"Do you have anything to drink? I could use a drink this morning."
"There's some vodka in the freezer."
"When did you start keeping vodka in the freezer?"
"Don't ask."
"Okay," he said. "I won't ask."
He got out the vodka and poured some into a cup he found on the
counter.
She said, "Are you just going to drink it like that, out of a cup?" She
said, "Jesus, Burt. What'd you want to talk about, anyway? I told you
I have someplace to go. I have a flute lesson at one o'clock."
"Are you still taking flute?"
"I just said so. What is it? Tell me what's on your mind, and then I
have to get ready."
"I wanted to say I was sorry."
She said, "You said that."
He said, "If you have any juice, I'll mix it with this vodka."
She opened the refrigerator and moved things around.
"There's cranapple juice," she said.
"That's fine," he said.
"I'm going to the bathroom," she said.

Carver's characters know a good deal less than the author does.
They don't share his wide perspective, and they don't often go in for
analysis or philosophical speculation. The intelligence of the stories is
communicated over their heads, so to speak, from author to reader,
and it is this quality that has led more than one critic to observe a
note of condescension in some of the stories. But in his best work,
Carver's voice serves to reinforce the world of his characters. His is an

almost journalistic kind of accuracy; his voice is the voice of experience.

"All of my stories have in some way to do with my own life," Carver says. But he is firm in his assertion that he doesn't engage in outright autobiography. The germ of a story is a single sentence, he explains, a sentence that offers a million possibilities. "It's a process of connections," he says. "Things begin to connect up. A line here. A word there. Stuff I heard or saw when I was 16 years old or 40 years old. There's no way I could ever write a story about my neighbor Art. But I may some day write a story and use him wandering onto his porch and saying, 'I'm doing my spring cleaning.'

"That picture may appear in my head later with yet another character, who is half his age. 'I'm doing my spring cleaning. What a beautiful day.' That may get into the story. It may have to do with a black man who is 30 years old, doing just that. Or the fact that I heard not so long ago that Art was urinating blood. There was something wrong with his bladder. I won't forget that. And some character in my story, one I'm very close to, he may be urinating blood."

The difference between the lives Carver writes about and the life he has lived is clear. Recently, he wrote an introduction to *On Becoming a Novelist,* a book by his former mentor, John Gardner, published posthumously. In the midst of fond recollections and considerable gratitude, Carver describes his own desire to be a writer as having always been "so strong that, with the encouragement I was given in college, and the insight acquired, I kept on writing long after 'good sense' and the 'cold facts'—the 'realities' of my life—told me, time and time again, that I ought to quit, stop the dreaming, quietly go ahead and do something else."

That desire, coupled with his long years of blue-collar living, has created a dual impulse in Carver, to be both artist and Everyman. As he assesses his chosen work: "If I write a story and somebody connects up with it in some way, is moved by it and reminded of his humanness, then I'm happy. What more can I want? It's important to do the work because somebody needs to do it. It's important to be reminded that we're human. I know I make more of it than I should, but I think it's a noble undertaking, this business. It beats a lot of other things I can think of."

Port Angeles rests against the Strait of Juan de Fuca, a pretty blue
sluice that separates Washington's Olympic Peninsula from British
Columbia. It's a town of blue-collar homes and trim lawns, bars and
takeout restaurants and motels. People who live here work outdoors,
in the woods or on the water; vacationers pass through and fish, hike
or ski in the mountains close by. It's an odd place for a writer
enjoying success, neither a cultural center nor a genuine retreat. Port
Angeles is the home town of the poet Tess Gallagher, the woman
Raymond Carver has been living with for five years.

They met in El Paso, while Carver was teaching there, the first job
he landed after getting sober, but they are keeping house long-
distance at the moment. She is in Syracuse, where she teaches and
where they keep another home. Their lives have been hectic lately.
"Traffic, traffic, commerce, you know," Carver says, too distracting
for him to work well, and that is why he is out here alone. Tess
Gallagher helped design this house, which sits on an abrupt bluff,
and this afternoon it is full of light streaming in through a dozen
windows. It faces north, across the water, and the air is clear enough
today that the city of Victoria, 22 miles distant, is plainly visible.

Throughout the afternoon, Carver has been nibbling, the sort of
instant stuff that nourishes his characters—shrimp cocktail, supermarket cake, breakfast cereal, canned soda. And there are other signs
of well-established habits. Dirty dishes are piled up on the kitchen
counter, and the place is generally littered, with paper, books, record
albums, a typewriter, all absently put down on available surfaces and
left there. The whole scene is actually charming, a man creating his
natural life in a better place than he is used to.

Times change, writers continue to write. Carver's stories about life
as it used to be may be spent. Many critics have noted that the stories
in *Cathedral* are fuller, more generous and more optimistic than those
in his previous books. Two stories in particular, the title story and one
called "Fever," end on notes of resounding uplift. Also, many of his
personal wounds have healed. He is back on amicable terms with his
first wife and with his children. And his recent projects have taken
him in directions he hasn't explored before. There are these poems,
spilling out in droves, he says, "better poems than I've ever written
before." Later on this year, Carver will be the feature poet in a special
issue of the literary magazine *Tendril*. He has a novel underway, but it

is incomplete and dormant at the moment. And last fall, he completed a long screenplay with the director Michael Cimino about the rehabilitation of juvenile felons. "I spend just a few minutes a month in the past," Carver says. "I have my children now, and I know them now on this basis in this new life. And I can't wish for things to be different."

Standing, looking out the window over the bright water, Carver bites into a sweet roll. "Nietzsche has a phrase, *Amor fati,*" he says. "Love what is."

An Interview with Raymond Carver
Larry McCaffery and Sinda Gregory/1984

To be inside a Raymond Carver story is a bit like standing in a model kitchen at Sears—you experience a weird feeling of disjuncture that comes from being in a place where things *appear* to be real and familiar, but where a closer look shows that the turkey is papier-mâché, the broccoli is rubber, and the frilly curtains cover a blank wall. In Carver's fiction things are simply not as they appear. Or, rather, things are *more* than they appear to be, for often commonplace objects—a broken refrigerator, a car, a cigarette, a bottle of beer or whiskey—become transformed in Carver's hands, from realistic props in realistic stories to powerful, emotionally charged signifiers in and of themselves. Language itself undergoes a similar transformation. Since there is little authorial presence and since Carver's characters are often inarticulate and bewildered about the turns their lives have taken, their seemingly banal conversations are typically endowed with unspoken intensity and meaning. Watching Carver's characters interact, then, is rather like spending an evening with two close friends who you know have had a big fight just before you arrived: even the most ordinary gestures and exchanges have transformed meanings, hidden tensions, emotional depths.

Although Carver published two books of poetry in the late 1960s and early '70s (*Near Klamath* in 1968 and *Winter Insomnia* in 1970), it was his book of stories, *Will You Please Be Quiet, Please?*, published in 1976 and nominated for the National Book Award, that established his national reputation as a writer with a unique voice and style. Pared down, stark, yet intense, these stories can perhaps best be compared in their achievement to work outside literature, Bruce Springsteen's album *Nebraska*. Like Springsteen, Carver writes about troubled people on the outs—out of work, out of love, out of touch—whose confusion, turmoils, and poignancy are conveyed through an interplay of surface details. His next collection, *What We Talk About When We Talk About Love* (1981), takes this elliptical, spare style even further. With just enough description to set the scene, just enough interpretation of motivation to clarify the action, these stories offer the illusion of the authorless story in which "reality" is transcribed and meaning arises without mediation. This move toward greater and greater economy was abandoned by Carver in *Cathedral* (1983); as the following conversation indicates, changes in his personal life affected his aesthetics. While still written in his distinctive voice, these stories explore more interior territory using less constricted language.

This change (mirrored as well in his most recent collection of poems, *Ultramarine* [1986]) is apparent not just in style but in the themes found in *Cathedral*, which contains several stories of hope and spiritual communion. As we drove to Carver's home outside Port Angeles, Washington, we were still formulating questions designed to reveal why *Cathedral* was less bleak, less constricted. But nothing very devious or complex was required. Sitting in his living room, which offers an amazing vista of the blustery Strait of Juan de Fuca, Carver was obviously a happy man—happy in the home life he shares with Tess Gallagher, his work, his victory over alcohol, and his new direction. Replying to our questions in a soft, low voice with the same kind of direct honesty evident in his fiction, Carver seemed less like an author of three collections of stories; a book of essays, short stories, and poems (*Fires,* 1983); and three volumes of poetry than he did a writer starting out, eager to begin work, anxious to see where his life would lead.

Larry McCaffery: In an essay in *Fires* you say, "To write a novel, it seemed to me, a writer should be living in a world that makes sense, a world that the writer can believe in, draw a bead on, and then write about accurately. A world that will, for a time anyway, stay fixed in one place. Along with this there has to be a belief in the essential *correctness* of that world." Am I right in assuming that you've arrived at a place, physically and psychologically, where you can believe in the "correctness" of your world enough to sustain a novel-length imaginary world?

Raymond Carver: I do feel I've arrived at such a place. My life is very different now than it used to be; it seems much more comprehensible to me. It was previously almost impossible for me to imagine trying to write a novel in the state of incomprehension, despair, really, that I was in. I have hope now, and I didn't have hope then—"hope" in the sense of belief. I believe now that the world will exist for me tomorrow in the same way it exists for me today. That didn't used to be the case. For a long time I found myself living by the seat of my pants, making things terribly difficult for myself and everyone around me by my drinking. In this second life, this post-drinking life, I still retain a certain sense of pessimism, I suppose, but I also have belief in and love for the things of this world. Needless to say, I'm not talking about microwave ovens, jet planes, and expensive cars.

LM: Does this mean you have plans to try your hand at a novel?

RC: Yes. Maybe. Maybe after I finish this new manuscript of poems. Maybe then I'll return to fiction and do some longer fiction, a novel or a novella. I feel like I'm reaching the end of the time of writing poetry. In another month or so I'll have written something like 150-180 poems during this period, so I feel like I'm about to run out this string, and then I can go back to fiction. It's important to me, though, to have this new book of poems in manuscript in the cupboard. When *Cathedral* came out, that cupboard was absolutely bare; I don't want something like that to happen again. Tobias Wolff recently finished a book of stories that he turned in to Houghton Mifflin; he asked me if it was hard for me to start work again after finishing a book, because he was having a hard time getting going again. I told him not to worry about it *now*, but that he should make sure he's well along on something by the time his book is ready to come out. If you've emptied all your cupboards, the way I had after *Cathedral,* it can be difficult to catch your stride again.

Sinda Gregory: Your newfound "belief in and love for the things of this world" is very evident in some of the stories in *Cathedral,* especially in the title story.

RC: That story was very much an "opening up" process for me—

I mean that in every sense. "Cathedral" *was* a larger, grander story than anything I had previously written. When I began writing that story I felt that I was breaking out of something I had put myself into, both personally and aesthetically. I simply couldn't go on any farther in the direction I had been going in *What We Talk About When We Talk About Love*. Oh, I *could* have, I suppose, but I didn't want to. Some of the stories were becoming too attenuated. I didn't write anything for five or six months after that book came out. I literally wrote nothing except letters. So it was especially pleasing to me that, when I finally sat down to write again, I wrote *that* story, "Cathedral." It felt like I had never written anything that way before. I could let myself *go* in some way, I didn't have to impose the restrictions on myself that I had in the earlier stories. The last story I wrote for the collection was "Fever," which was also just about the longest story I've ever written. And it's affirmative, I think, positive in its outlook. Really, the whole collection is different, and the next book is going to be different as well!

LM: What does it mean to a writer like you to find yourself, relatively suddenly, in such a different frame of mind? Do you find it difficult today to write about the despair, emotional turmoil, and hopelessness that is so much a part of the vision of your earlier fiction?

RC: No, because when I need to open this door to my imagination—stare out over the window casement, what Keats called his "magic casements"—I can remember exactly the texture of that despair and hopelessness, I can still taste it, feel it. The things that are emotionally meaningful to me are still very much alive and available to me, even though the circumstances of my personal life have changed. Merely because my physical surroundings and my mental state are different today doesn't mean, of course, that I still don't know exactly what I was talking about in the earlier stories. I can bring all that back if I choose to, but I'm finding that I am not driven to write about it exclusively. That's not to say I'm interested in writing about life here, where I live in Four Seasons Ranch, this chichi development. If you look carefully at *Cathedral*, you'll find that many of those stories have to do with that other life, which is still very much with me. But not all of them do, which is why the book feels different to me.

LM: A striking example of the differences you're referring to can be seen when you compare "A Small, Good Thing" (in *Cathedral*) with the earlier version, "The Bath," which appeared in *What We Talk About*. The differences between the two versions are clearly fundamental.

RC: Certainly there's a lot more optimism in "A Small, Good Thing." In my own mind I consider them to be really two entirely different stories, not just different versions of the same story; it's hard to even look on them as coming from the same source. I went back to that one, as well as several others, because I felt there was unfinished business that needed attending to. The story hadn't been told originally; it had been messed around with, condensed and compressed in "The Bath" to highlight the qualities of menace that I wanted to emphasize—you see this with the business about the baker, the phone call, with its menacing voice on the other line, the bath, and so on. But I still felt there was unfinished business, so in the midst of writing these other stories for *Cathedral* I went back to "The Bath" and tried to see what aspects of it needed to be enhanced, redrawn, reimagined. When I was done, I was amazed because it seemed so much better. I've had people tell me that they much prefer "The Bath," which is fine, but "A Small, Good Thing" seems to me to be a better story.

SG: Many of your stories either open with the ordinary being slightly disturbed by this sense of menace you've just mentioned, or they develop in that direction. Is this tendency the result of your conviction that the world *is* menacing for most people? Or does it have more to do with an aesthetic choice—that menace contains more interesting possibilities for storytelling?

RC: The world is a menacing place for many of the people in my stories, yes. The people I've chosen to write about *do* feel menace, and I think many, if not most, people feel the world is a menacing place. Probably not so many people who will see this interview feel menace in the sense I'm talking about. Most of our friends and acquaintances, yours and mine, don't feel this way. But try living on the other side of the tracks for a while. Menace is there, and it's palpable. As to the second part of your question, that's true, too. Menace does contain, for me at least, more interesting possibilities to explore.

SG: When you look back at your stories, do you find "unfinished business" in most of them?

RC: This may have to do with this newfound confidence, but I feel that the stories in *Cathedral* are *finished* in a way I rarely felt about my stories previously. I've never even read the book since I saw it in bound galleys. I was happy about those stories, not worried about them; I felt there was simply no need to mess around with them, make new judgments about them. A lot of this surely has to do with this whole complicated business about the new circumstances in my life, my sense of confidence in what I'm doing with my life and my work. For such a long time, when I was an alcoholic, I was very *un*-confident and had such very low self-esteem, both as a person and as a writer, that I was always questioning my judgments about everything. Every good thing that has happened to me during the last several years has been an incentive to do more and do better. I know I've felt that recently in writing all these poems, and it's affecting my fiction as well. I'm more sure of my voice, more sure of *something*. I felt a bit tentative when I started writing those poems, maybe partly because I hadn't written any for so long, but I soon found a voice— and that voice gave me confidence. Now when I start writing some- thing, and I mean *now* in these last few years, I don't have that sense of fooling around, of being tentative, of not knowing what to do, of having to sharpen a lot of pencils. When I go to my desk now and pick up a pen, I really know what I have to do. It's a totally different feeling.

SG: What was it that made you return to poetry after all those years of focusing exclusively on fiction?

RC: I came out here to Port Angeles with the intention of bringing to completion a long piece of fiction I had started back at Syracuse. But when I got out here, I sat around for five days or so, just enjoying the peace and quiet (I didn't have a television or radio), a welcome change from all the distractions going on at Syracuse. After those five days I found myself reading a little poetry. Then one night I sat down and wrote a poem. I hadn't written any poetry in two years or more, and somewhere in the back of my mind I was lamenting the fact that I hadn't written any—or really even given any serious thought to poetry writing for a long time. During the period when I was writing the stories that went into *Cathedral*, for example, I was feeling I couldn't have written a poem if someone had put a gun to my head. I wasn't even *reading* any poetry, except for Tess's. At any rate, I wrote this first poem that night, and then the next day I got up and

wrote another poem. The day after that I wrote *another* poem. This
went on for ten straight weeks; the poems seemed to be coming out
of this wonderful rush of energy. At night I'd feel totally empty,
absolutely whipped out, and I'd wonder if anything would be left the
next morning. But the next day there *was* something—the well
hadn't gone dry. So I'd get up, drink coffee, and go to my desk and
write another poem. When it was happening I felt almost as if I were
being given a good shaking, and suddenly my keys were falling out of
my pockets. I've never had a period in which I've taken such joy in
the act of writing as I did in those two months.

LM: You've said that it no longer matters where you are living as
far as your writing is concerned. Has that feeling changed?

RC: I'd certainly retract that statement nowadays. Having this
place here in Port Angeles has been very important to me, and I'm
sure coming out here helped me get started writing poetry. I think it
was getting clear away from the outdoors and my contact with nature
that made me feel I was losing whatever it was that made me want to
write poetry. I had spent the summer of 1982 out here (not in this
house, but in a little cabin a few miles from here), and I wrote four
stories in a fairly short period of time, although they took place
indoors and didn't have anything specifically to do with this locale.
But without question my poetry came back to me because of this
relocation. It had been increasingly difficult for me to work in Syracuse, which is why I pulled up stakes and came out here. There was
just too much going on back in Syracuse, especially after *Cathedral*
came out and there was so much happening in connection with the
book. There were people coming in and out of the house, and a lot
of other business that never seemed to end. The telephone was
ringing all the time, and Tess was teaching, and there were a certain
number of social obligations. This might only mean having an
occasional dinner with dear friends, whom it was always a pleasure to
see, but all this was taking me away from my work. It got to the point
where even hearing the cleaning woman, hearing her make the bed
or vacuum the rug or wash the dishes, bothered me. So I came out
here, and when Tess left to go back to Syracuse on September 1, I
stayed on for another four weeks to write and fish. I did a lot of work
during those weeks, and when I got back to Syracuse I thought I
could keep up that rhythm. I did manage to for a few days, but then I

found myself limited to editing the stuff I had written out here. Finally, the last few weeks or so, it was all I could do to make it from day to day. I would consider it a good day if I could take care of my correspondence. That's a hell of a situation for a writer to be in. I wasn't sorry to leave, even though I have some dear friends there.

SG: In the *Esquire* article you wrote about your father, you mention a poem you wrote, "Photograph of My Father in His 22nd Year," and comment that "the poem was a way of trying to connect up with him." Does poetry offer you a more direct way of connecting to your past?

RC: I'd say it does. It's a more immediate way, a faster means of connecting. Doing these poems satisfies my desire to write something, and tell a story, every day—sometimes two or three times a day, even four or five times a day. But in regard to connecting up to my past, it must be said of my poems (and my stories, too) that even though they may all have some basis in my experience, they are also *imaginative.* They're totally made up, most of them.

LM: So even in your poetry that persona who is speaking is never precisely "you"?

RC: No. Same as in my stories, those stories told in the first person, for instance. Those "I" narrators aren't me.

SG: In your poem "For Semra, with Martial Vigor," your narrator says to a woman, "All poems are love poems." Is this true in some sense of your own poetry?

RC: Every poem is an act of love, and faith. There is so little other reward for writing poems, either monetarily or in terms of, you know, fame and glory, that the act of writing a poem has to be an act that justifies itself and really has no other end in sight. To *want* to do it, you really have to love doing it. In that sense, then, every poem *is* a "love poem."

LM: Have you found it a problem to move back and forth between genres? Is a different composition process involved?

RC: The juggling has never seemed a problem. I suppose it would have been more unusual in a writer who hadn't worked in both areas to the extent that I have. Actually I've always felt and maintained that the poem is closer in its effect and in the way it is composed to a short story than the short story is to a novel. Stories and poems have more in common in what the writing is aiming for, in the compression of language and emotion, and in the care and control required to achieve their effects. To me, the process of writing a story or a poem has never seemed very different. Everything I write comes from the same spring, or source, whether it's a story or an essay or a poem or a screenplay. When I sit down to write, I literally start with a sentence or a line. I always have to have that first line in my head, whether it's a poem or a story. Later on everything else is subject to change, but that first line rarely changes. Somehow it shoves me on to the second line, and then the process begins to take on momentum and acquire a direction. Nearly everything I write goes through many revisions, and I do a lot of backing up, to-and-froing. I don't mind revising; I actually enjoy it, in fact. Don Hall has taken seven years to write and polish the poems that make up his new book. He's revised some of the poems a hundred and fifty times or so. I'm not *that* obsessive, but I do a lot of revising, it's true. And I think friends of mine are a bit dubious about how my poems are going to turn out. They just don't think poems can or should be written as fast as I wrote these. I'll just have to show them.

LM: One possible source of interaction between your poetry and fiction has to do with the way the impact of your stories often seems to center on a single image: a peacock, a cigarette, a car. These images seem to function like poetic images—that is, they organize the story, draw our responses into a complex set of associations. How conscious are you of developing this kind of controlling image?

RC: I'm not consciously creating a central image in my fiction that would control a story the way images, or an image, often control a work of poetry. I have an image in my head but it seems to emerge out of the story in an organic, natural fashion. For instance, I didn't realize in advance that the peacock image would so dominate "Feathers." The peacock just seemed like something a family who lived in the country on a small farm might have running around the house. It *wasn't* something I placed there in an effort to have it perform as a symbol. When I'm writing I don't think in terms of developing symbols or of what an image will do. When I hit on an image that seems to be working and it stands for what it is supposed to stand for (it may stand for several other things as well), that's great. But I don't think of them self-consciously. They seem to evolve, occur. I truly invent them and *then* certain things seem to form around them as events occur, recollection and imagination begin to color them, and so forth.

SG: In an essay in *Fires,* you make a remark that perfectly describes for me one of the most distinctive things about your fiction: "It's possible, in a poem or a short story, to write about commonplace things and objects using commonplace language and to endow those things—a chair, a window curtain, a fork, a stone, a woman's earring—with immense, even startling power." I realize that every story is different in this regard, but how *does* one go about investing these ordinary objects with such power and emphasis?

RC: I'm not given to rhetoric or abstraction in my life, my thinking, or my writing, so when I write about people I want them to be placed within a setting that must be made as palpable as possible. This might mean including as part of the setting a television or a table or a felt-tipped pen lying on a desk, but if these things are going to be introduced into the scene at all, they shouldn't be inert. I don't mean that they should take on a life of their own, precisely, but they should make their presence *felt* in some way. If you are going to describe a spoon or a chair or a TV set, you don't want simply to set these things into the scene and let them go. You want to give them some weight, connecting these things to the lives around them. I see these objects as playing a role in the stories; they're not "characters" in the sense that the people are, but they are *there* and I want my readers to be aware that they're there, to know that this ashtray is here, that the TV is there (and that it's going or it's not going), that the fireplace has old pop cans in it.

SG: What appeals to you about writing stories and poems, rather than longer forms?

RC: For one thing, whenever I pick up a literary magazine, the first thing I look at is the poetry, and then I'll read the stories. I hardly ever read anything else, the essays, reviews, what have you. So I suppose I was drawn to the *form,* and I mean the brevity, of both poetry and short fiction from the beginning. Also, poetry and short fiction seemed to be things I could get done in a reasonable period of time. When I started out as a writer, I was moving around a lot, and there were daily distractions, weird jobs, family responsibilities. My life seemed very fragile, so I wanted to be able to start something that I felt I had a reasonable chance of seeing through to a finish—which meant I needed to finish things in a hurry, a short period of time. As I just mentioned, poetry and fiction seemed so close to one another in form and intent, so close to what I was interested in doing, that early on I didn't have any trouble moving back and forth between them.

LM: Who were the poets you were reading and admiring, perhaps being influenced by, when you were developing your notions of the craft of poetry? Your outdoor settings may suggest James Dickey, but a more likely influence seems to me to be William Carlos Williams.

RC: Williams was indeed a big influence; he was my greatest hero. When I started out writing poetry I was reading his poems. Once I even had the temerity to write him and ask for a poem for a little magazine I was starting at Chico State University called *Selection*. I think we put out three issues; I edited the first issue. But William Carlos Williams actually sent me a poem. I was thrilled and surprised to see his signature under the poem. That's an understatement. Dickey's poetry did not mean so much, even though he was just coming into his full powers at about the time when I was starting out in the early '60s. I liked Creeley's poetry, and later Robert Bly, Don Hall, Galway Kinnell, James Wright, Dick Hugo, Gary Snyder, Archie Ammons, Merwin, Ted Hughes. I really didn't know anything when I was starting out, I just sort of read what people gave me, but I've never been drawn to highly intellectualized poetry—the metaphysical poets or whatever.

LM: Is abstraction or intellectualism something that usually turns you off in a work?

RC: I don't think it's an anti-intellectual bias, if that's what you mean. There are just some works that I can respond to and others operating at levels I don't connect with. I suppose I'm not interested in what you might call the "well-made poem," for example. When I see one I'm tempted to react by saying, "Oh, that's just poetry." I'm looking for something else, something that's *not just* a good poem. Practically any good graduate student in a creative writing program can write a good poem. I'm looking for something beyond that. Maybe something rougher.

SG: A reader is immediately struck with the "pared down" quality of your work, especially your work before *Cathedral*. Was this style something that evolved, or had it been with you from the beginning?

RC: From the very beginning I loved the rewriting process as much as the initial execution. I've always loved taking sentences and playing with them, rewriting them, paring them down to where they seem solid somehow. This may have resulted from being John Gardner's student, because he told me something I immediately responded to: If you can say it in fifteen words rather than twenty or thirty words, then say it in fifteen words. That struck me with the force of revelation. There I was, groping to find my own way, and here someone was telling me something that somehow conjoined with what I already wanted to do. It was the most natural thing in the world for me to go back and refine what was happening on the page and eliminate the padding. The last few days I've been reading Flaubert's letters, and he says some things that seem relevant to my own aesthetic. At one point when Flaubert was writing *Madame Bovary,* he would knock off at midnight or one in the morning and write letters to his mistress, Louise Colet, about the construction of the book and his general notion of aesthetics. One passage he wrote her that really struck me was when he said, "The artist in his work must be like God in his creation—invisible and all powerful; he must be everywhere felt but nowhere seen." I like the last part of that especially. There's another interesting remark when Flaubert is writing to his editors at the magazine that published the book in installments. They were just getting ready to serialize *Madame Bovary* and were going to make a lot of cuts in the text because they were afraid they were going to be closed down by the government if they published it just as Flaubert wrote it, so Flaubert tells them that if they make the cuts they can't publish the book, but they'll still be friends. The last line of this letter is: "I know how to distinguish between literature and literary business"—another insight I respond to. Even in these letters his prose is astonishing: "Prose must stand upright from one end to the other, like a wall whose ornamentation continues down to its very base." "Prose is architecture." "Everything must be done coldly, with poise." "Last week I spent five days writing one page." One of the interesting things about the Flaubert book is the way it demonstrates how self-consciously he was setting out to do something very special and different with prose. He consciously tried to make prose an art form. If you look at what else was being published in Europe in 1857, when *Madame Bovary* was published, you realize what an achievement the book really is.

LM: In addition to John Gardner, were there other writers who affected your fictional sensibility early on? Hemingway comes immediately to mind.

RC: Hemingway was certainly an influence. I didn't read him until I was in college and then I read the wrong book (*Across the River and into the Trees*) and didn't like him very much. But a little later I read *In Our Time* in a class and I found that he was marvelous. I remember thinking, This is *it*; if you can write prose like this, you've done something.

LM: In your essays you've spoken out against literary tricks or gimmicks—yet I would argue that your own works are really experimental in the same sense that Hemingway's fiction was. What's the difference between literary experimentalism that seems legitimate to you and the kind that isn't?

RC: I'm against tricks that call attention to themselves in an effort to be clever or merely devious. I read a review this morning in *Publishers Weekly* of a novel that is coming out next spring; the book sounded so disjointed and filled with things that have nothing to do with life, or literature as I know it, that I felt certain I wouldn't read it except under pain of death. A writer mustn't lose sight of the story. I'm not interested in works that are all texture and no flesh and blood. I guess I'm old-fashioned enough to feel that the reader must somehow be involved at the human level. And that there is still, or ought to be, a compact between writer and reader. Writing, or any form of artistic endeavor, is not just expression, it's communication. When a writer stops being truly interested in communicating something and is only aiming at expressing something, and that not very well—well, they can express themselves by going out to the streetcorner and hollering. A short story or a novel or a poem should deliver a certain number of emotional punches. You can judge that work by how strong these punches are and how many are thrown. If it's all just a bunch of head trips or games, I'm not interested. Work like that is just chaff: it'll blow away with the first good wind.

LM: Are there out-and-out experimentalists whom you *do* admire? I was wondering about your reaction to Donald Barthelme's work, for example.

RC: I like his work. I didn't care much for it when I first started reading it. It seemed so strange that I stopped reading him for a while. Also, he was, or so it seemed to me, the generation right

ahead of mine, and it wouldn't do at the time to like it all that much!
But then I read *Sixty Stories* a couple of years ago. He's terrific! I
found that the more I read his stories, the more regard I began to
have for them. Barthelme has done a *world* of work, he's a true
innovator who's not being devious or stupid or mean spirited or
experimenting for experimenting's sake. He's uneven, but then who
isn't? Certainly his effect on creative writing classes has been
tremendous (as they say, he's often imitated but never duplicated).
He's like Allen Ginsberg in that he opened a gate, and afterward a
great flood of work by other people poured through, some of it good
and a lot of it awful. I'm not worried that all that bad stuff which has
followed after Barthelme or Ginsberg will push the good stuff off the
shelves. It will just disappear on its own.

SG: One of the nontraditional aspects of your own fiction is that
your stories don't tend to have the "shape" of the classically rendered
story: the introduction/conflict/development/resolution structure of so
much fiction. Instead there is often a static or ambiguous, open-
ended quality to your stories. I assume you feel that the experiences
you are describing simply don't lend themselves to being rendered
within the familiar framework.

RC: It would be inappropriate, and to a degree impossible, to
resolve things neatly for these people and situations I'm writing
about. It's probably typical for writers to admire other writers who are
their opposites in terms of intentions and effects, and I'll admit that I
greatly admire stories that unfold in that classic mode, with conflict,
resolution, and denouement. But even though I can respect those
stories, and sometimes even be a little envious, I can't write them.
The writer's job, if he or she has a job, is not to provide conclusions
or answers. If the story answers *itself,* its problems and conflicts, and
meets its *own* requirements, then that's enough. On the other hand, I
want to make certain my readers aren't left feeling cheated in one
way or another when they've finished my stories. It's important for
writers to provide enough to satisfy readers, even if they don't
provide "the" answers, or clear resolutions.

LM: Another distinctive feature of your work is that you usually
present characters that most writers don't deal with—that is, people
who are basically inarticulate, who can't verbalize their plights, who
often don't seem to really grasp what is happening to them.

RC: I don't think of this as being especially "distinctive" or non-

traditional because I feel perfectly comfortable with these people
while I'm working. I've known people like this all my life. Essentially, I
am one of those confused, befuddled people, I come from people
like that, those are the people I've worked with and earned my living
beside for years. That's why I've never had any interest whatsoever in
writing a story or a poem that has anything to do with the academic
life, with teachers or students and so forth. I'm just not that interested. The things that have made an indelible impression on me are
the things I saw in lives I witnessed being lived around me, and in the
life I myself lived. These were lives where people really *were* scared
when someone knocked on their door, day or night, or when the
telephone rang; they didn't know how they were going to pay the
rent or what they could do if their refrigerator went out. Anatole
Broyard tries to criticize my story "Preservation" by saying, "So the
refrigerator breaks—why don't they just call a repairman and get it
fixed?" That kind of remark is dumb. You bring a repairman out to fix
your refrigerator and it's sixty bucks to *fix* it; and who knows how
much if the thing is completely broken? Well, Broyard may not be
aware of it, but some people can't afford to bring in a repairman if it's
going to cost them sixty bucks, just like they don't get to a doctor if
they don't have insurance, and their teeth go bad because they can't
afford to go to a dentist when they need one. That kind of situation
doesn't seem unrealistic or artificial to me. It also doesn't seem that,
in focusing on this group of people, I have really been doing anything
all that different from other writers. Chekhov was writing about a
submerged population a hundred years ago. Short story writers have
always been doing that. Not all of Chekhov's stories are about people
who are down and out, but a significant number of them deal with
that submerged population I'm talking about. He wrote about doctors
and businessmen and teachers sometimes, but he also gave voice to
people who were not so articulate. He found a means of letting those
people have their say as well. So in writing about people who aren't
so articulate and who are confused and scared, I'm not doing
anything radically different.

   LM: Aren't there formal problems in writing about this group of
people? I mean, you can't have them sit around in drawing rooms
endlessly analyzing their situations, the way James does, or, in a
different sense, the way Bellow does. I suppose setting the scene,

composing it, must be especially important from a technical standpoint.

RC: If you mean literally just setting the scene, that's the least of my worries. The scene is easy to set: I just open the door and see what's inside. I pay a lot of attention to trying to make the people talk the right way. By this I don't mean just *what* they say, but *how* they say it, and *why*. I guess *tone* is what I'm talking about, partly. There's never any chit-chat in my stories. Everything said is for a reason and adds, I want to think, to the overall impression of the story.

SG: People usually emphasize the realistic aspects of your work, but I feel there's a quality about your fiction that is *not* basically realistic. It's as if something is happening almost off the page, a dreamy sense of irrationality, almost like Kafka's fiction.

RC: Presumably my fiction is in the realistic tradition (as opposed to the really far-out side), but just telling it like it is bores me. It really does. People couldn't possibly read pages of description about the way people *really* talk, about what *really* happens in their lives. They'd just snore away, of course. If you look carefully at my stories, I don't think you'll find people talking the way people do in real life. People always say that Hemingway had a great ear for dialogue, and he did. But no one ever talked in real life like they do in Hemingway's fiction. At least not until after they've *read* Hemingway.

LM: In "Fires," you say that it is not true for you, as it was with Flannery O'Connor or Gabriel García Márquez, that most of the stuff that has gone into your fiction had already happened to you before you were twenty. You go on to say, "Most of what now strikes me as story 'material' presented itself to me after I was twenty. I really don't remember much about my life before I became a parent. I really don't feel that anything happened in my life until I was twenty and married and had the kids." Would you still agree with that statement? I say this because we were both struck, after we read the piece about your father in *Esquire*, with how much your description of your childhood and relationship with your father seemed relevant to your fictional world in various ways.

RC: That statement certainly felt true when I wrote it—it simply didn't seem that much had truly happened to me until I became a father, at least the sorts of things I could (or wanted to) transform in my stories. But I was also just gaining some perspective on various aspects of my life when I wrote "Fires," and by the time I wrote the piece on my father for *Esquire* I had even more perspective on things. But I see what you're saying. I had touched on something in a very close way in regard to my father when I wrote that essay, which I wrote very quickly and which seemed to come to me very directly. I still feel, though, that the piece on my father is an exception. In that instance I could go back and touch some "source material" from my early life, but that life exists for me as through a scrim of rain.

SG: What kind of a kid were you in that earlier life?

RC: A dreamy kid. I wanted to be a writer and I mostly followed my nose as far as reading was concerned. I'd go to the library and check out books on the Spanish conquistadors, or historical novels, whatever struck my fancy, books on shipbuilding, anything that caught my eye. I didn't have any instruction in that regard at all; I'd just go down to the library once a week and browse. All in all, I'd say my childhood was fairly conventional in many respects. We were a poor family, didn't have a car for the longest while, but I didn't miss not having a car. My parents worked and struggled and finally became what I guess you'd call lower middle class. But for the longest while we didn't have much of anything in the way of material goods, or spiritual goods or values either. But I didn't have to go out and work in the fields when I was ten years old or anything of that sort. Mainly I just wanted to fish and hunt and ride around in cars with other guys. Date girls. Things like that. I sponged off my folks as long as I could. The pickings were slim at times, but they bought me things. They even bought me my cigarettes the first year or two I was smoking; I didn't have a job and I guess they knew I would have gone out and stolen them if they didn't buy them for me. But I did want to write, which might have been the only thing that set me apart from my friends. There was one other kid in high school who was my friend and who wanted to write, so we would talk about books. But that was about it. An undistinguished childhood.

SG: Was your father much of a storyteller?

RC: He read to me a little when I was a kid. Mainly Zane Grey stories that he'd read when I'd ask him to (he had a few of those books in the house). But he also told me stories.

LM: You've referred to the bad times you went through with your drinking in the '60s and '70s. In retrospect, was there anything positive at all that came out of those experiences?

RC: Obviously my drinking experiences helped me write several stories that have to do with alcoholism. But the fact that I went through that and was able to write those stories was nothing short of a miracle. No, I don't see anything coming out of my drinking experiences except waste and pain and misery. And it was that way for everybody involved in my life. No good came out of it except in the way that someone might spend ten years in the penitentiary and then come out of that and write about the experience. Despite that comical remark Richard Nixon made about writing and prison at the time when he was about to be impeached, you have to take it on faith that prison life is not the best for a writer.

LM: So you never used any of those confessional stories that one hears at AA meetings as the starting point for one of your stories?

RC: No, I never have. I've heard a lot of stories in AA but most of them I forgot immediately. Oh, I recall a few, but none of them ever struck me as material I wanted to use for a story. Certainly I never went to those meetings thinking of them as possible source materials for my work. To the extent that my stories have to do with drinking, they all pretty much have some starting point in my own experience rather than in the funny, crazy, sad stories I heard at AA. Right now I feel there are enough drinking stories in my work, so I'm not interested in writing them anymore. Not that I have a quota in the back of my mind for any particular type of story, but I'm ready to move on to something else.

SG: I wonder if you're ready to move on to writing more about the outdoors or nature once again. Those elements seem to be missing from your recent work.

RC: I began writing by wanting to write about those things like hunting and fishing that played a real part in my emotional life. And I did write about nature quite a lot in my early poems and stories: you can find it in many of the stories in *Furious Seasons* and in some of the ones in *Will You Please Be Quiet, Please?* and in a lot of the poems. Then I seemed to lose that contact with nature, so I haven't set many of my recent stories in the outdoors—although I suspect I will in the time to come, since a lot of the poems I've recently been writing are set outside. The water has been coming into these poems, and the moon, and the mountains and the sky. I'm sure this will make a lot of people in Manhattan laugh! Talk of tides and the trees, whether the fish are biting or not biting. These things are going to work their way back into my fiction. I feel directly in touch with my surroundings now in a way I haven't felt in years. It just so happened that this was channeled into what I was writing at the time, which was poetry. If I had started a novel or some stories, this contact I've reestablished would have emerged there as well.

SG: Who are the contemporary writers you admire or feel some affinity with?

RC: There are many. I just finished Edna O'Brien's selected stories, *A Fanatic Heart.* She's wonderful. And Tobias Wolff, Bobbie Ann Mason, Ann Beattie, Joy Williams, Richard Ford, Ellen Gilchrist, Bill Kittredge, Alice Munro, Frederick Barthelme. Barry Hannah's short stories. Joyce Carol Oates and John Updike. So many others. It's a fine time to be alive, and writing.

Poetry, Poverty and Realism Down in Carver Country

Gordon Burn/1985

A different version of this interview appeared in *The Times* [London], 17 April 1985, 12. Reprinted by permission of Gordon Burn and *The Times*. Conducted Spring 1985.

I sat on the left in the train travelling north from New York to Syracuse, watching the ranch-style houses and four-bedroom colonials of Cheever country slowly give way to the non-deluxe tract homes and trailer parks that for a growing number of devotees are coming to mean Carver country.

Underclass America is a territory which, in just three volumes of short stories, Raymond Carver has made so distinctively his own that you feel you can almost hear the baby wails, vacuum-cleaner squeals and recriminatory, ketchup-hurling brawls emanating from the trackside dwellings as the train flies past.

Sitting on the left of the train was advice I had remembered from "Cathedral," the title story of Carver's latest collection, in which a man reluctantly welcomes a blind friend of his wife's into his home.

"Did you have a good train ride?" the narrator asks the blind man on arrival. "Which side of the train did you sit on, by the way?" To which the blind man replies: "Right side. I hadn't been on a train in nearly forty years. Not since I was a kid. With my folks. That's been a long time. I'd nearly forgotten the sensation."

"Have a good train ride?" Carver, a big, unexpectedly fleshy man in a duffle-coat and almost-Earthshoes, enquired politely when he collected me at Syracuse. "Did you sit on the left? You get the best views over the Hudson that way," he went on, having squeezed himself behind the wheel of a VW Beetle suffering from terminal rust. "I hadn't been on a train in years till we moved here. Not since I was a kid."

Raymond Carver's genius for forging meaning out of the day-to-day chaos of directionless and otherwise meaningless lives has established him as one of the most influential and popular short-story writers in America. He has evolved a spare, ruthlessly cut-back prose style that derives its power as much from what is left out as what is put in—"the landscape just under the smooth (but sometimes broken and unsettled) surface of things."

"Dirty realism" is what *Granta,* the magazine that first championed it in this country, christened the work of Carver and such American contemporaries as Richard Ford, Barry Hannah, Denis Johnson, Jayne Anne Phillips, and Bobbie Ann Mason, all of whom share a common subject matter—in Carver's words, "People who don't succeed at what they try to do, at the things they most want to do, the large or small things that support the life."

The following paragraph, from a story called "Where Is Everyone?," is classic Carver, both in its style and its preoccupations:

> During those days, when my mother was putting out to men she'd just met, I was out of work, drinking, and crazy. My kids were crazy, and my wife was crazy and having a "thing" with an unemployed aerospace engineer she'd met at AA. He was crazy too. His name was Ross and he had five or six kids. He walked with a limp from a gunshot wound his first wife had given him. He didn't have a wife now; he wanted my wife. I don't know what we were all thinking of in those days.

The simplicity is deceptive. "Carver's fiction," as Frank Kermode has pointed out, "is so spare in manner that it takes a time before one realizes how completely a whole culture and a whole moral condition is represented by even the most seemingly slight sketch."

It is only recently, since he received an American Academy of Arts and Letters award worth $35,000 a year, that Carver has been able to write full-time. The "No Visitors" sign is regularly posted outside the house in Syracuse where he lives in suburban anonymity with the poet Tess Gallagher, and he occasionally takes off alone for the house they have had built on the West Coast, in Washington State. On a recent visit there, more than a hundred poems poured out of him in sixty-five days. "Something happened," he said, still vaguely bemused. "I was writing poems at the rate of two or three or four a day. Which was a completely new experience for me. I felt . . . electrified."

Carver turned to short-story writing originally because short stories were all he could fit into his life as a husband and father. "I had to sit down and write something I could finish now, tonight, or at least

tomorrow night, no later, after I got in from work." It often meant
sitting outside in the car, scribbling on a pad on his knee. But he has
finally started on the extended piece of fiction (he is reluctant to call it
a novel) which the circumstances of his life always prevented him
from attempting until now.

Carver was born in 1938 and grew up in a small town in Washington State, where his father worked at a sawmill and his mother took
whatever jobs she could get. He married young and had two children
by the age of twenty. "In those days," he has written, "I always
worked some crap job or another, and my wife did the same. . . . I
worked sawmill jobs, janitor jobs, delivery man jobs, service station
jobs, stockroom boy jobs. . . . Time and again I reached the point
where I couldn't see or plan any further ahead than the first of next
month and gathering together enough money, by hook or by crook,
to meet the rent and provide the children's school clothes."

Almost willfully, like his father and many of the characters in his
fiction, Carver took to the bottle. He became an alcoholic. In the
fifteen months following the publication in 1976 of *Will You Please Be
Quiet, Please?,* his first collection of stories, he was in and out of
hospitals and other institutions and ended up in a rehabilitation centre
that had once been a hospital for the criminally insane.

"I couldn't do anything without alcohol," Carver said. "I couldn't
imagine teaching class unless I was drunk. I had a half-bottle in the
drawer of my office, one in my briefcase, one in the car, another in
the hedge at home. . . . I was going downhill fast. My life as a writer
was receding further and further into the yeasty distance. But then
the compulsion to drink left me as though it had never been there.
That was a real blessing."

June the second, 1977, was the last time he touched a drop. For
the past six years he has led a life of abstemious domesticity, mostly
on or around the Syracuse University campus. But the focus of his
writing hasn't shifted. He still writes about short-order cooks,
supermarket cleaners, travelling salesmen, brake-and-fender men
and other "marginal" people, trawling a past that he says he knows in
his bones to be inexhaustible.

"I wish my life had been different," he said. I wanted a different
and better life for my wife and my kids. We just got caught in a
whirlpool of some sort and couldn't get out."

David Sexton Talks to Raymond Carver

David Sexton/1985

From *Literary Review* [London], no. 85 (July 1985), 36-40.
Reprinted by permission of *Literary Review.* Conducted Spring
1985.

Raymond Carver was born in 1938 in Clatskanie, Oregon.
He grew up in 'a little two-bedroom house' in Yakima, a
small town in Eastern Washington. After school he worked
for six months in the same saw-mill his father worked in,
beginning a series of jobs that included 'janitor jobs, delivery man jobs, service-station jobs, stockroom boy
jobs. . . .' He married young and had two children—'I
was eighteen, she was sixteen and pregnant'.

He managed to put himself through college, and got a
B.A. degree from Humboldt State, after being taught at
Chico State by John Gardner to whom he pays tribute in
Fires. He also attended the Iowa Writers' Workshop for a
year on a five hundred dollar scholarship but did not stay
on to complete his M.F.A. degree. Later he worked as
night janitor at the Mercy Hospital in Sacramento. He
began to publish his stories and poems in small and then
national magazines.

In 1967 he got his first white-collar job working for a
text-book publishing firm in Palo Alto. After re-organiza-
tion he was fired, and managed a year of writing on the
severance pay and unemployment compensation. But by
now he was drinking heavily, as his father had done, and
he began fighting a ten-year battle with alcohol: 'I was out
of control, almost as good as dead. . . . My life was a
wasteland, I destroyed everything I touched'. He suffered
'blackouts, the whole business', and ended up in a rehabilitation centre that had formerly been a hospital for the
criminally insane.

In 1976 his first collection of stories, *Will You Please be
Quiet, Please?* had been published by Knopf. Fifteen
months later, June 2nd 1977, he stopped drinking. 'I'm
prouder of that than I am of anything in my life', he says;
'I'm a recovered alcoholic. I'll always be an alcoholic, but
I'm no longer a practising alcoholic'.

In 1983 he was given an American Academy of Arts and

Letters award worth $35,000 a year, and now writes full-time. He lives with the poet Tess Gallagher, outside Syracuse, New York, and in a house they have built on the West Coast in Washington State.

Raymond Carver's stories have been presented in Britain under the 'dirty realist' label fashioned by Bill Buford of *Granta,* which has also been applied to such writers as Bobbie Ann Mason, Jayne Anne Phillips, Elizabeth Tallent, Richard Ford and Tobias Wolff.

Raymond Carver came to England in May for the joint publication of *Fires,* a collection of essays, stories, and those poems previously published in America which he wishes to preserve, and of the Picador *Stories,* a bargain compendium of the two collections that have previously been published here, *What We Talk About When We Talk About Love* (1982) and *Cathedral* (1984), plus the one that has not, *Will You Please Be Quiet, Please?*.

It was his first visit to this country, and when we met at the Belgravia-Sheraton he was still tired from the plane. Raymond Carver is a large man, but in a way oddly amorphous, and very softly spoken.

David Sexton: In the first essay in *Fires* about the death of your father, there is this last sentence about these 'beautiful voices out of my childhood', saying 'Raymond', his name and yours. Your father is connected with the fact that you write, isn't he? Did he tell you stories?

Raymond Carver: He did. We had the Bible in our house but the family did not read. We didn't have books in the house, but now and again I would see father reading a book in bed. He'd take this book to bed with him to read—it was a Zane Grey western, as I recall. He would be reading these Zane Grey books and this seemed to me to be a private life that he had in a family that didn't really appreciate privacy. We lived in a very small house. But I would see him reading these books from time to time, and I was struck by this little world he had while reading this book. So sometimes I would sit on the bed and ask him to read to me. I'd like the things that he read to me. And he told me stories: stories about when he was a kid, and stories about my grand-father, who had fought in the Civil War—fought for a while on the Southern side, and then when the Southerners began to lose the war he became a turncoat and went to fight with the North, shooting at his friends. He told me that, and he told me a lot of stories about hunting and fishing, and encounters with bears and giant snakes and such. Stories that he'd lived through or stories that had been passed on to him. The stories made an impression on me, but Dad was not much of a reader, and he didn't live long enough to see the work that I began to publish.

He died in 1967. I like to think that he would have approved of what's happened.

DS: What were the very first things you wrote? Did you write as a child?

RC: I wrote as a child. I wrote and tried to imitate to a degree what I was reading. What I was reading was science fiction. So my early attempts had to do with people who became animals and animals who became people, and spooky stories—things like that. As I said there were no books in the house. I had no one to tell me what to read, so I just followed my nose. I'd go to libraries, to the public library in our town, and just check out books on pirate treasures, people looking for gold in South America, historical novels. Just whatever came to hand. I read everything—nothing very elevated or highbrow.

DS: You still have a lot of stories with a fishing or shooting setting. Do you do these things yourself?

RC: I do when I have the chance to do so. For many years I did not do any fishing or any hunting when I was living in the cities. But for the last year and a half I've been doing a lot of salmon fishing where I live now. But most of what you're talking about—the poems that have to do with fishing or hunting—were written prior to the time of my salmon fishing. Obviously those things made a large dent in my emotional life because some of these things still come back.

DS: After school you went into the saw-mill your father worked in. Was that more or less an automatic thing?

RC: Yes, it was. I wasn't encouraged to go to college, or, as it were, discouraged. Nobody told me what I had to do with my life. It was assumed that I had to earn a living and the way I could earn a living was to get a job at the mill where my father worked. When I went to work in the mill I went to work as what they call a common labourer. But it didn't take too long for me to understand that I didn't want to do that for the rest of my life. It was very hard work and not much satisfaction. But I had to do it.

DS: And then when you were very young you were married and had children. One of the extraordinary things about *Fires* is the expressions you have about the 'ferocious years of parenting', describing the children's influence as a 'negative one, oppressive and often malevolent', and again as 'heavy and often baleful'.

RC: That was all true then. I'm happy to say that I have a different relationship with my children now. But it was very difficult then for a number of reasons. My wife and I did not have any money. We did not have any skills. We did have a lot of dreams. When we had the children we were not grown up ourselves, and as it turned out we had all this staggering amount of responsibility. It was incumbent upon me to try to earn a living and at the same time I wanted to go to school. I'd be trying to write and trying to earn a salary. It was difficult. We seemed to bear up under it in our twenties. Maybe we had more strength and more idealism. We thought we could do it all. We were poor but we thought that if we kept working, if we did the right things, the right things would happen.

By the time we got to our thirties we were still poor, still trying to do the right things, but the life we had hoped for was not coming to pass. It was receding further and further. So somewhere in there in my early thirties I began to drink too much. And the children were coming into their own at that time—they were thirteen or fourteen. It became difficult.

DS: How much of the oppressive influence they had was economic, or was it also psychological? In a story—hardly a story, it's a situation—'The Father', in *Will You Please Be Quiet, Please?*, the child asks 'Who does Daddy *look* like?' and the children argue 'Daddy doesn't look like *anybody!*'; 'But he has to look like *somebody*'. He's suddenly faced with being on his own.

RC: Well, for many years I felt that my wife and I had no problems that money wouldn't solve. That was true for a long time, and then later in our thirties when we were still poor, we understood that it wasn't *just* money. There was a period of ten years when we were horribly poor, we were the working poor, we worked all the time, night and day—I worked nights and went to school days, and this went on for years. We still believed that if we worked hard and did the right things. . . . This is the American dream, what you're told when you're young: that if you work hard things will work out all right.

The economic thing was always a problem. So much theatre drama and movies and novels are built on the premise of family troubles, the breakdown in relationships. If you had these problems but at the same time were having to worry about putting food on the table or paying a doctor's bill or paying your rent . . . everything is compounded.

I don't want to make it sound like it was all bad, because it wasn't. My wife and I had some very good years. It sounds corny to say: we were poor but we were happy. We had all these responsibilities, but we were young and strong and felt we could do everything. And we were very much in love.

But in the main it *was* economic. Nobody in my family had ever gone beyond sixth grade in school. They knew work and nothing else but work. Nobody in my wife's family was educated or had done anything or knew anything. And nobody ever bought so much as a pair of shoes for the kids. No one had money. My parents were fighting for their lives. Our respective families were living a very marginal kind of life. I talk about it in my essay on my dad. It would have been nice to have had some kind of respite. I used to dream of just having a week or two to be relieved of pressure. Impossible to find that.

DS: You say in *Fires* that you limited yourself to writing things that you could finish in one sitting. But you also say that to write a novel you need to see a world that will 'for a time anyway, stay fixed in one place'. Was the reason for the short stories also that the world was fractured for you?

RC: The world was very fractured, and the world I was living in didn't want to stay in one place. Not only did the people change—other than the characters in my family—but by dint of our moving around and hoping for a better job, in one case going to someplace 2000 miles away from our home where I'd been given a small scholarship to college, we moved too much. We were dislocated, dispossessed.

I wanted to write, so I wrote when I could. I wrote poems when I didn't have time to write a story—I could write a poem much quicker

than I could write a story. I didn't have time to work on anything
longer. Now the situation is different and I do have what I didn't have
then, time to write. Now it's a matter of choice that I write stories or
poems. My last book that was just published in the United States and
that Collins will publish here in England next year, *Where Water
Comes Together with Other Water,* is a book of poems.

DS: Your style has changed, hasn't it? The sentences have
become longer, you use more active expressions. It shows particularly
in the revision in *Fires* of three stories from *What We Talk About
When We Talk About Love.*

RC: That's true. And in the new book *Cathedral* the stories are
different somehow from the earlier stories. Especially different from
the stories in *What We Talk About When We Talk About Love* which
are so pared down. Everything I thought I could live without I just got
rid of, I cut out, in that earlier collection. It felt like I'd gone as far in
that direction as I wished to go. I felt I'd soon be writing stories I
wouldn't want to read myself. After I'd finished that book and it was
accepted for publication, I didn't write anything else for about six or
eight months. Then the first thing I wrote was 'Cathedral' and I knew
that story was different from anything I'd ever written, and all of the
stories after that seemed to be fuller somehow and much more
generous and maybe more affirmative. And the stories in *Cathedral*
were written in a shorter period of time than the stories in the other
books. All the stories were written over a fifteen month span of time,
from fall of 1982 to spring of 1983. The book was published in fall of
1983. The first collection of stories, *Will You Please Be Quiet,
Please?*, took me about fifteen years.

Things have changed in my life, and I think those changes have
been reflected to a degree in my work. My poems are different. I
rather think they're better. I feel closer to them now than to the
poems that are in *Fires.* I think that a writer shouldn't go on writing
the same thing over and over again. But it wasn't a conscious thing
on my part. Certain things were happening in my life that seemed to
have an influence that moved over into my work.

DS: Is it right that the extreme clipped precision of the earlier
work is in some sense influenced by alcohol? One gets a feeling that
this extremely controlled writing down of uncontrolled happenings
may be.

RC: No, because when I wrote the stories I was cold sober.

DS: I wasn't suggesting they were written under the direct influence—but that the view of the world given in this extremely poised style was indirectly influenced by alcohol.

RC: That's partly true. I hadn't thought of that. In a way you're right because alcoholism can manifest itself in many ways, and if your life is in shambles and chaos, there's the desire to be able to exercise some kind of control. And I think maybe I was doing that in the prose of those stories which I tried to make so precise and so exact. It was some arena, some place on the map where I could exercise complete and total control. Also I'm obsessive about saying exactly what I wanted to say.

DS: The use of ellipse, things left out, is also very precise.

RC: This goes back to Hemingway of course—it's all right to leave things out as long as you know what you're leaving out. I think that was one of his dictums. I hate to say, me too, but I did feel like I knew what I was leaving out. I talk about this a little in the essay 'On Writing'. I get bored easily and I get bored with prose that's too circuitous or overblown, and I just don't have much patience for stories of that sort. So I guess I was in a hurry to get on with the story. I left out unnecessary movements. I was interested in having stories that worked invisibly. They would work without the author obtruding. He would put things in motion and let the story assume a life of its own, and go on about its business. In life we sometimes take short-cuts, do things in such a fashion that there are little things that we don't need to pay attention to any longer. I didn't want to take short-cuts in my stories, but I wanted things to operate on their own, so to speak—as they so often do in life. Sometimes I might have taken out too much. That was when I was beginning to feel I was going too far in this direction.

Someone, meaning it as praise, called me a 'minimalist', and I didn't like that, it just made me uncomfortable. There are great minimalist painters, writers and composers I guess, but it made me uncomfortable. I thought, maybe I've taken out too much. So maybe I've relaxed a bit. Relaxed is not the right word. Begun to open up.

DS: Is that the motive behind the revision? Some of them are actually expanded as if the character had remembered more about the story.

RC: Yes. That's partly due to the fact I started looking at those differently. Some of the stories I went back to seemed like unfinished business to me. This is nothing too amazing. Frank O'Connor was a great one to revise his stories—even sometimes after they were in print. His great story 'Guests of the Nation' is published in about four different versions.

DS: But perhaps it's expected more of poets. In 'On Writing' you mention starting a story ('Put Yourself in My Shoes') with the sentence 'He was running the vacuum cleaner when the telephone rang', and you say that from there you made the story just as you'd make a poem, 'one line and then the next, and the next. . . .' 'Line' is a word usually used for poetry, isn't it? You use some material both as a poem and as a story, as with 'Distress Sale' and 'Why Don't You Dance?'.

RC: That's unusual. I don't think I've done it too often. That is the only case I can recall.

DS: When do you decide when something is going to be a poem or a story?

RC: Last spring when I wrote all the poems that make up this new book, everything that came to me seemed to want to be a poem. But I am sure that there are many, many stories buried in the poems.

DS: Can I ask you specifically then about how you write? Hemingway used to space out the words on the typewriter when he was writing fiction.

RC: He wrote his first drafts in longhand. I write my first drafts or rough draft in longhand. I write the first draft of a poem or of a story very quickly—I just get it out on the page. As Guy de Maupassant said, 'get black on white', get something down. Then everything is subject to change after that except for the first sentence—the first sentence or the first line of a poem or a story remains the same. Rarely if ever does that change. But everything else is subject to change. I get the bare bones of the thing down, then I feel like everything will be all right, eventually. I like to revise, to re-write. But I need something to go from, of course. So I guess there's always the fear that if I don't get it down in a hurry, I'll lose it. It goes back to the old days of having to write in such a hurry and in such peculiar circumstances. This is not true these days, of course, but I still tend to work that way—get something down very fast and type it up. And once I get it typed up I can begin to work it. I mean really work on it.

DS: Are endings a trouble? People always pick up on them, don't they? Yours are very carefully pitched between confirming the pattern and being oblique.

RC: I think I have overshot the end sometimes on some of the stories, and had to go back and work on it to get it right. Next to beginnings, endings are certainly the most important, most crucial, for poems or stories. I don't think endings have caused me any more trouble—any more hard work—than the rest of the story, but they've got to be done just right. It's often the last line or the last word of a poem or a story that really moves you in a certain way, that is meaningful to you. Most often I know how a story is going to end early on. I get the first line and the ending some way ahead.

DS: Do you still teach creative writing?

RC: No, I don't. I received this grant from the Academy of Arts and Letters. It's a tax-free annual income for 5 years, and it's renewable at the end of that time. The only stipulation is that I do not have any other form of employment—that I am not teaching or running a hotel or working for wages in a saw-mill or what-have-you. So I resigned my job the day I got this news. I finished the semester and said I wouldn't be coming back. I no longer teach but I don't miss it. I think I did a good job when I was teaching and I don't miss it at all. In fact I wonder how I got anything else done while I was teaching.

DS: What did you feel able to teach? In *Fires* you quote John Gardner as saying writers are made as well as born, but then add in brackets '(Is this true? My God, I still don't know)'.

RC: You can teach writers, putative writers, some of the things not to do. You can teach them the absolute necessity of being honest in the work, not faking it.

I think in writing, like playing the violin or playing the piano, or painting, certain things can be taught. Some of the most distinguished violinists or pianists today studied with masters, with maestros. This doesn't mean that everybody who studies with a maestro is going to become a great pianist or a great violinist or a great writer. But at least it keeps them on the right track. Michelangelo didn't jump up full-grown and do the Sistine Chapel—he worked as an apprentice with another painter for seven years. Beethoven learned to write his own music by studying with Haydn and other composers. I think this is an old and honourable relationship. You can't make a great writer or even a decent writer out of somebody who's incapable of writing, but I think certain things can be taught and passed along. And I think I was able to pass along some of these things to some students of mine, in the same way that certain things were passed along to me.

So I think by teaching writing or music or photography or architecture or any of the arts, young artists can be helped. They can also be hurt, but they can be hurt otherwise by not knowing anything at all. It is a phenomenon in our time over there—it's probably the single most important literary revolution that's come along. Yeats learned a lot from Ezra Pound, and Pound helped and taught Ernest Hemingway as well as Yeats. Guy de Maupassant learned from Flaubert. Flaubert read de Maupassant's stories in manuscript, and said, No, no, no, this will never do. Finally Guy de Maupassant gave Flaubert a story: 'Boule de Suif'. Flaubert said, This is a story, you've done it. So that kind of informal teaching has always been going on, and what has been done these days is to formalize it.

DS: Did you teach literature in your courses?

RC: Yes. I had a unique situation at Syracuse University; I taught one course in fiction writing and I taught another course in literature, but it could be a course of my own devising. Comparing an author's creative work in novels or short stories and a critical work by the same author seemed to work out very well.

DS: 'The Blue Stones' is a beautiful poem in *Fires,* which turns on its epigraph from Flaubert. It reveals something of your directly Flaubertian regard for the *mot juste.* When did you read him?

RC: I first read *Madame Bovary* many, many years ago. I've read it three times, most recently when I taught it two years ago. But that particular poem came from something that happened some time ago—the poem itself is not so old, I wrote it in 1978 or '79. Many years ago I read the journals of the Goncourt Brothers, and in the *Journals* there's this talk about Flaubert. The poem was based on a particular passage—Flaubert is talking to Edmond de Goncourt about writing *Madame Bovary* and how he would jack off at his desk when he was writing some of the love scenes in the novel. That stuck in my head.

DS: How much do you think literature can help readers make sense of their lives?

RC: I've read things, especially when I was younger, that made me know I was living my life in a very unbecoming way. I thought I could change my life, that I'd *have* to change my life after I put the book down. But it was impossible—impossible to go out and become a different man, or live a different life. I think literature can make us aware of some of our lacks, some things in our lives that diminish us, that have diminished us, and it can make us realize what it takes to be human, to be something larger than we really are, something better. I think literature can make us realize that our lives are not being lived to the fullest possible extent. But whether literature can actually change our lives I don't know. I really don't know. It would be nice to think so. Maybe a story or novel could change our lives, change our emotional lives, while we're reading it. Maybe if we do this enough a process of osmosis will take place, will help us with what lies ahead.

DS: I wonder what a Russian reading your work might think about America. Your stories aren't political, are they? They don't make that extension, and they're not set in a sharply particular time.

RC: No, it doesn't much matter who's running for President, they don't care what bill's before Congress, because whoever's President, whatever bill's before Congress, it's not going to make any real difference. And what other readers in other countries might make out of this I don't know, but I think there are enough other things in the stories that interested readers can connect up with.

But somebody attacked me last fall, a neo-conservative critic, saying that he was afraid my stories were going to give a false impression of America—to the Americans, as well as to people in other countries. (The stories have been translated into twenty or so languages.) Because under the Reagan administration, you see, people should be happy, people shouldn't be suffering, or out of work, or sick of their jobs. This critic was saying that we shouldn't write about people who are dispossessed and unhappy, and whose lives have gone bust. 'Let's put a happy face on things' was what he seemed to be wanting.

But I don't know. I read stories by Maxim Gorky and Chekhov, and a number of Italian writers and French writers, and Irish short story writers, and most often they're writing about the dispossessed, the submerged population. They're not writing about professional people who are having crises at their white-collar places of employment, or worried that something's happened to their Rolls-Royce. I'm not trying to take any political stance. I'm just writing stories, writing something about what I know about.

DS: A reviewer said of 'Where Is Everyone?': 'I laughed all the way through the story—but it was awkward, uneasy laughter'. He said he needed a couple of stiff drinks afterwards. Your humour is close to pain, isn't it?

RC: That's life, is it not? In a lot of instances the humour has a double edge to it. We laugh at it because if we didn't laugh at it—I don't mean to sound corny, but if we didn't laugh at it we could bawl our eyes out. I'm glad somebody does find humour in these stories. A story in *Cathedral* called 'Careful', about a guy who has his ear plugged up, is on the face of it a grim and desperate situation, but I read the story aloud at Harvard University last month—the first time I'd read it—and the people howled. They found it terribly funny in parts. They were not laughing at the last pages of the story, but there are places that are very funny. It's not the *Saturday Night Live* kind of humour, it's dark humour.

DS: The story 'Cathedral' really is the only one where people make contact, isn't it? In 'After the Denim' it's clear the Packers do love each other, but it's unusual in your stories, isn't it?

RC: The fact that there's not much love and connection made between my characters?

DS: Yes. You really make a jump at the end of 'Cathedral', when suddenly they move together instead of apart.

RC: Yes, and I like that a lot. When I wrote that story I knew the story was different in kind and degree than any story I'd ever written. And that was the first story I wrote for the book *Cathedral*. I think the story signals something for me that is not present in the earlier stories. I think that in the book *Cathedral* a lot of the stories are fuller and more interesting, for me anyway, than any of the other stories. The story 'Fever' for instance—where the wife has gone away and left him with the kids. 'A Small, Good Thing', that's a story where people make connection after the baby has died.

But my life has changed and I think it's fair to say I'm becoming more optimistic. So I hope that's what you've detected in the work.

I do keep going back, however, for a lot of things that made a great impression on me when I was younger. I do go back to things that happened in my other life for material. It's still very much present for me, though my circumstances are different now of course.

DS: How autobiographical are the stories in fact?

RC: Stories don't just come out of thin air, they have to come from someplace. So everything I've written about—something in that story has really happened—or I've overheard something, I'm bearing witness to in some way. I imagine, I recollect, I combine—as any good writer does. Writers can't write strict autobiography—it would be the dullest book in the world. But you pull something from here, and you pull something from over here, well it's like a snowball coming down a hill, it gathers up everything that's in its way—things we've heard, things we've witnessed, things we've experienced. And you stick bits and pieces here and then make some kind of coherent whole out of it.

DS: Seeing all your stories together in one book brings out continuities, doesn't it?

RC: I think that a writer's signature should be on his work, just like a composer's signature should be on his work. If you hear a few bars of Mozart, you don't need to hear too much to know who wrote that music, and I'd like to think that you could pick up a story by me and read a few sentences or a paragraph, without seeing the name, and know it was my story. Even though it might be about living in London and commuting to Brussels, something I've never written about and probably won't.

So this is a bit strange. I started out writing stories and poems and I guess at the time my expectations were very low, so I don't know exactly how to relate to this. Carver stories—no one could be more surprised about this than I am. But I'm very pleased and happy, yes.

Raymond Carver
Nicholas O'Connell/1986

From *At the Field's End: Interviews with Twenty Pacific North-west Writers* (Seattle: Madrona, 1987), 76-94. Reprinted by permission of Madrona Publishers, Inc. Conducted Summer 1986.

Raymond Carver writes with uncommon power about commonplace things and commonplace people. His short stories operate by implication; every word, every gesture is fraught with significance. By choosing details judiciously, he endows objects as seemingly insignificant as a kitchen chair with startling power. In his hands, colloquial American English achieves such concision that a whole world view or moral condition can be summed up in a single sentence.

Through meticulous rewriting and revising, Carver gets underneath the veneer of ordinary lives, exposing the workings of the human heart at its best and worst. His stories concern people pushed to the edge—of bankruptcy, divorce, separation, eviction—people forced to reveal themselves through speech and action. Once he gets his hands on them, he can be absolutely pitiless in his examination of the nooks and crannies of their characters, but he does not condemn them. He approaches them with sympathy, and respect for their inherent mystery.

Carver portrays the American underclass with accuracy and compassion because he was once a part of it. Born in Clatskanie, Oregon, in 1938, he spent much of his early life in Yakima, Washington. At age eighteen he married Mary-ann Burk, and by the time he was twenty he had fathered two children. To support his young family, he worked a succession of what he describes as "crap jobs," including pumping gas, picking tulips, sweeping hospital floors, cleaning toilets. After years of such jobs, of family troubles, of problems with alcohol, his life hit rock bottom. Only after giving up drinking did things turn around for him. Gradually, Carver got his life back on track, and the memories of those troubled years made him better able to bear witness to those who have not yet found a way out of their difficulties.

Carver is the author of four collections of short stories:

133

Will You Please Be Quiet, Please? (1976), *Furious Seasons*
(1977), *What We Talk About When We Talk About Love*
(1981) and *Cathedral* (1983). He is also the author of *Fires:
Essays, Poems, Stories* (1983), *Dostoevsky: A Screenplay*
(1985) and five volumes of poetry: *Near Klamath* (1968),
Winter Insomnia (1970), *At Night the Salmon Move*
(1976), *Where Water Comes Together with Other Water*
(1985) and *Ultramarine* (1986).

In 1963, he received an A.B. from Humboldt State
College. He went on to study at the University of Iowa, and
eventually taught there and at a number of other univer-
sities around the country. Before coming to Port Angeles,
Washington, Carver lived in Syracuse, New York, where
he taught at Syracuse University. He has received numer-
ous awards, including the prestigious Mildred and Harold
Strauss Livings Award, 1983; the National Book Critics
Circle Award nomination in fiction, 1984, and the Pulitzer
Prize nomination in fiction, 1984, both for *Cathedral.*

The interview took place in the summer of 1986 at
Carver's house in Port Angeles, which he shares with the
poet Tess Gallagher. The house is in a quiet, residential
neighborhood, and overlooks the Strait of Juan de Fuca.
Carver is a tall, soft-spoken man, shy in manner, who is
very meticulous about getting his wording right.

Why do most of your stories take place indoors?
I don't know. They do though, don't they? That's probably partly
due to the fact that I spend most of my time indoors, and really the
stories have something to do with the engagement or involvement
between men and women, and these moments or little dramas are
better played-out indoors than outdoors. It's healthy out-of-doors,
and there are always some vapors hanging around indoors—fetid air.

*Could most of your stories take place in almost any town in the
United States?*
Sure, and have.

The physical place, the city and so on, isn't quite so important?
No, those kinds of landmarks and guides aren't terribly necessary
in my stories. There are always certain spins on these things, but you
could say that men and women behave pretty much the same

whether in Port Angeles, or Bellevue, or Houston, or Chicago or Omaha or New York City.

And I don't know if this is a good thing or bad thing in regard to my stories; there's no way to judge. I was rootless for so many years and didn't have any real *place* or location, some of the things that are so nurturing for a writer. I seem to have lost them in some great cyclone back in the '60s.

Where did you grow up?

I grew up in Yakima, on the other side of the Cascade Range. I was born in Oregon, and my parents moved to Yakima when I was two or three years old. I went to grade school and high school over there. My childhood was given over to fishing and hunting and baseball and those kinds of activities. And then I began going steady with this girl when I was seventeen. We were married about a year later and moved to California. I still have some relatives in Yakima, and I still like to go back there now and again. It's very different from this country over here, but it has its own particular beauty. My heart lifts up when I see the Yakima Valley.

I don't know what else to say about Yakima. I'm glad I left; it was much too small a place when I was a teenager, and I had to leave. I wanted to get out and see the world, where things were happening, where I thought things were happening.

So pretty quickly you moved to a larger city?

I just knew I couldn't live there forever, and I was very anxious to get away. But I don't think that's any different than what happened to a lot of other young people. I wanted to go places that were not familiar and do things that I was not in the habit of doing.

Were you ambitious?

I suppose I was, in a sense. I knew I wanted to write even then, but I was quite lazy in lots of other ways. I didn't want to work. I was offered a job in a hardware store in Yakima. It would have been comfortable; I'd just got married and it would have secured our life. I didn't take it. Furthermore, I've never liked physical labor; I've had to do it but I've hated it.

So I was ambitious in regard to the things that interested me, and extremely lazy and lackadaisical about the things that didn't. [Laughs]

Was writing one of the things that interested you?

Sure. I've wanted to write for as long as I can remember. When I got married, that life seemed to take over to a large extent, because we started having children early on and my family became the central focus of my life. I still wanted to write, but we had to cover the rent and the groceries and the school clothes.

Before you were married did you have plans of writing a novel?

Frankly, I was never all that much interested in writing a novel. I liked to write short stories. And the circumstances of my life dictated that I write the shorter forms, the things I could finish up in a few sittings. I like to read novels, but I've never been that interested in writing one.

My reading tastes were very unformed during this time. There was no one, absolutely no one, to give me directions or pointers in this; no one to tell me what or who I should be reading. So I sort of followed my nose. I used to go to the library and check out anything that interested me—fiction, of course, along with books about cattle drives and searches for buried treasure, history books of all kinds. There was less time to read, of course, after I got married, but I always liked to read in those early years. And it was during this period I felt I wanted to try to write. I made some halfhearted tries at it.

Was it poetry first?

I think it's poetry first with everyone; and it certainly was with me. Those first poems were awful, of course. Later on when I began writing more seriously I started sending the work out. Along in there somewhere I had a story and a poem accepted by two different magazines on the same day.

Did this happen a long time after you had started writing?

The acceptances came when I was twenty-three, and I'd been wanting to write since I was seventeen or eighteen, but I didn't have any serious work habits in those days.

Did you find it hard to reconcile family responsibilities with writing?

Yes, of course. It's harder when you're unformed and untried and untested yourself, and then suddenly you have certain heavy responsibilities like raising children and earning a living and all of that. It was difficult and it remained difficult until we all parted company.

It struck me in reading your stories that somebody couldn't have written them without going through a lot. Could you have written those stories without going through the things you did?

Well, probably not; I'm certainly a product of the things that formed me. Certain events made a very deep and abiding impression on me, but who's to say what I would have written had I not lived the life I did, given the fact that I wanted to write as badly as I did? I'm sure I would have found something else to write about.

The stories and poems I've written are not autobiographical, but there is a starting point in the real world for everything I've written. Stories just don't come out of thin air; they come from someplace, a wedding of imagination and reality, a little autobiography and a lot of imagination.

But the stories have taken a particular turn or are cast in a particular way because I know what I'm writing about; in that I'm no different from any author whose work you might admire. What you look for in a writer is someone writing with authority about his subject; you want to feel you can trust him, and put yourself in his hands, so to speak, and go with it.

Had I not had the life I did have, I wouldn't have written the particular stories I did, but I want to think that I would have written stories of equal interest and of equal merit. But who can say?

I asked that question because in reading your stories I noticed that you seem to have a lot of compassion for the downtrodden.

I hope so, I hope that comes through, because I cast my lot with those people a long time ago. Those are the people I grew up with and know best, and they still seem to be a source of most of my imaginative interest. I haven't written that much about people who haven't found it necessary to be tried in some way or another. I've been around academics off and on, and I've spent a lot of time on college campuses, but I've never once written anything about a college campus or about school. Never. That life simply never made a lasting emotional impression on me. I do know something about the life of the underclass and what it feels like, by virtue of having lived it myself for so long. I do feel more kinship, even today, with those people. They're my people. They're my relatives, they're the people I grew up with. Half my family is still living like this. They still don't know how they're going to make it through the next month or two. Believe it or not, but it's true.

Do you see yourself as a spokesman for these people?
I'm just bearing witness to something I know something about. Most things in the world I don't know anything at all about, and I couldn't care less. I'm bearing witness to what I can.

Did you feel compelled to write those stories?
Yes, or I wouldn't have written them.

Was this compulsion building up in you over the years when you didn't have much time to write?
If you look at the copyright dates of the stories that are in my first book of fiction, *Will You Please Be Quiet, Please?*, the first story was published in 1963, and the last story was published in 1975, and the book was published in 1976, so it took about twelve or thirteen years to put those stories together. I wasn't able to apply myself all that much, all that steadily.
The stories in *What We Talk About When We Talk About Love* were written between 1976 and '81, and the stories in *Cathedral* were all written in eighteen months.

So the stories in Cathedral *came a lot more quickly?*
Right, within eighteen months. And the first book took twelve or thirteen years to put together, partly because I was out of control for several years, and partly because of the vicissitudes of trying to earn a living and raise a family and write stories and go to school.

As an editor at The Seattle Review, *I read a lot of stories submitted to the magazine which are Raymond Carveresque stories. Are you aware of how influential your style has become?*
I was thinking about an anthology I saw recently. There are two parodies in it, good-natured parodies, parodies of my stories. And they recently had a Raymond Carver Write-Alike Contest at the University of Iowa. It was good-natured enough, but it was a real contest.
I'm aware of the fact that a lot of young writers are trying to write more or less the way I write. But a lot of young writers try to write like

somebody else. It's not all that bad if they're trying to write like me; they could have worse models. Some of the economy in the stories is good for young writers, and some of the care for what's being said. It's okay to try to write like somebody else. A lot of people used to try to write like Don Barthelme. Barthelme is a wonderful writer in many respects, but he isn't always the best kind of model for young writers. What he can do well, young writers who are not as smart and talented as he is would botch. And the results are usually pretty terrible.

Did it take you a long time to evolve your particular style?

It took a while to develop my style, sure. It took from the 1960s into the 1970s, writing stories and then rewriting them and continuing to work on a story. I was not at all that anxious to send a story out, because if I sent it out I'd just have to write another story, and stories were hard to come by in those days. It was a conscious thing and it just took a while. I didn't just start writing stories like "Feathers" or "Cathedral."

I think the newer stories are similar to the other stories, but different. And that pleases me, because you can't keep repeating yourself. This is not saying anything against the earlier stories, but the new stories are sufficiently different from the earlier stories that I'm pleased with the difference.

When you were starting out, did you learn by imitation?

I didn't, at least not in the way you might be thinking. I've heard stories about Frank O'Connor trying to write like Guy de Maupassant or studying de Maupassant's stories to see how the stories worked, and even copying them out. Somerset Maugham would do things like this, copying out whole passages of writers he admired, in an effort to improve his own style and assimilate what those writers could teach him.

I never did this, but there were certain writers who meant a lot to me and still do, writers like Chekhov, Hemingway, Tolstoy, Flaubert, to name a few. I read their books, novels and stories, and while I didn't try to write like these people, I certainly wrote more carefully, and better too, I think, because those were the kind of people I admired. But I never had any one particular writer over and above all the other writers, unless it was Chekhov. I think he is the best short story writer who ever lived. Isaac Babel is another wonderful writer.

He could take two or three pages and make the most wonderful little story.

Were you always a perfectionist, I mean in your writing?
My life was very sloppy. I guess I was looking for perfection in some area. As far back as I can remember I couldn't abide the sight of a messy manuscript. In those days I didn't have access to copy machines and typists and all that. I did all of my own typing. A story would come back from a magazine that I had submitted it to, and if I changed a few words or crossed something out, saw a paper clip mark on it, or a coffee stain, I would end up retyping the whole story. I might type twenty copies of a story, just trying to get it right, getting it where I wanted it to be. So I suppose the answer's got to be yes—a perfectionist in the writing, not the life.

And you don't send out anything until it's just right?
I'm in no hurry. I wrote a lot of stories this spring and the first part of the summer, but the stories never went out in a hurry. I have a story up there in a drawer right now that hasn't gone out. I'm working now with a typist who has a word-processing machine, so I can give her a manuscript and she can spend time with it, and give it back to me; and at the same time I found myself working on another story. So, often I find myself with two stories in the works at the same time. I like working that way.

Do you ever leave stories for six months or so?
I've never left them that long, but even recently I have left them for two or three weeks. It's good if a writer can do that because the story cools down a bit and the writer gets a bit of distance on it, and the emotional heat isn't as strong as it was earlier. I like it when my stories cool down enough that I can look at them very coldly.

Who was the first person to recognize that you had talent?
I suppose every beginning writer has to feel like he has talent, or he wouldn't be able to do what he has to do. You need something to sustain you, so certainly you have to believe in yourself. But I was just flying blind for the longest time, and without question my life changed when I found John Gardner as a teacher. He made a vast impression on me.

Did you pick up things from Gardner's style?

Not from his style, no. But I had never had anybody look at a manuscript of mine the way he did. And let me say I believe that things can be passed from one person to another. The association of a maestro and an apprentice is age-old: Michelangelo had a teacher, so did Beethoven. They were apprentices at one time or another, and then somebody showed them how, taught them their trade. If someone you knew had the desire to study the violin you would try to engage a really distinguished teacher to teach this person, you wouldn't put the person in the room with a violin and some sheet music. So certain aspects of writing can be taught.

Gardner was a wonderful teacher. He could show you things. He could take a story and tell you, "This is working and this isn't working and this is the reason why."

I was simply electrified. I'd never met a writer before. I was nineteen or twenty years old, and I'd never laid eyes on a writer. And he was a writer; even though he hadn't published at the time. He was cut out of different cloth from anyone else I'd ever met. He was very helpful. He showed me things, and I was at that particular point in my life where nothing was lost on me. Whatever he had to say went right into my bloodstream and changed the way I looked at things.

He made me understand that if you can say something in ten words, say it in ten words rather than twenty words. He taught me to be precise, and he taught me to be concise. Taught me a lot of other things, too; I learned a lot from him. My life was still pretty boxed in, but I'd learn things from him and even if I couldn't put these things into practice immediately, the things I learned were long-standing and abiding.

Did you see him outside of the classroom?

No, not really. He wasn't much older than I was. I was nineteen and he was probably twenty-five. But he was very busy; he was trying to write his own books, and *was* writing his own books, even though some of these books never got published for another fifteen years or so. *October Light,* for instance, was written when he was in his twenties but it wasn't published until six years or so ago. That's why it seemed he was so prolific; but much of the stuff that was published in the '70s was written in the '60s.

I associated writing with a high calling, a thing to be taken very,

very seriously, and he was very important in strengthening that, but there was very little off-campus association with him. Once in a while he would come to a party with the students but other than that I never saw him socially. I was just a squirt, and he was a grown-up with grown-up friends.

We resumed an acquaintanceship which became a friendship during the last year of his life. In the course of seventeen years we probably exchanged three or four letters, and then we got to know each other again after not seeing each other for a long time, and it was nice.

To what extent are you writing moral fiction as Gardner would define it?

For a long time I didn't want to read Gardner's book on moral fiction; I didn't want to find out that I was writing *immoral* fiction. But what Gardner was asking for was that writers be more serious in their approach to their work; you just didn't know what effect your works might have on somebody; somebody might be sick and dying of cancer, and your work might give them some kind of support or succor. There's enough stuff around that diminishes the human spirit.

John Cheever said the same thing to me once. He said that fiction should throw light and air on a situation, and it shouldn't be vile. If somebody's getting a blow-job up in the balcony of a theater in Times Square this may be a fact, but it's not a truth. There is a difference. Maybe some of my later stories would be considered life-affirming, linking us all together in a great enterprise, etc., but there are writers who will tell you that the act of writing itself is a moral act, and that that is enough in itself.

You said in one of your essays that moral fiction had a lot to do with being truthful and accurate in your writing.

Yes. In the same essay, I quoted Ezra Pound, "Fundamental accuracy of statement is the ONE sole morality of writing." That's as good a starting point as any; and then you go from there. But you can't say, "I want to write a moral story." You have to write what's given to you. And then there's the melody that comes out of you and comes out in the story too, if you're lucky; the story should certainly be a connecting up emotionally first, and then it should be an intellectual connecting up.

When I read and am moved by a story by Chekhov it's similar to listening to a piece of music by Mozart and being moved by that, or being emotionally moved by something by Edith Piaf. When something can reach across languages, and hundreds of years even, and move you, that's all you can ask.

Do you try to avoid making explicit statements in your work?
Yes. I'm incapable of doing that; I wouldn't know the first thing about making statements: the peach pickers aren't getting paid enough for picking a box of peaches, so put a character in there who shows that. No, nothing schematic or programmatic.

But there does seem to be a point to your stories. A reader comes away from them thinking someone has behaved badly, or somebody has behaved well.
Yes, absolutely. Many people behave badly and some people behave well in my stories but I'm not out to make a point, or illustrate anything.

So what you want to say is contained by the story?
Yes. The meaning of the story comes out of the story itself, and is not imposed on the story. I don't want to sound like a dope about my own stories. But sometimes I'm surprised by the stories, sometimes they veer away from what I had in mind and felt as I was writing them.

Is it more the emotional effect that you're interested in?
Yes.

In Chekhov, it seems that the meaning arises out of what is implied by the story.
Not something that was imposed by him. Of course he was in the driver's seat because he was giving you the information about these people in a given situation, so he took you where he wanted to take you.

Would you say that that's true of your stuff too?
I think so.

How do you go about writing a short story?
When I am writing, whether it's poetry or fiction—and I mean

this—virtually everything suggests itself as a story or as a poem.
Something that's said, something I see, something I overhear, an
image or even a line or dialogue, transfers itself to an image, and I
feel a necessity to start writing.

When I start writing, I tend to write very quickly. And of course at
that time I'm looking for someplace quiet, someplace where the
phone isn't ringing. And then I try to write the story as quickly as I
can. I don't think I've ever written more than two or three stories
where it's taken more than two days to write the first draft. Usually I
just plunge on, even though I don't always know what I'm doing, and
try to get something out on the page.

And then when I feel like I've exhausted it, that's the time I'll go
back and type it up and see what I have. Sometimes I'm quite
surprised, even when I read the story in longhand and am typing it
up. Sometimes I won't know what's coming next. I'm quite surprised
to see what I've written. I'll be reading something, and think, "Oh,
that's interesting. What's going to happen now?"

I'm not saying the early drafts are written unconsciously, in a trance
or daze, but they're written in some kind of condition whereby
you've taken leave of normal things, and the stories have kind of
taken over and directed me somehow.

I don't have very many wasted stories, or stories that don't work or
come off. I know a lot of writers who make a lot of false starts. That
rarely happens with me. I have a few that I've finished that are
drafted that I don't have much interest in, but I don't have very many
stories that I feel I didn't know where I was going or what would
happen.

And then, after the story is typed up and I have worked on it for
several drafts, I'll show it to Tess, get a response from her, and then
it's usually back to the typewriter again. Eventually that story will find
its way to a typist, she will type it up, and then the real work begins:
the rewriting, the tinkering around, that kind of thing.

Does that usually mean compressing the story?
In the past it's always been compressing and taking out, but lately
I'm putting in as much or more than I'm taking out. It used to be that
the story was ten pages long in manuscript, but when I first wrote the
story and had it typed up it was twice that long. I just rendered it

down. Now a story is twenty pages to begin with and twenty pages in manuscript, though the substance might have changed. I'm putting in as much as I'm taking out. Cross a line here, and add a line somewhere else.

Why are you adding more things to the stories now?
That's hard to say. I feel it's necessary or I wouldn't be doing it. The stories, most of them, are larger somehow and I'm simply putting flesh on more things, putting color in the cheeks, rather than trying to take all the color out. I'm sure this has something to do with my own frame of mind and getting older, etc. But now I'm adding to the characters, and adding to the situation itself, making it larger, making the stories give more, making them more generous.

Are you moving toward writing a novel?
I don't know. All the stories I'm writing these days seem to be 5,000 words or so, which is certainly longer than they used to be. I'm not consciously moving towards a novel. I could get a contract to write a novel tomorrow if I wanted—I'm under contract to write this book of stories—but I waited to sign the contract to write stories until I felt I wanted to write stories again. And for two years I didn't write stories; I wrote poems and some essays. My agent was very per-turbed with me, I think, because I wasn't writing any fiction, but maybe I'll write a novel someday, and again maybe I won't. It's no big thing. I'll either write a novel or I won't. I'm not going to worry about it. I don't have to write a novel for money or for glory or anything else.

It seems that together the stories create a world in much the same way a novel does.
I've been told that. I'm always interested in hearing such things. I don't know if that's good or bad or simply a matter of interest. There are more things in this life that I don't have an opinion on than I do.

In these longer stories are you trying to show more sides of your characters?
Yes, and the characters' relations with other characters.

I really noticed that with the stories in Cathedral. *The characters seemed to be more sculpted.*

True, and that's good. That, too, was a conscious thing. It wasn't part of a program, but I felt I wanted to get back in the world more.

To what extent are your characters general types?
I don't think that there are any types. In fact when I'm talking about characters in stories, I tend not even to talk about characters, I tend to talk about the people in the stories; they're individuals, after all.

Many of them seem recognizable, as if they were people you would know.
That's good.

So you're trying to create specific personalities for your characters?
I try to write them as individuals, sure. If I weren't trying to write them as individuals, I don't think you'd have this feeling that you do. If I somehow failed to make them believable, I don't think you could have made the remark you just made. They're not types, they are individuals.
Physically for the most part, you don't know what they look like. I'm not good at, or very interested in, physical description, how somebody wears his hair or her hair, or if they're pale or ruddy or have hair on their forearms or what they're wearing. But emotionally I think I struck them right, and that is what you recognize. I was never interested in great long descriptions of characters in Victorian novels, page after page of how he was dressed or how she walked and held her parasol.

You were more interested in what they were thinking?
Not so much what they were thinking, but what they were doing, what they were saying to each other, what they *weren't* saying, what they were saying as opposed to what they were doing, and what they were doing and not saying much about. People's actions seem to be of most interest, finally, than *why* they do things.
I'm not really interested in what makes torturers in Chile or Iran do what they do. As far as the psychology of what brought them around to become torturers, I don't care. The fact is that they're torturers; that's what's important, and so awful.

So that through their actions they show . . .

What they are. Who cares what made the Green River killer kill thirty-five people or however many? The fact that he killed thirty-five women because of something in his past is of little interest to me. What could bring someone to do this? I don't even want to know. The fact is people do things, people commit terrible acts, acts of public or domestic violence. I don't need to go back on a twenty-year expedition to what brought this man to punch his wife in the eye, or this woman to hit her husband with a skillet.

How do you come up with your stories?
Ideally the story chooses you, the image comes and then the emotional frame. You don't have a choice about writing the story. I think that writers reach a point where they realize most areas of experience are not available to them—through lack of interest, lack of knowledge, lack of emotional involvement. I would be quite incapable of writing a story about young politicians, or even old politicians, or lawyers, or the world of high finance and fashion.

There's a filter at work which says this is or is not a story. And maybe there will be some little something, the germ of an idea, which will strike some kind of chord and begin to grow. I think a story ideally comes to the writer; the writer shouldn't be casting the net out, searching for something to write about.

In one of your essays you talked about how short stories offer a glimpse of life. Do you try to pick incidents for your stories which can sum up a whole life?
Sure. Again it's not part of the program, it's not a conscious thing, but readers are certainly free to draw inferences from certain fictional situations, and do. I've been beaten over the head by some critics, mainly conservative critics. Someone wrote a long essay against my work in *The New Criterion* a year or so ago, saying that the picture I portray of America is not a happy one; that my characters are not real Americans; that they should be happier and find more satisfaction in this life; that I'm concentrating on showing the dark underbelly of things. This was a real political interpretation of my stories. They said I didn't know anything about the workingman; that I've probably never held a blue-collar job in my life, which is amusing.

Then I have some people, especially foreigners, tell me that my

stories are without question an indictment against the American capitalist system, because they show the failure of the American capitalist
system—people out of work, people drinking too much, and so forth.

I'm not following any kind of formula or program for myself. I
don't have any goals, and I don't have any plans worked out; I'm just
writing stories.

Somebody was trying to give me a strange reading on one of these
New Yorker stories recently. You get the strangest kind of letters in the
mail; people write and tell you what your stories mean. I named a
character Bud in one of the stories, and someone told me it really
must be short for Budweiser and the good times. [Laughs]

Has Port Angeles been a productive place for you to work?

Yes, it's good to work out here, especially in the winter when the
days are short and there're no interruptions, and there's nothing to
do but work, and everything is at a great remove—from about
December to March. It's good to be here then. We're isolated, and
that's good when you're working. But for myself, I get cabin fever if
I'm here too long. I need to get out every now and again. It's a little
different for Tess because it's her home; she grew up here and has
family here.

Did your writing change as a result of moving back here?

Well, it changed a lot in that book of poems. I wrote that book in
Port Angeles when I was out here by myself, during that time when
Tess was back in Syracuse, teaching. I've never had an experience
quite like it in my life. I wrote one, two, three and sometimes four
poems a day. I wrote from sunup until sundown. I did this every day
for six weeks. I wrote the whole book in six weeks. I've never had
anything like that happen in my life. When I had finished the book
and was ready to go back to Syracuse, I felt like I'd been through
some kind of astounding experience, something I'd never been
through in my life.

The poems came in this burst of energy and activity, and they were
a real opening out for me. I hadn't written any poems in quite a long
time and there was nothing I wanted more at the time than to write
those poems. And so, of course, it helped to be here.

That was January of 1984. I came out here with the expressed
intention of writing fiction. *Cathedral* had come out that fall and there

was still so much happening in connection with that book that it was very hard to get back on the track and writing again; there were a lot of distractions. I came here with the intention of being out here for a couple of months and working in utter quiet and solitude on fiction. I didn't write anything for a week, and then I started writing poems. I can't imagine I would have written those poems had I stayed in Syracuse or had I gone someplace else. So it's changed my writing in that regard, yes, and also my life.

My fiction I don't know, maybe so. I'm not the best judge. Maybe if I were in San Francisco the stories would be the same, but maybe not.

Why did writing poetry appeal to you?

I hadn't written any poetry in a long time, as I said, and I was beginning to feel I wouldn't write any more poems—ever. And so the poems were just a great gift and completely unexpected. Whatever the merits of the poems, and I think that some of them are pretty good, they allowed me to write something every day and something I wanted to write more than anything else. They satisfied my story-telling instinct; most of the poems in there have a narrative line to them. And it was just wonderful to write them; there was just nothing else like it. And I did it because I wanted to, which is the best reason for doing anything.

And the same thing with the second book of poems?

Yes. I had some poems left over that were not going to be published in the first book, and some more poems that I wanted to write, and so in that instance I sat down with the intention of writing poems. I wrote poems and more poems and pretty soon I saw another book taking shape.

Was it a relief to get away from writing short stories?

No, it was a relief just to be working, and to be working on something I wanted to work on. Had I been writing stories I'm sure I would have been just as happy. It felt good to be working again and it felt wonderful to be writing poems again. When I was writing those poems, I felt that there was nothing in the world more important than writing them. I didn't know if I'd ever write another story or not, and it was okay, it didn't matter.

Do you and Tess help each other with each other's work?

We're the best readers that we'll ever have. I read her stuff with a very cold eye and she reads my stuff the same way. As I said earlier, I'll write four or five drafts of a story and show it to Tess and usually I'm back at my typewriter the next day; she has made some good suggestions. She's a very good reader.

Has she changed the direction of your writing?

I'm quite sure of it. There is more of a fullness as a result of Tess's good eye and encouragement. We met, and then with her encouragement and suggestions and my own sense of my life and what I wanted out of it, my life began to open up.

Are you happier now?
Than when?

Ten or twenty years ago.

Oh, sure. There was a long period in my life when I was writing and had children and so forth; it was hard, but it was a life, it was my life, and even though it was hard, I was, I'm sure, happy. And then there was a very dark period for several years of emotional assaults on each other before the marriage ended.

There's no question that I'm better off now, but comparisons are difficult to make, and I'd rather just say that I've had two lives: one life that ended when my drinking ended, and another life, a new life, that started after I quit drinking and met Tess. This second life has been very full, very rewarding, and for that I'll be eternally grateful.

What We Talk About When We Talk About Literature: An Interview with Raymond Carver

John Alton/1986

From the *Chicago Review*, 36 (Autumn 1988), 4-21. Reprinted by permission of *Chicago Review*, copyright © 1988. Conducted 15 October 1986.

This interview with Raymond Carver was conducted October 15, 1986, the night after his reading at Virginia Tech in Blacksburg, Virginia.

Raymond Carver was born in Clatskanie, Oregon, in 1938. He was educated at Humboldt State College (now California State University, Humboldt) and University of Iowa. He then taught at the Iowa Writers' Workshop as well as at University of California, Santa Cruz; University of California, Berkeley; Goddard College; University of Texas, El Paso; and Syracuse University. He published four books of poetry, but is best known for his short stories, collections of which include *Will You Please Be Quiet, Please?* (1976), *Furious Seasons* (1977), *What We Talk About When We Talk About Love* (1981), *Cathedral* (1983), and a collection of what he considered his best stories, *Where I'm Calling From* (1988). Carver won several awards for his writing. Among these are a National Endowment for the Arts Discovery Award for poetry (1970); a Wallace E. Stegner Creative Writing Fellowship, Stanford University (1972-73); a Guggenheim Fellowship (1978-79); and a National Endowment for the Arts Award for fiction (1980). Carver received a Pulitzer Prize nomination and a National Book Award nomination, both for *Cathedral*. In early August of this year, Raymond Carver died at the age of fifty.

John Alton: When a person writes a story based on personal experiences—which you've emphasized in the past—for publication in a national magazine, the implication is that the writer is trying to make his experience appeal to a general audience. To what extent

151

was this a motive when you were writing the stories in *Will You Please Be Quiet, Please?*

Raymond Carver: If you look at the stories in *Will You Please Be Quiet, Please?*, the copyright dates on the stories go from 1962 or 1963 to 1976. The stories were written by the seat of my pants over a twelve or fifteen year period. The stories in the other books come closer together. I was simply trying to write the best stories I could write, and, of course, to some extent I drew on personal experience, yes. I wouldn't say it was a *motive*, however; it was really more a way of working.

JA: Were you using models of stories by other writers whom you admired? Was that the standard you used?

RC: I think every writer does that to some extent. He is unconsciously setting his own stories against stories of writers he most admires—Chekhov or Tolstoy or Ernest Hemingway or Flannery O'Connor, or whomever. But by the time I was finished with each of my stories, the original model was so far removed, so far back in the misty past, that the finished product bore no resemblance to what I had started out with. This may be partly due to the fact that I revise my stories a lot. But when I began writing stories I had no audience in my mind or even any sense of an audience. I figured the only audience I had a chance to reach was the audience that read the little magazines, the magazines I was reading at the time. I had no aspirations that my stories would ever be read by people who read *Esquire, The Atlantic, Harper's, The New Yorker.* I just wrote the best stories I could and tried not to bore the reader.

JA: So you weren't really conscious of an audience then?

RC: No.

JA: How about now?

RC: I am now, sure. It's inevitable. But that doesn't mean I tailor my stories to suit a particular publication, such as *The New Yorker* or *The Atlantic.* As always I'm just trying to write the best stories I can. Of course, I'm more conscious of the fact that more people are interested in my stories, more magazines, more editors are interested—I can't help but know that.

JA: Did you read a lot of literary journals in the old days?

RC: Yes, I did.

JA: So you would recommend that kind of reading to young writers?

RC: Of course I would. I was introduced to them by John Gardner, who brought a box of them to class one day. I was nineteen or twenty years old, it was a small, unsophisticated, state-supported school, and I'd never seen magazines like those. He said this was where 90 percent of the best fiction and 98 percent of the best poetry in the country was being published. Those magazines had short stories, poems, and criticism of living authors, *by* living authors. It was a terrific discovery for me.

JA: In "Fires," you say that your style may be "nothing more than a working marriage of necessity and convenience"—that is, that your memory recalls only specific, basic details and that your family life didn't leave you time to write. Do you see this [minimalism] as a strength or a condition thrust upon you that you're working your way out of?

RC: I don't like the term "minimalism." It's been used to tag a number of excellent writers at work today, but I think that's all it is, a tag.

JA: Certainly you have stories that are not minimalist.

RC: Yes, for sure. But I don't like that term [minimalism] at all. Like a lot of other things, this too will pass. A few years from now all the writers being labeled "minimalist" will be labeled something else, or not. They may still be writing in a "minimalist" sort of way, but the tag will drop away.

JA: I often hear the question, "Why doesn't he supply an effluence of detail, as Faulkner does?" In other words, you supply general, very brief descriptions. My response to this is with another question: Doesn't that generality of detail make your stories more universal?

RC: Well, I hope so, but it's not the point or intent; it's an effect. Whether it makes them more universal or less, I'm not the one to judge, and it would be presumptuous of me to do so. Faulkner? Faulkner is Faulkner. But there's also an awful lot of rhetoric in Faulkner, and there are certain writers—not just Southern writers— who tend to pile on the rhetoric when they write fiction. And I generally have a hard time with that brand of work.

JA: In your essays "On Writing" and "Fires," you discuss the way your personal life forced you to adapt to the short form of the story and the poem, yet you don't explicitly discuss the way your personal life affected aspects of your work such as *theme* or *conflict*. Could you respond to this?

RC: Of course many of the stories, especially in the early books, parallel to a degree some of the things that might have happened and pressed down on the life I've had. That is the "conflict" part of your question. For me the theme is implicit in the material and in the way the writer addresses himself to that material.

JA: Would you classify most of the conflicts as domestic?

RC: Some people have called them existential conflicts, but to a degree domestic conflicts can quickly escalate into existential conflicts. I don't want to be putting more on it than there is. But I've written a good deal about a great many aspects of domestic life, yes.

JA: So an external and an internal conflict exist simultaneously?

RC: Yes, I feel so, and I'm not just writing autobiography, understand. But many of those stories were suggested to me not by books, or by just "thinking up" things to write about, but by events that in fact did happen in real life. For instance, the story called "A Serious Talk," the one where the main character breaks the key off in the front door lock. We once lived in a house where the key had broken off in the lock. But most of the rest of that story is put together with some things that happened at various other times and in other places.

JA: So when you write you don't think so much in terms of an ideal theme or conflict?

RC: No. I never start with an idea. I always see something. I start with an image, a cigarette being put out in a jar of mustard, for instance, or the remains, the wreckage, of a dinner left on the table. Pop cans in the fireplace, that sort of thing. And a feeling goes with that. And that feeling seems to transport me back to that particular time and place, and the ambience of the time. But it is the image, and the emotion that goes with that image—that's what's important.

JA: Do you re-see it with detachment?

RC: Yes, I think you have to have a detachment if you're going to be a writer at all. Chekhov said something in a letter once that may be pertinent: "The writer's soul must be at peace, or he can't be impartial." On another occasion he told a writer not to begin writing until he felt "as cold as ice." That's detachment.

JA: When did you first achieve that ability to be detached from your feelings? A lot of the feelings you elicit in the reader are negative, about which it's difficult to be objective.

RC: The first time, I suppose, would have been in some of the poems. Some of the poems in *Fires*. As far as the first story is concerned, perhaps "They're Not Your Husband" was an early example.

JA: It's more comic, at least I think so, than most of your other stories.

RC: It is, yes. But about that time the idea of people looking on, or people looking *through* something at someone else—a real and a metaphorical frame for the story—that notion began to appeal to me. And I used a frame somewhat similar to that in several stories, written more or less during the same period. In the story "Fat," for instance, there's a woman telling the story to another woman, and she frames the story. I can remember the circumstances under which I wrote that story. In the first place, it was suggested to me by my former wife, who was a waitress at the time. She told me about waiting on a fat man who addressed himself as "we." It struck me, and stayed with me. I didn't have time to write the story then, but I did write it years later. When I finally sat down to write the story, I decided it should be from the waitress's point of view.

JA: And that was a way of objectifying what had happened?

RC: Yes, it was. Maybe this goes back to your question about "detachment."

JA: In "On Writing," you assert that a writer's tone or "unique and exact way of looking at things" is more important to a writer's greatness than craft or talent. How would you describe the tone of your early work?

RC: Tone is a very hard thing to talk about objectively, but I feel that a writer's tone is his signature, not just the way he crafts his stories. I can tell you what my tone isn't. It's never satirical. And it isn't ironic, clever, or glitzy. The tone is serious, by and large, though obviously some of the stories are humorous in places. I don't think a *tone* is just cobbled up by a writer. It's the way the writer looks at the world, and he brings his view to bear on the work at hand. And it can't help but infuse nearly every line he writes. Insofar as *craft* is concerned, I think craft can be taught. One can be taught certain

things that one should or should not do in writing. One can be made
to understand how one's sentences can be written better. But I don't
think that this attitude toward one's work—tone—can be handled like
that. Because if it isn't *your* tone, if it's somebody else's tone or
philosophy you're trying to pick up, it'll be disastrous.

JA: If you had to name your tone, what name would you assign it?

RC: I think my stories often have to do with loss, and as a result
the tone is, well, not somber, but severe. Grave, maybe, and somewhat dark—especially the early stories. But the story I read last night
("Whoever Was Using This Bed") had a dark side to it. I suppose
generally the tone is *grave*. But life is a serious business, isn't it? It's
grave, life is, tempered with humor.

JA: It seems to me that there is a tremendous sympathy on your
part for the characters.

RC: I hope so. I feel there is, at any rate. In all the books so far, I
could never have been condescending to those characters and felt
myself any sort of writer at all. I have to care for the people in the
stories. These are my people. I can't offend them, and I wouldn't.

JA: That's interesting. So when you create characters, you imbue
them with characteristics from your past and that elicits in you a
powerful sympathetic emotional response?

RC: I don't know how powerful it is, but it's considerably
necessary to me. So I suppose it's powerful.

JA: Recently E. L. Doctorow commented that the business of a
writer is to record the movements of power in the writer's own time.
Do you agree?

RC: That's pretty fancy. I know Doctorow, and I have a lot of
regard for his writing. But if you read all of Doctorow's work, what
he's saying and what he's doing are sometimes two different things.
That may be the way he sees his calling, and that's fine. But I can
think of a hundred good writers who don't see it that way. What
about his novel *Welcome to Hard Times?* What does that have to do
with movements of power in the writer's own time?

JA: I suppose it may be archetypal. Isn't it about a town in North
Dakota?

RC: It takes place in an Old West town. It may be North Dakota.

JA: It's an analysis of the psychology of a town, a treatment of brute force, and people's responses. So you don't see yourself doing this kind of thing?

RC: What I think, with all due respect to Doctorow, who is a marvelous writer of the first order, is this: what an interesting, unusual idea. But that's all I think: what an interesting notion, really quite novel. And it's good for Doctorow—it works for him. And that's fine; that's what it's all about, making it work for you.

JA: But one thing you can say about your work is that the characters seem powerless—I can think of just a couple of exceptions to that—and the powerlessness of your characters and the fact that they're all from a certain level of American society suggests that, at least indirectly, you're recording the *absence* of power, if not the movement of it.

RC: That's a legitimate response, sure. I was thinking of it in a different sense, but, yes, that's okay. Yes, I see what you're saying, and I agree with that, except that the situations in the earlier stories are different from that of many of the later stories. The characters in the later stories are not destitute or trapped or beaten up on by circumstances. It's a life that they may have asked for once, but simply don't want any longer. They make decisions.

JA: In "Fires" you seem to imply that luck or a kind of synchronicity affects your stories—for example, the character Nelson in "Vitamins." In your stories your characters also seem often to be at the mercy of luck, which is an aspect of the great naturalist literary tradition at the turn of this century. I've often wondered if you feel a philosophical sympathy with writers like Dreiser, Dos Passos, and Steinbeck? Do you feel you share a similarity of tone with these writers? The concern with social issues, the plight of the poor, and so forth?

RC: Most of the people I've written about in the early books are the working poor, and I know that life very well indeed. But most of the naturalist writers you mentioned—I can't read them. It isn't because of their concern with socialism. It's because they're such bad, line-by-line writers. Steinbeck is rather a different cast. Some of his work means a great deal to me.

I've been accused—and praised—for taking, or not taking, a social stand in my work. It's been said that I portray people struggling in a society that is oppressing them, and so this society—the society we're living in—is corrupt, it's bad, the system has failed us, and so on. And on the other hand, I've been accused of making "political" statements that are harming the republic in some way by not putting a happy face on things, by presenting an image that isn't going to redound to our credit, which isn't going to be in our best interests abroad. However, some other critics have praised what they regard as my "political" awareness and the "stance" I'm taking. But really all I'm trying to do is write stories, and for the most part write stories about what I know about.

JA: What's your reaction to people who hold you socially responsible for our image abroad?

RC: It's silly! I'm annoyed in general at these neoconservative critics who think all's right with the country, but things could be even better if certain people would stop criticizing it in the stories they write or the canvases they're painting. I think the whole thing's no good, that right-wing outfit. I don't like right-wing politicians, and I don't like right-wing critics. There's a whole group of critics now who are very cozy with certain powers that be in the administration. Erich Eichman and Bruce Bawer, for instance, are a couple of wormy characters. *The New Criterion* magazine is their stronghold. They're offended by my work. They're offended by the writing of a number of writers whose work I happen to admire.

JA: The critics loved *Will You Please Be Quiet, Please?* How do you feel about that? Do you feel mystically or naturalistically lucky?

RC: Well, I certainly don't feel mystically lucky and I don't feel naturalistically lucky either, though maybe luck plays a part in all this. Who knows? It's a piece of luck that we're both still alive and able to talk about these things in Blacksburg, Virginia. If you're talking about the conjoining of the publication of that book and the fact that certain people liked it and talked about the book, I don't know if that could be called *luck* so much as it should be called fortuitous. Luck plays a role in a million small, everyday things. But I don't understand luck, you know, not really. I feel I'm a lucky man, personally. But the concept, the notion of luck is an abstraction to me, and I don't know how it can be sensibly talked about.

JA: So you don't even think in those terms? You don't go around thinking, what if this or that had happened to me?

RC: No. You mean thinking on the order of, What if I had taken that job that was offered to me in 1962? Would I still be with my wife? Where would I be living now? Would my kids' lives have turned out differently? No, I don't. The past is all over. I do live very much in the present.

JA: So if your characters aren't existential, you are. Do you practice it to any extent?

RC: I suppose so. But I don't feel I'm emphasizing the dark side of things. I don't call myself an existentialist and I don't feel like an existentialist—whatever that feels like. I don't know how to explain it. I'm a writer, that's all, and I'm not consciously politically engaged in my writing.

JA: In your essays, you demonstrate a willingness to examine the link between your personal life and your work, which many critics feel is their province. How do you feel about literary critics?

RC: You mean when it applies to my own work or just in general?

JA: Just in general. Harold Bloom, for example.

RC: I haven't read Harold Bloom, but I have read Alfred Kazin, who I think is a wonderful critic; and there's another critic and essayist whom I have the highest regard for, V. S. Pritchett. He's wonderful. I think John Updike is a wonderful critic. He's first-rate. But I don't think I know anyone who is any better at it than V. S. Pritchett.

JA: Do you read a lot?

RC: I wish I could read more. I'd like to read more than I do. We should all read the masterworks by all the great writers. I love to read, but when I'm writing, I don't read books.

JA: You said you don't really think about the way critics respond now, but does it ever cross your mind how a hypothetical critic one hundred years from now might see your work?

RC: I feel lucky to be able to look ahead for just a short period, a few weeks or a few months. I can't imagine what they'll say a hundred years from now, if anything. I have no sense of that. It'd be presumptuous, not to say foolish, to think very much along those lines.

JA: By the way, do you know much about the deconstructionists?

RC: A little. Enough to know that they're crazy. They're a very strange bunch. They really don't have that much to do with literature, do they? They don't even *like* literature very much. I don't think they do, anyway. They see it as a series of texts and textual problems and writers as signifiers and such like.

JA: It may be literary inflation, but I think some of the things they have to say are philosophically interesting.

RC: But I don't know what that has to do with literature and the things we've been talking about.

JA: It seems to be a way of critiquing criticism.

RC: So? I think their interests are antithetical to literature as we know it. They're an interesting bunch, yes. They all—most of the deconstructionist critics I know—they're all very cordial, very smart, immaculate dressers, and all that, but we're not even talking about the same thing when we talk about literature. And they're certainly not interested in the writers I'm interested in. Furthermore, they don't read or understand or care about poetry. Their way of thinking is very arcane. Sometimes it's downright creepy.

JA: It's very unemotional.

RC: Right. Very unemotional, and far, far out, brother. I like some of them personally, but we don't share any common assumptions about anything having to do with literature.

JA: Have you ever learned anything about your work from a critic?

RC: No. No review I've ever read concerning my work has changed the way I've written or even changed the way I've thought about myself or my stories.

JA: It doesn't tell you anything new?

RC: No, it doesn't. And if you start to believe the laudatory reviews, then you have to believe the other ones as well, perhaps.

JA: So the primary concern you have is telling the truth the way you see it?

RC: Yes.

JA: Leonard Michaels used the expression "terrifying vision of ordinary human life in this country" to describe *Will You Please Be Quiet, Please?* What's your reaction to this?

RC: I liked that remark back when I first saw it, when my editor sent me the quote that would appear on the book. I felt I'd done something right in the stories, and I was pleased with what Michaels said. He is a writer whose work I hold in high regard.

JA: He used the word "vision"; what do you see as your vision of ordinary human life in this country? Do you accept that as an epithet?

RC: The vision now, today, is, I suppose, more hopeful than it once was. But for the most part, things still don't work out for the characters in the stories. Things perish. Ideas and ideals and people's goals and visions—they perish. But sometimes, oftentimes, the people themselves don't perish. They have to pull up their socks and go on.

JA: From the details of your personal life, which you freely admit bear a direct influence on your work, it can be said that during the composition of the stories that made up the first two collections, you were living a lower-middle class life.

RC: Working class, lower-middle class, sure. Then it became not just lower-middle class, it became the very desperate, very populous substratum of American life. The people who can't meet their financial and moral obligations and responsibilities. That's where I lived for a very long while.

JA: The "desperate" class you call it?

RC: Yes. I remember when I was watching the movie *Ordinary People* (which I thought was a good movie), but at the time I thought, what would happen if the people in the movie had the problems they have in the movie, but what if, in addition to those considerable problems, they didn't know how they were going to pay their rent the next month? What if, in addition to everything else, their car was going to be taken away from them, or they didn't have any food in the refrigerator? In addition to the terrible family problems they had, what if they also had overwhelming financial worries?

JA: So in writing your stories, it's safe to say that what you did was distill an archetypal experience for a whole class?

RC: Maybe. You said it. I didn't.

JA: We could call it, then, the lower-middle class, and include the desperate class in with them: those who get the VISA card and overdo it, and worse.

RC: My father and all my father's friends and family were working-class people. Their dreams were very circumscribed. They were people in a different social situation than the people you and I hang out with today, and they didn't seem to have the same sets of problems. Problems and worries, yes, but they were different. For the most part they worked their jobs and took care of their property and their families.

JA: You call them working class, but technically speaking—in terms of their incomes—they would be lower-middle class. They have a different environment, that is, they're not office clerks, but their income level is in that (lower-middle class) range so that they can buy a new car every six years, and end up sharing the same troubles as the office clerk. In "Neighbors" and in "The Ducks" I see similar things at work. So would it be reasonable to say that the lower-middle class, as I've described it, is your subject matter?

RC: It's certainly the subject matter for many of the stories in the earlier books. "The Ducks," as you pointed out. But in "Put Yourself in My Shoes," Myers and his wife are people who have more going for them. Myers is a writer. (And, incidentally, it's the only story about a writer I've ever written.) So not all the stories fall into that category. But the majority of them do, I guess.

JA: A recent statistic I ran across was that something like 75 percent of the people in this country are considered lower-middle class. How does it feel to be the spokesperson for 75 percent of America?

RC: One of the spokespersons.

JA: Who else would you include?

RC: I would include Bobbie Ann Mason, Richard Ford, especially his short stories, Louise Erdrich, Alice Walker. There are many others, of course. I hate to make lists and, you know, I don't really feel like a spokesperson. I feel awkward being considered in that position.

JA: Are you uncomfortable with the implication of importance? That it seems to inflate your importance?

RC: Yes, it just makes me uncomfortable. It makes me uncomfortable to think of myself as a spokesperson.

JA: Your stories seem to represent emotional maps of lower-middle class life, and there are recurring motifs of characters caught in self-destructive behavior. One of those is eating or overeating. Obviously this is not a problem limited to the lower-middle class, but in your lower-middle class world, eating is featured prominently. Could you elaborate?

RC: It's interesting you picked that out of the stories, that you noticed that. John Cheever once said that the characters in my stories always seemed to be eating. It's partly true, I guess. Poor people, disenfranchised people, they can never get enough to eat. They're always putting too much on their plates and then not able to eat it. I'm not trying to demonstrate anything, however, or make any kind of point.

JA: It's an observation?

RC: It's just an observation, and I suppose it's something I know about myself. I'm guilty of that myself, still.

JA: Does it indicate to you a symptom of frustration, a way of relieving anxiety?

RC: No, I don't read it that way at all. It's simply that they don't have enough, or can't get enough, of what they need to sustain them. So they like to pull up a chair to the table and eat, and sometimes they put too much on the plate when they do.

JA: In surveying the predicaments of your characters in your first two collections, the major problems the characters face seem to be isolation, physical and emotional exhaustion, and sexual aberrance. Could you expand on the causes of each of these conditions and the relations between them?

RC: I'm not sure about the sexual aberrance.

JA: Well, for example, the voyeurism in "The Idea." And there are strong suggestions of frigidity, or just disinterest in sex, on the part of many of the characters throughout.

RC: If it's true, I suppose it comes from the physical and emotional exhaustion. Of course, the characters in "The Idea" are an elderly couple, but as far as the treatment of sex is concerned, I'm fairly conservative there in that there aren't really that many sexually attractive or available people in my stories.

JA: I'm thinking of "What's in Alaska?" The couple in that story.

RC: Yes. There's an affair going on between the husband's friend and his wife. That's true.

JA: The woman wants to have sex at the end of the story, but they end up on opposite sides of the bed. And in the story "Fat," Rudy makes love to the narrator against her will.

RC: I see what you mean. Certainly I think that loneliness and isolation and physical exhaustion are true of my people, or many of them anyway. It was true for me during a period of my life, and it

seemed to be true for the people I associated with. These things
could not help but find their way into my stories.

JA: Another question along those lines. You have a dream motif in
many stories. You do this in the earlier stuff—"The Student's Wife,"
for example—but I've noticed it in a couple of recent *New Yorker*
stories, "Elephant" and the one you read last night ("Whoever Was
Using This Bed"). There are several more that involved dreams
occurring, and I wonder what importance you place on the unconscious mind and its relation to the kind of surface reality you record.
You get at the unconscious only in an indirect way, and seem to show
a relation to the waking, everyday world. I wonder if you think about
it much.

RC: I don't think about it very much. It may be one of those things
you don't think about but that's sometimes relevant to your work.

JA: But there seems to be a relationship between the unconscious
and the physical, the surface, much like the one you acknowledged
earlier where physical exhaustion and isolation create internal, even
sexual problems. That's being recapitulated in the dream motif. The
people are disturbed by their circumstances and they dream about it.
It shows up in their dreams.

RC: Yes, for sure, it's there. In truth, though, I hadn't thought
about it. But I think you're right.

JA: It seems you come down on the side of the unconscious. You
seem to suggest that's where importance lies, and your stories involve
a sort of hatching out, like the couple in "Whoever Was Using This
Bed." The man and woman hatch out internal troubles that had been
there for quite a while.

RC: That's right, and they work through it all. This discussion led
into that, but they never did get to the truth. Yes. That's good. I like
that observation.

JA: In *Will You Please Be Quiet, Please?* in particular, there's a
definite motif that the men are particularly affected by the conditions
we've talked about in the stories, more so than the women. Could
you comment? Is that just happpenstance?

RC: Well, I suppose there are more male or male-point-of-view
characters in that first book than in the others. There are several
stories written from the first person point of view of a woman. "Fat"
and "The Idea," for instance, are two that come to mind.

JA: But, for example, the woman in "Fat" is more sympathetic than Rudy, a male figure; and toward the end of the book, starting with "Jerry and Molly and Sam"—the character's name is Al—he seems like an archetypal male failure I see recurring there. Were you making a sexual distinction?

RC: No. I didn't intend that.

JA: But the women seem stronger.

RC: I think they are perhaps. At least they're more apt to survive.

JA: Last night, in hearing you read the essay on your father ("My Father's Life"), it occurred to me that your mother seemed to have a real strength, a willingness to endure. Is that where that story motif comes from?

RC: Probably so. I hadn't thought about it. Also, it's just that I felt like I knew more of what I was talking about in the beginning—I needed the confidence—when I gave the stories a male point of view. But I feel I know something about women, and I felt I could be deeply sympathetic, and involved, in taking a woman's point of view. So I embarked upon telling a story from a woman's point of view. But, yes, I think men do get hit hard in many of the stories.

JA: Is that because they're more often in positions of responsibility?

RC: And can't meet their responsibilities. Yes, sure.

JA: In your stories, the characters encounter something strange— sometimes exotic or beautiful—but the effect on the characters is often destructive. This happens sometimes in your early work, but I'm thinking especially of "Feathers," from *Cathedral*, where the narrator and his wife seem poisoned by the beauty they witness—the altruism between the hosts and the peacock. What is your point here? Are you saying the lower-middle class should be kept out of art museums?

RC: No, not at all, of course not. It's just that these people, the narrator and his wife, meet a couple, a truly happy couple, and the implication is that later they compare and contrast their own lives to that ideal life they witnessed, the life belonging to that other couple. A couple who are surrounded by beauty, if you will. The man who is telling the story says, "More's the pity for us." Things began to happen to them after that evening. She cuts her hair. They have a child, and it's a conniving child, etc., and things tend to go to hell for them afterwards. But it's no more and no less than that. I wasn't trying to set up dichotomies, or rules to govern lives.

JA: Would it be safe to say that lower-middle class conditions—isolation, physical and emotional exhaustion, the drain on the internal life—somehow deplete the capacity for an appreciation of beauty, or alter the effect that beauty has on people?

RC: I think those people you're talking about don't have time to go to museums, and they—most of them, at any rate—don't have time to read books, and they don't have time to go to lectures and concerts.

JA: But they are affected in the story. The couple who go to dinner at Bud and Olla's house.

RC: Yes, right, but that situation is so transparent and looms so large because of the peacock. I don't want to make any more of it than that.

JA: Still, the observation remains.

RC: Yes, and it's an interesting observation.

JA: Many of your stories conclude with an ambiguous character change. Are you simply recording an impression derived from personal experience or is there some principle guiding these artistic touches?

RC: Frankly, I don't know what the principle is, and I'm not writing autobiography, as I've said. It just seems that that's the way the stories should end. It's the way that they aesthetically satisfy my demands, my requirements for the story, and also maybe just the way I see things.

JA: In some ways this question resembles the notion that beauty can affect the lower-middle class in a strange way. Your characters seem more tantalized by change than anything else. Is this a widespread condition that accounts for your characters' perplexity? Because they want out of their circumstances, but the chances of getting out are slim.

RC: Yes. I like that. I like that notion. I think that's fair to say.

JA: So change—a condition basic to life—is a tantalizing thing?

RC: Yes. You'll get no argument from me about that. That's an important aspect of things.

JA: I noticed recently you're using clichés in your characterizations, and I wonder if you're just observing, or recording the way a mind works.

RC: It's there for a purpose; it's working for me, I think, not against me. Or at least I hope and assume this is the case!

JA: Often in your stories clichés trigger more profound responses, as transitions work themselves out. Something will happen, a character will say something that's a cliché, and the next thing you know it leads to a more profound way of thinking.

RC: Right. Okay.

JA: In the first book, the most striking thing is the powerlessness of the people, their helplessness. It shows us a huge span of our cul- ture—people who can't deal with their lives. That's what's terrifying. But in your new work you seem to be focused on the way people wrest salvation from adversity, like "A Small, Good Thing," for example, and "Cathedral." The latest collection, *Cathedral*, seems different in several ways from *Will You Please Be Quiet, Please?* The narratives are fuller, but most strikingly your tone seems much more optimistic. I'm thinking of a comparison between "A Small, Good Thing" and the original version entitled "The Bath." Would you please expand on this and talk a little bit about what brought on this change?

RC: I suppose it has to do with the circumstances of my life, a number of things coming together, my getting sober, and feeling more hope—feeling that there was life after alcohol—meeting and beginning to live with Tess Gallagher. Not only the internal circumstances of my life changed but the external circumstances changed as well. I suppose I became more hopeful, somewhat more positive in my thinking. Also, I simply didn't want to continue to write the same stories over and over again. So a number of things were at play when I began writing those stories, and all of them, as you know, were written in an eighteen-month period.

JA: When you wrote the more negative, bleaker stories, do you feel as though it hurt you? If you go back and brood morbidly, does it take something out of you now?

RC: I don't ever fall into those moods of brooding and depression that I used to have in my teens and twenties.

JA: And you don't attach any artistic value to brooding?

RC: No! Some with suffering. A little suffering goes a long way, you know, and for ten years I was a practicing alcoholic. I had a full measure of suffering then. There are things I wouldn't know anything about if I hadn't been an alcoholic, or my life hadn't been in chaos for so long. But I wouldn't recommend it to anyone.

I'm glad you think the new stories are different from the others, the ones that came earlier. They are different. But then I'm different too.

Carver's World

Roxanne Lawler/1986

From the *Peninsula Daily News* [Port Angeles, WA], 9 November 1986, sec. C, 1, with supplementary material transcribed and edited from the reporter's unpublished audiotape. Printed by permission of the Port Angeles *Peninsula Daily News* and Roxanne Lawler. Conducted October 1986.

Raymond Carver sits back in an easy chair, one hand cupping his head, one knee draped casually over the other.

Dressed in nubby brown sweater, white jeans and slippers, he appears as comfortable as old shoes. This, after all, is where he lives, in this room that has given birth to many poems and short stories.

Currently at the forefront of American fiction, Carver has been able to devote himself full-time to his art in the past few years. In 1983, he won the Mildred and Harold Strauss Livings Award, which pays him $35,000 a year for five years to do nothing but write.

He's been using the time to do just that. After living in California, Iowa, New York and Texas, he's settled on Port Angeles as a place compatible with his work.

Beyond him in the spacious study of his West Port Angeles home stands a large oak desk with a couple of ashtrays on top and a scattering of notes. Before it, a swivel chair stands ready for duty. To the left, a typewriter on a separate stand. Just up from the desk, a window overlooks Ediz Hook and Port Angeles Harbor.

"It's a good room for writing," Carver says, with an unassuming simplicity that might typify one of his characters.

It's apparently a good room for reading, too. The books in his study take up two walls of the room.

They lean against each other, filling six shelves of two wood bookcases on either side of the desk. Mostly stories and poetry, they reflect the enduring passion of a man who never outgrew a boyhood love of literature.

Growing up in Yakima, the young Carver sampled whatever caught his eye during weekly trips to the library—historical novels, stories about Spanish conquistadors, books about shipbuilding.

Then he went home and had his head filled with stories told by his father.

Eventually he would try his hand at writing some stories of his own. And he would keep trying, while struggling to keep a marriage intact, raise a family, make ends meet—and fight alcoholism.

His marriage and family fell apart. Alcoholism ruled his life until he decided to stay sober nine years ago.

But the perseverance paid off. Today, when he looks at the books on his shelves, he takes pride in knowing that many were written by him.

On a Tuesday afternoon, the glow from a lamp beside Carver warms the gray fall light filtering in from outside. Behind him on a shelf are a dozen copies of his most recent publication, *Ultramarine*. The collection of poetry is his second in two years, for a total of five poetry collections, three books of short stories and a collection of poems, essays and stories.

Known primarily as one of America's top short story writers, Carver has written poetry along with his fiction over the years. He's especially pleased with the new book.

"I feel like I haven't written any better poems," he says of the book, which represents 18 months of work. Indicative of its success is word that even prior to publication, the publisher sent it back to the press for a second printing.

Carver credits Port Angeles with providing much of the inspiration for the new work. Since 1980, he's spent a good portion of each year in Port Angeles with his companion, nationally known poet Tess Gallagher, who grew up in Port Angeles. The two are going abroad next year when a book of Carver's poetry is published in London, but they plan to keep Port Angeles as their home base.

For Carver, 48, Port Angeles has been a good place to work. Moreover, it has exerted a definite influence on his work.

Asked about those influences, he lights a cigarette, thinks a moment. Then fixes you with direct, intent blue eyes—eyes looking for honesty and truth. Always a question in them.

"You know, the process of writing is mysterious, and I can't really tell you why the poems started coming," he says, somewhat mystified himself. "But I know it had something to do with this landscape here and the water.

"I seriously doubt I would have written these poems had I been

living someplace else. I would've written something, I don't know
what. But I doubt that I would've written the number of poems that I
did and worked with the intensity that I worked on them."

The Port Angeles influences don't show up in every poem, but
they're there—in a cloudy mountain range in "The Rest," in
strapping on snowshoes in "The White Field," in trolling a coho fly in
"Cutlery," and in netting a silver salmon in "Evening."

The poems have a number of fishing references, in fact, testimony
to Carver's one great temptation locally. A big man with a gentle
bearing and hair peppered with gray, he has been hunting and
fishing since his youth.

Salmon-fishing itself came to him rather late, but now he's hooked.
He's got a 16-foot boat in the harbor.

"That's the one thing that interferes with my writing," he says, in
his quiet, gravelly voice. "When the salmon come in, I have trouble
staying at my desk then. It's probably my downfall. I'll fish very hard
for a few days, then turn down any invitations to go, then go back
out again."

He's also fished in the local Salmon Derby. His best day of fishing
was when he caught a 32-pound salmon with Morris Bond,
Gallagher's brother, off Ediz Hook.

His worst day?

"When I lost two about that size—and maybe they were even
bigger," he says with a grin.

Fishing for stories and poems is a little more predictable. Although
even there, Carver generally starts by spinning out a line.

"I start with the first line." He says it definitely, emphatically.

"Usually that first line comes to me, and everything else is usually
subject to change, except that first line usually remains the same.

"And I don't know where the first lines come from. Sometimes
they're generated by an image, something in my head, or just by a
line that seems to be floating around in my head. And that goes
down on the page."

Once uneasy that anyone should know about his approach to
writing, Carver eventually learned that many other writers also go
through this process of "discovery."

"It's a process of, how do I know what I want to say until I see what
I've said?" he explained, one finger scratching his cheek. "That's why

most of my stories go through a lot of drafts. And I'm no different than most of the writers of my acquaintance."

Carver said he knows of no writers "worth their salt" who don't rewrite their novels five or six times—or their short stories 10 or 15 times, or their poems 20 or 30 times.

"And most writers have infinite patience for that kind of work."

Carver has had many outside commitments in the last few weeks. At one point during the interview, he says he's tired of talking about himself. But when he talks about literature, his eyes show excitement.

His speech is both spontaneous and hesitant. The words rush out in a gust at times, haltingly at others—as if Carver is choosing them as carefully as when he writes.

He compares rewriting to the rehearsals preceding a ballet or concert. "Think of all the rehearsals that went into that," he says. "And I think those rewrites and revisions are dress rehearsals for the finished product."

Neither does he view rewriting as an onerous task.

"No, not at all, I love to do it, I love to do it!" he says, the words tumbling out. "And lots of painters work this way, too. You know, they'll paint something, and then they'll cross it out, and then they'll paint something else, and it becomes something else, and they just keep working at it."

An example from Carver's own work is the poem, "The Minuet," from Ultramarine, which he says he revised about 25 times.

Such patience for detail may explain why each Carver story and poem is so perfectly crafted, with no extraneous words. The result is a deceptive simplicity of style that reflects Carver's wish to write in the language people use.

One of Carver's early teachers was novelist John Gardner. From him, Carver learned to use "common language" to convey a clarity and precision in his work.

"I place a high premium on clarity and simplicity, not simple-mindedness—which is quite different," he says.

He believes that some of the most complex thoughts "can be expressed in the simplest and clearest language." To have one language for the educated elite and another in which we communicate with people, would go against his grain, he says.

"We'd have to have a class system, is what it would amount to."

And so you have Holly in the story "Gazebo," who says, "Something's died in me. It took a long time for it to do it, but it's dead. You've killed something, just like you'd took an axe to it. Everything is dirt now."

Or Sam in "I Could See the Smallest Things," when he says, "Slugs. . . . Everywhere you look around here at night. I lay out bait and then I come out and get them. . . . An awful invention, the slug. I save them up in that jar there."

But the obsession with "the right word" began even earlier than Carver's college days.

He sighs, puffs on his cigarette.

"I suppose it goes back to when I was a kid in Yakima. I'd hear words at home, things my dad might say. And I'd repeat these words or expressions and get laughed at by other kids because I was pronouncing the words wrong. And this made me want to get the words right. I just didn't want to be laughed at, I guess.

"So I put a premium on finding the right word for what I wanted to say."

Carver agrees that most people who aren't writers probably underestimate what it takes to be a writer, namely "a great deal of hard work."

His own hard work began in his early 20s, when he decided that if he was really going to be a writer, he'd better start writing something.

His "red letter day" came as a college undergraduate in about 1962. On that day, he had a poem and story accepted for publication in different magazines. Like brand-new parents showing off their baby, he and his wife drove all around town showing the letters of acceptance to their friends.

But his real struggle was yet to come. In his 30s, he started drinking, and "went off like a rocket." In half a dozen years or so, alcoholism brought his family life crashing down around him and his writing almost to a standstill.

"It was a mess," he says, recalling the memory as if it were from another life. "The family life just became a wasteland. It was a disaster toward the end."

During his last two or three years of drinking, Carver was doing little in the way of writing, and publishing even less. And he'd just about quit thinking about writing as a serious endeavor.

"The light, if you will, had just pretty nearly dimmed out toward the end of the drinking," he says. "A great amount of flickering, but to all intents and purposes, I was finished. . . . The liquor just had me on my back, and I was incapable of doing much of anything at all."

After visits to one treatment center after another, Carver made a firm decision—on June 2, 1977, he notes quickly—to quit drinking. Soon, his health returned. But not, however, his desire to write.

"When I got sober, I was so grateful to have my health back that it didn't matter if I ever wrote again or not."

A Guggenheim fellowship and encouragement from Gallagher renewed his interest in writing. Carver decided that he would use the grant to write short stories, and that was that.

"I simply said I'm going to start writing short stories. And one story led to another."

Carver has been sober ever since. In that time, he's continued to write the stories and poems that have placed him on an eye-level shelf of the American literary world.

He says his life has improved dramatically since meeting Gallagher, and that now he can't imagine living with someone who is not a writer. He can't imagine life with someone "who doesn't share the same, larger goals and aspirations, and somebody who, like Tess, understands my need for privacy and solitude, as I understand hers."

His book of poetry out, Carver has once again turned to short stories. But he plans to return to poetry. When the need arises. When he needs to deal with things that are perhaps more intimate.

"The poems seem closer to me somehow, more personal," he says, lighting another cigarette. "Even though I'm not writing autobiography in the poems any more than I am in the fiction."

He does, however, see a closer relationship between short stories and poems than between short stories and novels—because of the need to make every word count for something.

On leave for the past few years from his teaching post at Syracuse University in New York, Carver still has advice for young writers. First, they must "write about things that matter, about what counts." Then they must learn that all the great writers revise, and that the young writer must learn to revise, also.

"He has to love it," Carver says earnestly. "He has to love the act of writing, the sound of the typewriter, the smell of the ink, whatever. And he has to make it his world, no one else's."

The interview concludes as the afternoon draws to a close.

Outside Carver's home, dusk drops a dark curtain.

A couple of dogs bark. Wood smoke rises from chimneys. The Olympics are outlined sharply in the crisp fall air.

Nearby in one yard rests an old junk car. In another yard, a beat-up rubber tire.

It could be a scene from a Carver story.

In a well-lit kitchen with curtains not quite right, somebody is reaching for a beer. Down the street, a millworker is planning to take his girlfriend out for dinner. Across the street, somebody is smoking a cigarette, listening to a friend.

Somewhere out there, a Carver story is taking place.

Q: What got you back to writing after you stopped drinking?

A: It was the Guggenheim fellowship and Tess's encouragement and the fact that I had the desire to write again. That desire had not been with me when I first got sober. I might even have in some subconscious way blamed some of the things that had happened in my family on my wanting to write. I had taken my family on strange odysseys one place or another trying to find the ideal writing situation, the ideal job, and the ideal place to live. So I think I might have unconsciously blamed the writing for some of the things that happened. I could certainly imagine life without writing, as I could now, if it comes down to that. I feel like I'm writing in one sense to bear witness. And if it ever comes down to the point where I feel I'm not bearing witness any longer, I could stop writing. I hope that never happens, and with any luck at all it won't happen.

Q: Do you feel that with each story or poem written more are generated?

A: Yes. And every poem or story counts, becomes a part of you. I'm not talking about adding to one's reputation or one's glory. It becomes a part of the writer, part of his witness to his time here on earth. The older I get the more I feel that I am part of something, that I am making a contribution, being a conduit, yes, or an instrument. I don't mean in a religious sense. You find yourself feeling like you're sharing things not just with living writers or artists, but with the dead writers as well. I think it was Ezra Pound who said, "It's important that great poems get written. It's not important who writes them."

Q: What about the idea that artists need to drink, use drugs, or be mad?

A: I don't hold with that at all. Quite the contrary. I think that most of the best work of the past and of the present was done by people who were not alcoholics and not maniacs. It was Flaubert who said you should be sane and sober in your everyday life so that you can be wild and inventive in your writing. I've never written a single poem or story or anything else under the influence of anything. What little writing I got done in the days when I was drinking was done when I was sober.

Q: What would be your assessment of the health of the short story today?

A: I truly think there is a renaissance of the short story. I don't think it's a faddish thing. The serious readership has always been there, and now there is an audience for the short story. Many writers are setting out to write short stories and nothing but short stories with the expectation of having a book of short stories published. This was something unheard of even ten years ago. Beginning short-story writers could not give away their collections. First of all, they had to publish one or two or three novels. Now publishers are bringing these books out, and people are reading them and reviewing them seriously.

Q: If you were still teaching, what would be your advice to young writers?

A: First of all, I'd tell them they have to write. They can't just talk about writing. They have to be willing to write as if their lives depended on it and be able and willing to go the course. I had a writing teacher tell me, "Are you ready to starve for ten years and work menial jobs and take all kinds of rebuffs and rejections and setbacks? If at the end of ten years you're still writing, maybe you're going to be a writer." I wouldn't tell them that, but I would tell them that they have to write and they have to be honest. Write about what counts, what's important, and if you're lucky someone will read it.

Matters of Life and Death
William L. Stull/1986

From *The Bloomsbury Review*, 8 (January/February 1988), 14-17; reprinted in *Living in Words: Interviews from* The Bloomsbury Review *1981-1988,* ed. Gregory McNamee (Portland, OR: Breitenbush, 1988), 143-56. Supplementary material has been transcribed and edited from the unpublished audiotape that was the source of the published interview. Printed by permission of William L. Stull, Gregory McNamee, and *The Bloomsbury Review.* Conducted 11-12 November 1986.

These days, Raymond Carver and his companion Tess Gallagher shuttle between two houses in Port Angeles, a mill town and low-key resort atop Washington's Olympic Peninsula. Carver's house is a handsomely restored Victorian in a working-class neighborhood west of town, not far from the truck route, harbor, and log dump. There, in November of 1986, we discussed his fiction, with Carver stoking the wood stove against the autumn damp. The next afternoon we shifted to Gallagher's residence, an elegant contemporary in a development to the east of Port Angeles. With his back to the deepening blue of the Strait of Juan de Fuca, Carver talked about his recent poetry, much of which had been written in the glass-walled study downstairs.

Raymond Carver is the author of five collections of short stories, two chapbooks, and three volumes of poetry. He and Gallagher have collaborated on a screenplay, *Dostoevsky,* and in 1986 Carver served as guest editor of the annual *Best American Short Stories.* In 1983 the American Academy and Institute of Arts and Letters selected Carver for one of its first Mildred and Harold Strauss Livings. His more recent honors include a Pulitzer Prize nomination for *Cathedral* and the 1985 Levinson Prize from *Poetry* magazine. Carver is now editing a book on Byron for Ecco Press's Essential Poets series. He spent the winter of 1987 in Syracuse, New York, working on a third book of poems and more short stories. (Raymond Carver died on August 2nd, 1988, as this book was going to press.)

The Bloomsbury Review: It's been four years since you received your Strauss Livings. Has the fellowship agreed with you?

Raymond Carver: The award changed my life dramatically and irrevocably. It's let me see myself as a full-time writer. Of course, they gave me the award on the basis of my fiction, and the first thing I did was write two books of poems. But I am writing fiction again. I came out here in January of 1984 with the intention of writing fiction. After *Cathedral* was published in October 1983 there was a real hubbub going on in Syracuse, and this hubbub extended right on into the new year. It wasn't entirely unpleasant, but I was thrown off my stride, and I couldn't find my way back to my work. And I had emptied out my cupboards. I had no new work in hand after *Fires* and *Cathedral* appeared. I didn't have anything new that I was working on, and everything seemed to conspire against my writing new work. The phone was always ringing. I was trying to work, but I simply couldn't see my way clear to do it in Syracuse. For a while I thought I would try to find an apartment to work in. But then Tess suggested I come out here and work. This house was sitting empty. So I came out here with the intention of writing fiction. But when I got here I just sat and was very quiet and still for a week. I did some reading. Then on about the sixth day I wrote a poem. I can't really tell you why. I think I picked up a magazine and read some poems and thought I could do better. I don't know if that's the best motive for writing a poem, but I think it is what prompted me to begin to write poems. The next day I wrote another poem, and the next day I wrote a couple more. In two weeks I had twenty poems or so, and I just kept writing. No one could have been more surprised than I was, because I hadn't written any poetry in over two years. I would write myself out every day, and then at night there was nothing left. The bowl was empty. I went to bed at night not knowing if there would be anything there the next morning, but there always was. So somewhere in there, after I had fifty or sixty poems written and was still going, I thought, jeepers, maybe I'm going to write a book of poems. Lo and behold, I wrote poems for sixty-five days, including a poem on the day I left here. I wrote a poem in the morning and left on an early afternoon flight to go back to Syracuse. And I had my book, *Where Water Comes Together With Other Water.* In September of 1984 I started writing poems again. And I kept writing poems until February or March, and for all intents and purposes I had the poems that went into *Ultramarine*. I went back to writing stories last winter, and now all those poems seem like a great gift. I can't really account for how they happened.

TBR: Elsewhere you've said that a poet needs something more than talent in order to stand out from the crowd of MFA program graduates. What is that something?

RC: It's something to be got at beyond the poetry. I'm not sure just what it is, but it's something unmistakable in the work and it always declares itself when it's there. Rilke is quoted as saying, "Poetry is experience." That's partly it. In any event, one always recognizes the real article from the trumped-up ersatz product which is so often top-heavy with technique and intellection and struggling to "say" something. I'm tired of reading poems that are just well-made poems.

TBR: Who are some contemporary poets who achieve what you're talking about?

RC: I admire the work of Philip Levine. I like Robert Hass's poetry. He's writing about things that matter in a very beautiful, straightforward manner. Galway Kinnell is another. Hayden Carruth, Philip Booth, William Heyen, Mary Oliver, Don Justice, Louis Simpson, Tess, to name just a few. There are lots of others.

TBR: In a good many instances, you've approached what seems to be a single incident from two angles, treating it in both poetry and prose. Are there limits on a writer's experience?

RC: I don't feel I'm short on things to write about. But some things, I'm thinking of "Distress Sale" now, that poem, or the story "Why Don't You Dance?"—the yard sale situation—the idea, the image of the yard sale made such a strong impression on me that I dealt with it first in a poem and then in a story. The same thing is true with regard to the poem "Late Night with Fog and Horses" and the story "Blackbird Pie." In each instance I wrote the poem first and then wrote the story, I suppose, because I apparently felt a need to elaborate on the same theme.

TBR: Is narrative, the storytelling element, what links the genres for you?

RC: Yes. And just as I'm more interested in representational art as opposed to abstract art, I'm more interested in poems with a narrative or story line to them than in free-associating poems that don't have any grounding in the real world.

TBR: Dennis Schmitz was one of your teachers in the late sixties. Recently he commented that your poetry gets at the figurative possibilities of everyday living—seeing a snail on the garden wall or locking yourself out of the house.

RC: I'm interested in that kind of poetry, and I'm pleased with Schmitz's remark. He was for many years—and still is—an inspiration to me, even though our poetry is very different.

TBR: Your new poetry openly celebrates intimacy, and in some poems the walls between life and art seem very thin. Is there a risk of sentimentality or embarrassment in that?

RC: Any right-thinking reader or writer abjures sentimentality. But there's a difference between sentiment and sentimentality. I'm all for sentiment. I'm interested in the personal, intimate relationships in life, so why not deal with these relationships in literature? What about intimate experiences like those recounted in "A Haircut" or "The Gift"? Why can't such experiences be turned into poetry? These little experiences are important underpinnings in our daily lives, and I don't see any problem in turning them into poems. They are, after all, something that we all share—as readers, writers, and human beings.

TBR: You're not inclined to treat mundane matters ironically, then?

RC: No. I can't imagine treating them ironically or denigrating them in any way. I don't think there should be any barriers, artificial or otherwise, between life as it's lived and life as it's written about. It's only natural to write about these things. The things that count are often intimate things. I'm embarrassed for the people who are embarrassed by the idea of someone writing about things such as haircuts and slippers and ashtrays and hominy and so on.

TBR: Still, for a long time, and even to an extent today, the facts of everyday living, things like getting haircuts and picking up the mail, were thought by some to be subjects beneath the poet's dignity.

RC: But see where that's gotten us. So much of our poetry has become like something you see in a museum. You walk around and politely look at it and then go away and discuss it. It's been given over to teachers and students. And it also seems to me that of all the art forms, poetry is probably the one with the worst press, if you know what I mean. It's got the largest number of hanging judges involved on the peripheries. So many people who don't even read poetry often make pronouncements about it. These people feel that standards have been thrown out the window, the barbarians are at the gate, and nothing is sacred any longer. I don't have sympathy for guardians, so-called, of sacred flames.

TBR: You don't hold with the modernist notion that poetry needs to be difficult?

RC: Of course not. I'm saying just the opposite. My friend Richard Ford recently passed along a remark he'd heard from Joyce Carol Oates. She told him, "Ray's poems are arousing resentment in some quarters because he's writing poetry that people can understand." I take that as a compliment. I don't have a whole lot of patience with obscurity or rhetoric, in life or in literature.

TBR: Three years ago, when you reviewed Sherwood Anderson's *Selected Letters* for *The New York Times,* you quoted Anderson as saying, "Fame is no good, my dear, take it from me." What do you make of all the attention you've received?

RC: It's not unpleasant. I haven't gotten blasé about it. I don't think I'm a different person. The good things that have happened are a spur that makes me want to do more. I don't want to rest on my laurels, as it were, comfortably or uncomfortably. I feel everything is yet to be done. Speaking of his work a year or so before he died, John Gardner said, "When you look back there's lots of bales in the field, but ahead it's all still to mow." I feel that way.

TBR: In your essay "Fires" you acknowledge John Gardner and Gordon Lish as influences on your writing. Gardner was your teacher at Chico State, and in your foreword to his posthumous book *On Becoming a Novelist* you write about what he taught you. Lish was your editor at *Esquire* and later, for a time, at Knopf. What did you learn from him?

RC: In much the same way as John Gardner, he gave me some good advice and counsel on particular stories. He was a stickler for the right word. In that sense, I had two of the best teachers a writer could possibly have. He had a wonderful eye, an eye as good as John Gardner's, even though he and Gardner were completely different in other ways. Gardner said don't use twenty-five words to

say what you can say in fifteen. This was the way Gordon felt, except
Gordon believed that if you could say it in five words instead of
fifteen, use five words. One of the things that was so helpful about
Gordon was that he believed in me as a writer when I needed that,
when I had no other contact with the great world, living as I was in
Sunnyvale and Cupertino, California. He championed my work. He
was constantly reading it aloud at conferences and even reprinting it
when he had the opportunity. I owe him a real debt of gratitude.

TBR: Gardner and Lish may have taught you not to waste words,
but you carried verbal economy to new extremes in revising the
stories for *What We Talk About* from their magazine versions. You've
said that you cut your work to the marrow, not just to the bone.
Later, when you published alternate versions of the stories in *Fires*,
you restored many of the excisions. What led you to perform such
radical surgery in the first place?

RC: It had to do with the theory of omission. If you can take
anything out, take it out, as doing so will make the work stronger.
Pare, pare, and pare some more. Maybe it also had something to do
with whatever I was reading during that period. But maybe not. It got
to where I wanted to pare everything down and maybe pare too
much. Then I guess I must have reacted against that. I didn't write
anything for about six months. Then I wrote "Cathedral" and all the
other stories in that book in a fairly concentrated period of time. I've
said that if I had gone any further in the direction I was going, the
direction of the earlier stories, I would have been writing stories that I
wouldn't have wanted to read myself.

TBR: The Strauss award bought you time to write, but many of
your recent poems suggest that time seems shorter than ever to you.

RC: I've become more aware of this in the last two or three years.
But any changes that have come about in my life because of the
grant have been for the good. My life seems more interesting, for one
thing. I suppose I'm living the life now, and I'm usually not aware of
this on a conscious level, but I'm living the life that as a young writer I
often dreamed about but never in my wildest imaginings thought
could come true. Now that I'm in that life, it's fine, it's very agreeable.
But I know there's a great responsibility, too.

TBR: To what?

RC: To my work. I feel like I have an extraordinary opportunity,
and there's so much work to be done. When a few days go by and I

don't write, things don't seem quite right, no matter how good it is otherwise. I don't feel responsible to the American Academy of Arts and Letters or beholden to anyone or any institution, you understand. I just feel it's imperative that a writer keep writing. That *I* keep writing. I can't imagine not writing. Oh, I suppose I could, if I felt I didn't have anything else I wanted to say. I could stop then, sure. But as long as I feel that I can write and bear witness, I intend to do so.

TBR: Writers have traditionally worked alone, but for almost ten years you've lived, worked, and collaborated with Tess Gallagher. How has this worked out?

RC: It's been very good for me, and I daresay I can speak for Tess as well. When we first got together back in 1978 she was writing and I wasn't writing. I was in the process of recovering my life. I had my health back, I was no longer drinking, but I wasn't writing. After my two books came out in 1976, there was no new work being written. And there was no new work for a good while after I got sober either. At that time I felt it was okay, it really was, if I never wrote again. I was just so grateful to have my wits back, you know. I'd been brain-dead for such a long time. And suddenly I had this other life, another chance at things. And in this new life it wasn't all that important if I wrote or not. But Tess was writing, and that was a good example for me. I was patient, and I simply waited to see what would come along, if anything.

TBR: Recently, neorealist fiction, yours included, has been faulted from the left. Some critics urge a return to the literary experimentalism of the late sixties and early seventies. How do you react?

RC: It's strange, because a number of right-wing, neoconservative critics say I'm painting too dark a picture of American life. I'm not putting a happy face on America. That's the stick they swing at me. As for the experimental fiction of the sixties and seventies, much of that work I have a hard time with. I think that literary experiment failed. In trying out different ways of expressing themselves, the experimental writers failed to communicate in the most fundamental and essential way. They got farther and farther away from their audience. But maybe this is what they wanted. Still, I think when people look back on that period fifty years from now it's going to be looked on as an odd time in the literary history of the country, an interruption, somehow.

TBR: An interruption in the course of realism?

RC: I don't really think in those terms, but now that you ask me, yes. For someone like myself, a writer in the realist tradition, it just seems that fiction about fiction or about the experience of writing fiction is not very viable or lasting. What are we doing if we're not writing about things that count, matters of life and death, as it were, to use the title of Tobias Wolff's anthology? I don't go around thinking of myself as a realist writer. I simply think of myself as a writer. But, it's true, I am trying to write about recognizable human beings who find themselves in more or less critical situations.

TBR: What makes your writing uniquely your own?

RC: Well, certainly, the tone in the work, I suppose. Geoffrey Wolff said in a review of my first book of stories that he felt he could pick out a story of mine without seeing my name attached to it. I took that as a compliment. If you can find an author's fingerprints on the work, you can tell it's his and no other's.

TBR: Where do those fingerprints lie? In subject? In style?

RC: Both. Subject and style, the two are pretty much inseparable, right? John Updike once said that when he thinks of writing a story only certain areas of writing and experience are open to him. Certain areas, and lives, are completely closed. So, the story chooses him. And I feel that's true of myself. Speaking as a poet and story writer, I think that my stories and poems have chosen me. I haven't had to go out looking for material. These things come. You're called to write them.

TBR: You're sometimes discussed as a social realist who focuses on the downside of working-class life. But, if your people are beat, they're seldom beaten. It's been suggested that your abiding subject is human endurance. Would you agree?

RC: That's a preoccupation, yes, and a writer could do worse. I'm saying he could set his sights lower. Most things that we care for pass away or pass by in such a rush that we can scarcely get a fix on them. So it's really a question of enduring and abiding.

TBR: Your work, especially the work in *What We Talk About*, is now associated with what a number of critics have termed "minimalist fiction." In 1985, *Mississippi Review* devoted a special issue to the topic, and it featured your essay "On Writing." A few years earlier, however, you tried to shake off the "minimalist" tag. What makes it stick?

RC: The more special issues of magazines that are devoted to this, the longer it's going to be around. I'll be glad to see the appellation fade so that writers can be talked about as writers and not lumped together in groups where they usually don't really belong. It's a label, and labels are unattractive to the people attached to the labels. I've stopped paying it any mind, frankly. It was an annoyance for a while, and now it's not. I admire much about many of the writers who've been labeled minimalists, and yet they're all different from each other. Each offers up his or her own pleasures.

TBR: Some critics believe that if there's one thing uniting these writers and setting them apart from other postmoderns, it's their distaste for irony. Does that ring true to you?

RC: I think they mean that these writers, the so-called "minimalists," are not ironists in the sense that there are no secrets between the sophisticated writer and the writer's sophisticated audience. And I would agree with them there. I see irony as a sort of pact or compact between the writer and the reader in that they know more than the characters do. The characters are set up and then they're set down again in some sort of subtle pratfall or awakening. I don't feel any such complicity with the reader. I'm not talking down to my characters, or holding them up for ridicule, or slyly doing an end run around them. I'm much more interested in my characters, in the people in my story, than I am in any potential reader. I'm uncomfortable with irony if it's at the expense of someone else, if it hurts the characters. I don't think that's in my stories, and I really don't see much of it in the writers who are talked about as minimalists. I strive not to do that. I think I'd be ashamed of myself if I did.

TBR: Endurance seemed about the most one could hope for in *What We Talk About When We Talk About Love*. But in *Cathedral* things began to change. In that book some of your characters seem to prosper in spirit, if not in hard cash.

RC: Yes, and as a writer and a very interested bystander, I'm pleased to see this happening. A writer doesn't want to go on repeating himself, using the same characters in the same circumstances, time and again. It's not only desirable, it's healthy to move on. I'm not working any kind of conscious program in my stories, no, of course not. But it seems like every time I've finished a book there's been a clear line of demarcation. There's always been a time after I finished putting together a book manuscript when I haven't worked for a while on stories. After I finished *What We Talk About* I didn't write stories for a good long while. Six months or so. Then the first story that I wrote was "Cathedral." It happened again after *Cathedral* came out. I didn't write a story for nearly two years. It's true. I wrote poems. The first story that I wrote and published after *Cathedral* was "Boxes," which appeared in *The New Yorker.* Then five or six stories came very close together. And I feel these new stories are different from the earlier ones in kind and degree. There's something about the voice, yes. Again, speaking just as an outsider or bystander, I'm glad to see these changes at work.

TBR: What common denominators do you see in the new stories?

RC: Well, for one thing, they've all been written in the first person. It's nothing I planned on. It's just the voice I heard and began to go with.

TBR: If every story is a fresh start, is a writer's development really cumulative?

RC: I feel it's cumulative in that you know you have written other stories and poems. Work begins to accumulate. It gives you heart to go on. I couldn't be writing the stories I'm writing now if I hadn't written the ones I have written. But there's no way in the world I could go back now and write another "Gazebo" or another "Where I'm Calling From" or for that matter anything else I've written.

TBR: You wrote many of the stories in *Will You Please Be Quiet, Please?* during 1970 and 1971, when you were on your first NEA Fellowship. What did you learn about writing during that year of concentrated work?

RC: Well, to put it simply, I discovered that I could do it. I had been doing it in such a hit-or-miss fashion for so long, since the early sixties. But I discovered that if I went to my desk every day and applied myself I could seriously and steadily write stories. That was probably the biggest discovery I made. Somehow, I suppose at some deeper level, I was tapping into some things that were important to me, things I'd wanted to write about and finally was able to, without a sense of grief or shame or confusion. I was able to confront some things in the work head-on. Call it subject matter. And I suppose during that time I fastened onto or discovered a way of writing about these things. Something happened during that time in the writing, *to* the writing. It went underground and then it came up again, and it was bathed in a new light for me. I was starting to chip away, down to the image, then the figure itself. And it happened during that period.

TBR: What's next?

RC: I have a contract for the new book of stories, and I'm in a story-writing mood. I can't wait until I can get back to my desk and stay there. I have a lot of stories I want to write. I'm wild to get settled in here and be still.

TBR: In both narrative and imagery, there's considerable overlap between your poems and your stories. What else, to your mind, connects your poetry and fiction?

RC: For one thing, it's the economy and unity. There's nothing extraneous or baggy or shapeless about the story or poem as there sometimes is with a novel. And I write my stories and poems in the same way, building from one word to the next, one line or sentence to the next. There's also the spirit. You're trying to capture and hold a moment. A novel is an accretion of detail that may cover weeks or months or years—generations, God forbid. The story takes place in a much smaller compass of time, just like the poem. The impulse is to say it now, get it into the corral rather than let it roam around the range.

TBR: It's possible to read a number of your stories in more than one published version. I'm thinking of pairs like "Where Is Everyone?" and "Mr. Coffee and Mr. Fixit." Do you count those one story or two?

RC: Two stories. And there are about four versions of "So Much Water So Close to Home." The version that appeared in *Spectrum* and then in *The Pushcart Prize* anthology is different from the versions in both *What We Talk About* and *Fires*. They're all different stories, and they have to be judged differently. That was a period when I rewrote everything. I haven't done that in some years now. I don't know if I've gotten lazier, or more confident, or less interested in the work after it's published—or simply more eager to get on with something new. But I haven't done any of that in years. Now when I'm through with something, I tend to lose interest in it, as I said. It's not painful for me to reread it, but it's simply not something I'm interested in doing. Also, and I hadn't thought of this until now, maybe I was afraid to look ahead too far in those days. I didn't know what was around the next corner. Maybe it was an empty square, or maybe a nice courtyard. Or else simply a closed door.

TBR: In the past, your stories have focused mainly on fathers and sons, husbands and wives. Two of your new stories, "Boxes" and "Elephant," focus on other sides of the family: mother and son, brother and brother. What do you make of this?

RC: At this moment I don't know what kind of story is going to come next. I mean that. But I don't feel I'm at the end of something. And that's a good feeling. It's just that some other things have been made available to me, been given to me.

TBR: A story of yours called "Intimacy" appeared in *Esquire* last August. The characters looked a lot like people we've read about in your autobiographical essays. Was the story fiction?

RC: Fiction, yes. There never was such an encounter between any people I know. The story isn't autobiographical, but the emotion of the story is true, in every line.

TBR: "Intimacy" is very spare, nearly all dialogue. In another of your recent stories, "Blackbird Pie," the narrator offers all kinds of background and asides. Is your approach to storytelling changing?

RC: I wrote those two stories no more than two or three weeks apart from each other, and it was a time of discovery. It was a high tide. I like what's happening, and there are many more stories I want to write. In truth I feel like all the stories I've written in the past six or eight months were not really, in some strange way, they were not the stories I intended to write. The other stories, the ones I will write, are the harder stories. But we'll see. I feel I'm just beginning to make some discoveries about what I can do with a short story, about what I want to do with *my* short stories. I'm more or less verging on finding out something, and that's exciting.

TBR: You wrote the poems for *Where Water Comes Together* and *Ultramarine* in separate sessions, but the time between the two periods of composition was fairly short. Beyond the fact of separate publication, what sets the two books apart?

RC: *Ultramarine* feels closer to me now than the other book, having just been published two weeks ago. It may be the stronger of the two books. But in preparing for the Poetry Day reading in

Chicago last week I went back to *Where Water Comes Together With Other Water,* and I found myself very interested in many of the poems. I hadn't looked at any of them in a long while. Probably if I were doing the book over again there are some poems I wouldn't include, but I found twelve or fifteen poems, at least, that I still think are very good. *Ultramarine* seems more considered, somehow, more careful in certain ways. Also, a lot of the poems in *Where Water Comes Together* came after not having written poetry in a long while and feeling very much out of touch with myself. And they were all written in the space of two months and two weeks. The newer book was written over a longer period of time, six or eight months. So you see there is a difference that way, too. I like both books, but the poems in *Ultramarine* may be richer because they deal with relation-ships with other people in ways that the poems in *Where Water Comes Together* sometimes do not.

TBR: Many of the poems in *Where Water Comes Together*— "Energy," "Wenas Ridge," "The Fishing Pole of the Drowned Man"—tell and retell a family story, perhaps a family myth. Is the speaker working off a family curse?

RC: I feel a little uncomfortable in responding to that. I don't want to be seen as making myths, as it were. Let's just say there were some rather dreadful and frightening things that happened in those days. I guess I wanted not just to bear witness to some of those events but to explore them and to reach some conclusions, if possible. In "Anathema" I say that "the house was pulled down, / the ground plowed up, and then / we were dispersed in four directions." There *is* something biblical-sounding about that, I suppose. The poem is not simply a cataloging of horrific events whose significance is lost on the speaker. The whole book is, in its way, maybe, a story of a life. The final poem, "For Tess," is a love letter, and a poem of affirmation.

TBR: But even in "For Tess," for a minute or two before the speaker opens his eyes and goes back to "being happy," he lies down and imagines himself dead. For all its affirmations of love, life, and intimacy, your new poetry seems death-obsessed in a way none of your previous poetry was.

RC: Mortality weighs on you when you reach your mid-forties in ways that it doesn't in your mid-twenties and thirties. Poetry, finally, is a matter of life and death. Basically, I have little interest in poetry that only talks about fruit and nice decor. I'm interested in poetry that talks about the larger issues, life and death matters, yes, and the question of how to behave in this world, how to go on in the face of everything. Time is short and the water is rising.

TBR: *Ultramarine* is already in its second printing. Is poetry winning a wider audience?

RC: Poetry lost its audience years ago, and this is tragic. I don't know if the situation is going to change in the years to come. I'd like to see a wider readership, but let's face it, poetry is never going to have the readership that novels and books of short stories have. Let's just say that it would be a more desirable situation for poetry if it could reach a larger number of people than it does at present.

TBR: If there's any truth to the "house of fiction" analogy, the room that many readers associate with poetry seems to be the study. Can poetry open other doors?

RC: The door to the kitchen, the door to the living room, the door to the closet. Even the bathroom! And if it's locked, why not open it? Cesare Pavese wrote poems about daily life in Italy. He wrote in an Italian that was not the Italian of the educated, literary class, and he wrote about subjects that were not often, not ever, I'm told, written about in literary Italian. I read his poems years ago. I don't think I'm the first poet to write about life, my word, no.

TBR: How do you picture the audience for your poetry?

RC: I think every writer is writing to please himself, and if he pleases himself he might have some chance of pleasing some other good readers. I don't visualize an audience any more with my poetry than I do with my fiction, except perhaps the audience that John Cheever said he wrote for, the audience of intelligent, grown-up men and women. My poetry is not simply a matter of self-expression. A writer wants to communicate, and communication is a two-way street between writer and reader. It doesn't matter if the writer is writing poems or short stories, he's writing about matters of the heart, matters that are of concern and close to him. He simply needs to find the right form, the right way of saying these things in the hope of communicating what he's feeling to the reader.

TBR: Some of your new poems, "The Garden," for example, are stanzaic, while others, sometimes longer ones, are single sweeps, long verse paragraphs. What determines the shape of your poems?

RC: Most of my poems are narrative and don't need to be set in perfect stanzas. The form that each poem took seemed to me the most natural form available to it. If I had to do it all over again, I'm sure I'd do it exactly the same way. And yet I think that there is enough variety for the eye and ear to prevent the reader from becoming bored. They don't all look alike on the page. Stanzas, numbers of syllables, lines per stanza—I'm not so interested in these things. It's more important that the poems be lively and that they look lively and right on the page.

TBR: One form that recurs is the listing pattern of Smart's "Jubilate Agno" and Ginsberg's *Howl,* initial repetition.

RC: There are several poems like that, yes. Poems like "My Car" and "Fear" are in the tradition of the poem as a catalogue. These poems are open-ended. In a way, they're not over yet, though there is a closure at the end of each poem. But both those poems could still be added to. Witness today when that fuse blew out and I had to take the car down to the shop. And the things I fear I haven't even begun to touch on!

TBR: How do you know when a book of poems is completed?

RC: I felt a sense of closure with both books. I knew that "For Tess" ended *Where Water Comes Together with Other Water.* It also went back to the dedication at the beginning of the book. I felt I had a book, not just a collection of poems, but a coherent book. Each book has a beginning, middle, and end. "The Gift," which ends *Ultramarine,* could have been placed nowhere else in the book. I feel that when the reader gets there, to that last poem, there ought to be a sense that he's been somewhere, done something, experienced some of the life that went into the book.

De Minimis: Raymond Carver and His World

Francesco Durante/1987

From *Il Mattino* [Naples], 30 April 1987, 13. Reprinted by permission of Francesco Durante and *Il Mattino*. Conducted April 1987. Translated by Susanna Peters Coy.

He's a peculiar American. He smokes. He's not homosexual. He reminds you of some actor from the fifties, but you don't know exactly who. He drinks mineral water, at the most tonic, after having been for many years, almost to the point of no return, a drinking buddy of so many poor souls who, like him, were in and out of depressing alcohol rehab centers. Which is to say that he is one of the few who still recognize the role and mastery of the too-soon-forgotten (neither Beat nor minimalist) Charles Bukowski. "In *Fires,* I even dedicated a poem to him. It's titled 'You Don't Know What Love Is.' It's kind of the story of an evening that he spent at my house, and many lines are nothing more than phrases taken directly from what he said. . . . Well, Bukowski is a really strange guy; it's almost impossible to agree with him. I was in my early twenties and I told him that I liked his poems. He answered that I must have terrible taste."

Raymond Carver—with whom I am speaking—is perhaps the most "mythic" of today's American writers: the recognized master of that literary renaissance that is producing legions of fiction writers barely out of adolescence. He is the alchemist who has distilled, at an incomparable level of perfection, the quintessence of a genre that only ten years ago seemed in inexorable decline, the story, or better the "short story," understood at such a rarefied height as to make one suspect who-knows-what operations of stylistic mechanics, while he, Carver, claims to respect a single obligatory criterion: "to write about everyday things, and to speak not to the elite groups but to the people." "I say things in a few pages because words are all I have, so it's better if they're the right ones." "No cheap tricks. I tell about my world, only that, and it's his own world, more than his style, that sets one writer apart from another." From simple string, a golden rule: "Simplicity is the seal of truth. I think an ancient Roman said that. Maybe Seneca?"

Life, people, things, personal experiences, even if not strictly
autobiography. Carver the man possesses these goods in abundance.
To begin with, in fifty years he never rode in a limousine until two
years ago when he bought himself a Mercedes. No Hollywood-style
swimming pools, no big houses with patios, no high-society parties.
Vices, yes, but those of the poor: instead of coke, he went for beer
and whiskey.

The son of a sawmill worker and a waitress, he spent his childhood
and early youth in Yakima in Washington State; in sum, at the end of
the earth. After high school he too went to work in the sawmill, and
at eighteen, having gotten his sixteen-year-old girlfriend pregnant, he
got married. The young couple managed as best they could: they
studied and graduated. Ray was even awarded a scholarship at the
Iowa Writers' Workshop. But meanwhile, the children had become
two and the pay from his library job (his wife was a waitress) wasn't
enough. There followed three years as night custodian for a
California hospital. He would write in the morning when he got
home (and meanwhile his wife would have left on her rounds as a
door-to-door book saleswoman). Carver was twenty-nine when he
began his descent into the hell of alcoholism. He was arrested and he
underwent numerous hospitalizations as he unsuccessfully tried and
tried again to detox himself. His marriage was breaking up. He
emerged from this situation only in 1977, one year after the
publication of his first successful book, the story collection *Will You
Please Be Quiet, Please?*

Those stories—torn from him by literary agents in the course of
conversations at which Carver regularly turned up drunk—God only
knows how he wrote them: typed, on packing paper, in the kitchen,
the garage. They didn't bring him wealth, but they did bring a solid
reputation. The consecration was to come in 1981 with *What We Talk
About When We Talk About Love* and in 1983 with *Cathedral,* the
two books that have just been published in Italian editions, the first
by Garzanti (*Di cosa parliamo quando parliamo d'amore*) and the
second by Serra and Riva (*Cattedrale*; Mondadori had already
published this one in 1984 but it sold poorly).

Carver seems the opposite of the squalid, provincial, mysteriously
troubling characters of whom his stories speak. Today he is a shy,
mild-mannered man. He speaks softly and you have to listen intently

in order to understand his drawling English. He owes much—he says "everything"—to Tess Gallagher, the poet and fiction writer with whom he has lived since 1979, after separating from his wife. Tess is a sturdy, vivacious, and cheerful woman, with an Irish boldness. With her, Carver divides his time between Port Angeles, on the Pacific Ocean in the far northwest of the States, where he goes salmon fishing, and Syracuse, New York, which he doesn't much like and where, he says, he couldn't work.

Ray and Tess are giving a class today for a packed student audience from the Department of English Literature at the Sapienza. We are in the Villa Mirafiori on the Via Nomentana, a villa that the first king of Italy wished to give to a beautiful woman. Agostino Lombardo does the honors of the house, exchanging pleasantries with the ageless Fernanda Pivano. (She wrote the afterword to the Garzanti edition.) The young scholar and poet Riccardo Duranti also speaks. His translation of Tess's poetry will be brought out in the autumn by Labirinto, publisher of the review *Arsenale*.

Ray reads "Popular Mechanics," a two-page story, a little chilling, that describes a couple's argument during the moment of separation. He is packing his suitcase and wants the baby. She doesn't want to give it to him. He pulls from one side, she from the other. Here is the ending, at the least ambiguous: "In this manner the issue was decided." It would be foolish to call this scene sketchy, marked as it is by the excitement of a dialogue that cuts off the breath, even in the thin banality of the situation. To read is to believe.

"It's hard," says Carver, "to be simple. The language of my stories is the language people commonly speak, but it is also a prose that must be worked on to make it seem transparent. That's not a contradiction in terms. I subject a story to as many as fifteen revisions. The story changes with each of them. But there's nothing automatic; rather, it's a process. Writing is an act of discovery. As the person working on the writing, I have to search for the most productive solutions."

Questions are put to him. Must the fiction writer double himself in order to write poetry?

"For me, they're two related genres. I write stories as sparing as poems and poems that tell stories. Right now I'm writing only poetry and everything I see gives me material for poems."

What do you think of the creative writing programs from which come today's young American writers, including your student Jay McInerney?

"I think that they can teach mostly what *not* to do."

What are your working habits?

"I write and rewrite, first by hand, then by typewriter. Then a neighbor puts the story on her word processor and I correct and she recopies. The important thing, anyway, as Maupassant says, is to put black on white."

What influence has Hemingway had on your work?

"I don't feel his influence too much, even if I could take it as a compliment to be considered his descendant. Anyway, I don't write fishing stories."

Here, more clarification is needed. Chatting along, Carver tosses off a list of names. There's Chekhov and Flaubert and Tolstoy and even an occasional Italian: Moravia, Buzzati, Pirandello, even Verga—all short-story writers. "You have a great tradition in this area and, besides, Boccaccio invented the genre." And there's Flannery O'Connor, Singer, Updike, Donald Barthelme, Cheever. . . . He never mentions Faulkner or Salinger, but that's not to say he avoids them on purpose. On the other hand, he doesn't spare a dig at the postmodernists of the 1970s. ("What a shame, such an excess of ambition crowned by so little success.") And it's understandable why, since those writers are polar opposites to him and his world. He directs a special bit of irony toward John Barth and his bizarre, self-consoling theoretical inventions, according to which literary experimentalism goes hand in hand with the liberal spirit. It's as if Carver, the minimalist, with a companion who claims that "the very act of writing in a capitalist society like this already has a certain morality," were a Reaganite.

Ascendants and descendants. You want to see that Carver finally risks becoming a best seller even in Italy (Italian is the twenty-fifth language into which he's been translated), in the wake of his under-thirty epigones, the Ellises, the Leavitts, the McInerneys? The fact remains that the first Italian edition of *Cathedral* met with stony silence. Six hundred copies sold. . . .

"I have no opinion about that. Sure, it's distressing," he answers me, "to think that in 1984 my time hadn't yet come. And it's uncomfortable to be anybody's 'father.' I know something about that, because I have a daughter who's living with an unemployed fellow and who has her own two kids. At any rate, I'm not unhappy with the idea of becoming a best seller. As for taking on the role of head of a school, I'll pass. Maybe I've contributed to the resurrection, even in a commercial sense, of the short story, that's all. I don't even like to be labeled a minimalist. Let's say instead New Wave; it's more generic. . . . "

More or less when you started, the Talking Heads also began to cut records. And they eventually made *True Stories.* Some of these, like certain stories of yours, have very simple titles, like the names of objects and such. Is there any relationship between that work and yours?

"I listen to music, sure, but not while I'm writing. I also listen to the Talking Heads and Springsteen and Mozart and Charlie Parker and that splendid survivor, Tom Waits. He's survived self-destruction and bears his own witness. What we have in common is that we speak to the people, to all the people."

Then you must be interested in film, too.

"In 1982, Michael Cimino asked me to help him shape up a screenplay on Dostoevsky's life. I got Tess involved and we completely redid it. Now it's a book. I hope it becomes a movie. Anyway, a movie was made from a story in *Cathedral,* 'Feathers,' and many others are under option."

And your first, long-awaited novel?

"A novel? Maybe next year I'll write it, but now it's just not there. Who knows? In November, a collection of my poems was published, *Ultramarine.* In February 1988, another story collection will come out. It's provisionally titled *Where I'm Calling From.*"

A Conversation

Kasia Boddy/1987

From *London Review of Books,* 10, no. 16, 15 September 1988,
16. Reprinted by permission of Kasia Boddy and London Review
of Books Ltd. Conducted 10 June 1987.

RC: When I came to the writing of these poems [*In a Marine Light*] I
hadn't written any for about two years. I'd been writing stories, and I
didn't know if I'd ever write any more poems. I felt writing poetry
might have passed out of my life. I lamented that, but it didn't seem
as if there was anything I could consciously do about it. Then I went
from Syracuse, New York, out to Washington State, with the
intention of writing fiction. In the house in Washington, after I had sat
still for about a week, not writing at all, I wrote a poem one night.
And the next morning I got up and wrote another poem, and before
the day was over I had three poems. And I kept writing like this for, I
think, 65 days. And I had a book—a full book. I had about a
hundred and twenty poems—more than enough for a book. I quit
writing then and went with Tess on a trip to South America. Then
about three months later, back home again, I started writing poems
once more. I wrote the rest of the poems that make up the book. In
the space of about eighteen months—it was an extraordinary time—I
wrote two hundred and fifty to three hundred poems. I've never had
a time quite like it in my life. When I was writing these poems I was
entirely happy. I could have died then, and I would have died happy.
Then, for whatever reason, I stopped writing poems and went back
to writing stories, and it is likely I have enough stories now for a new
book. But I've started writing poems again recently! It's a good time
in my life right now. I'm writing stories, and I'm writing poems. When
I began writing stories again, all the poems that are in this book
seemed like nothing less than a great gift to me. It is a mystery to me
now where they came from. But I began as a poet. My first
publication was a poem. So I suppose on my tombstone I'd be very
pleased if they put 'poet and short-story writer—and occasional
essayist'. In that order.

KB: But in some ways your poems and stories are very similar.

Your stories are in many ways like poems, and your poems usually tell stories.

RC: True. Narrative poetry, poetry that has content, subject-matter—that's the poetry that most interests me. And some of my poems are very story-like. I do think there is a stronger relationship between a story and a poem than there is between a story and a novel. Economy and preciseness, meaningful detail, along with a sense of mystery, of something happening just under the surface of things.

KB: You say that the fiction you like to read usually contains an element of autobiography. Your poems seem to be more autobiographical than the stories.

RC: It's true. But the poems aren't autobiographical. Sometimes a little, maybe. But even if they were, that would be okay. I've just visited the house where Thomas Mann lived—it's a little museum now in Zurich. I don't think there's a more autobiographical writer in the world. *Buddenbrooks* is a generational novel about his family. It's more than that, of course, but it's the history of his family he is dramatising, making them come alive again by turning the whole show into literature. Certainly writers—the writers *I* most admire at any rate—make some use of their own lives. The poems let me do something that I can't do in fiction. I think I become more intimate in the poems, more vulnerable in ways I don't often allow myself to be in the stories. I'm a little more removed there, a little more distant, perhaps. I suppose the poems are closer to me somehow. They come from some place in the deepest interior region. The stories aren't like that, always. When I was writing all these poems, I felt that never in my life had I had a time like that before. I would sometimes write two or three in a day, if you can imagine. I'd go to bed at night and I wouldn't know if I had another poem left in me. I was exhausted. And I'd get up in the morning feeling empty but refreshed at the same time, and I'd go to my desk and begin writing poetry again. It was just wonderful. That's what I meant when I said: 'Take me now.' I could have died happy then.

KB: I read that you dislike the word 'theme', and prefer to speak of your 'obsessions'.

RC: Well, I suppose it goes back to being a student. I used to shy

away from 'theme' and 'symbol' and heavy-sounding words like
these. I think theme or the meaning of a story declares itself in the
work itself, and that it's finally impossible to separate the meaning of
the story from the content and the way things are worked out. For
better or worse, I am an instinctual writer rather than a writer working
out a programme or finding stories to fit particular themes. There are
certain obsessions that I have and try to give voice to: the relationships between men and women, why we oftentimes lose the things
we put the most value on, the mismanagement of our own inner
resources. I'm also interested in survival, what people can do to raise
themselves up when they've been laid low. I wish you could see
some of the new stories because the new stories are different in a lot
of ways—in ways I can't really articulate—from the stories that have
come before. I think all the stories in each of my books seem to be
somewhat different from the other, earlier stories. The stories in
Cathedral, for instance—most of them, at any rate—are vastly
different from the stories in the first book. They're fuller, more
generous, somehow. There's a new story about Chekhov and his last
days: I never would have written anything like that, I couldn't have,
five years ago.

KB: Critics talk about your stories—especially the first two collections—as being very bleak. I haven't felt that.

RC: I'm glad.

KB: There has always seemed to be something.

RC: There's some humour in the stories.

KB: In that sense, I didn't feel there to be that much of a jump
between *What We Talk About* and *Cathedral.* But maybe *Cathedral* is
more explicitly hopeful.

RC: I think it is. The stories in *Cathedral,* most of them—well,
some of them anyway—are finally more positive, more affirmative,
than the stories in the earlier collection. But I'm glad you don't find
all the stories so bleak.

KB: I found the reviews more depressing than the stories.

RC: Yes. But I think they're beginning to take a bit of a different
tack now. Writers shouldn't be criticised for their subject-matter,
should they? Samuel Beckett is about as dark as a writer could
possibly be. His work is very claustrophobic to me. And I have a

book in my coat pocket—a book of poems by Philip Larkin, and my God, Larkin is dark—isn't he? But he writes with such wonderful finesse.

KB: The other thing that the critics like to talk about is failure of communication as a theme. I felt that although the characters maybe don't communicate verbally, they usually manage to communicate in other ways.

RC: I think that's true. It's hard sometimes for people to talk and say what they really mean: either because they're not skilled enough at being initimate with other people, or just feel the need to protect themselves. But there are other ways of communicating. Things do happen, things do get done and said in the stories, even though sometimes people may be talking at cross-purposes at times, or seemingly to no good purpose.

KB: I'm interested in those stories which appear in different forms in different collections. Are they different versions of one story or different stories?

RC: I feel they're different stories. I'm certainly not the only writer who has ever rewritten stories after they were published. I read somewhere that Frank O'Connor was constantly changing his stories long after they were in print. He went through about three different versions of his great story 'Guests of the Nation'. For me, it was like conceiving a story and seeing it as unfinished business. The stories 'A Small, Good Thing' and 'The Bath' are really two different stories.

KB: You weren't happy with 'The Bath'?

RC: It won a prize when it appeared in a magazine, but I felt it was a minor league effort, and I'm not happy with it to this day. I'm going to be publishing a *Selected Stories* and I'm not going to include 'The Bath'. I am going to include 'A Small, Good Thing', of course. But I don't do that kind of rewriting much any more. I have more confidence in the stories now, or maybe it's just that I feel that I have more things to do than I have time to do them, and I tend now not to look back so much. I do all the revision when I'm writing a story, and once it's published I'm just not much interested in it any longer. I want to look ahead. I think that's healthy.

KB: I really like your 'Poem for Hemingway & W.C. Williams'. Do you agree with the suggestion that Hemingway could be called the model for your stories and Williams for your poems?

RC: They both influenced me when I was young and malleable. I had a great deal of admiration, and still do, for much of Hemingway's work and much of Williams's work.

KB: Williams's short stories as well?

RC: Yes, especially 'The Use of Force' and some later stories. But I did not read his stories, or very much of his poetry, until long after they could conceivably have had any influence on me, except that little story of his 'The Use of Force'. In fact, when I was reading his poems in my early twenties, it was like I was vaguely aware that he had written prose, but only knew him as a poet. He wasn't even taught at the college where I went to school. But I came upon his poetry because I was reading something about writers in Paris in the Twenties. About the same time I started a little magazine when I was going to college in California—this was when Williams was still alive, about 1958 or '59. And I wrote to him and asked for a poem for this magazine, and told him what admiration I had for his poems. And almost by return mail he sent me a poem. It was a great, great thrill for me. This poem, called 'The Gossips', was published in a post-humous book of his, *Pictures from Brueghel*. The poem had his signature across the bottom of it. It was a real treasure. Of course I lost it through a set of unfortunate circumstances. But it was so kind of him to send me a poem. He was my hero.

KB: I've heard him reading his poems on tape. He sounds nice. Laughing between poems.

RC: He was an extraordinary man. He sometimes wrote poems in between seeing patients.

KB: On his prescription pad. Are you conscious of making comments with your stories?

RC: What kind of comments?

KB: About your attitude towards your characters and how they live, about the society they live in.

RC: I write oftentimes about working-class people, and the dark side of Reagan's America. So in that regard I suppose the stories can be read as a criticism, as an indictment. But that has to come from outside. I don't feel I'm consciously trying to do that. And I don't have any programme for writing stories, as I've said.

KB: In an essay called 'The Post-Modern Aura' Charles Newman has spoken of 'Neo-Realism' in fiction as 'the classic conservative response to inflation—under-utilisation of capacity, reduction of inventory and verbal joblessness'. The essay was written just after *What We Talk About* came out, and he mentions your work as an example of 'Neo-Realism'. I think he's saying that when people don't have much they become thrifty, in all areas—literature as well as economics.

RC: When I wrote those stories I didn't have any money at all. I was as poor as a churchmouse. I didn't know how I was going to pay my rent. He may be right, although it's a pretty florid sentence. It's a theory. He may be right. Who knows? Who cares? The main thing is to get the stories written.

KB: Will you go back to teaching when your Strauss Livings Award runs out?

RC: If I do, it won't be full-time again: it'll just be a seminar here and there. But I hope I don't have to at all—not because I can't teach, or think it's a waste of time, but it's just that there are so many other things I'd rather be doing. But I didn't dislike teaching the way some writers do. I've had so many other worse jobs, lousy jobs, that when I was teaching I counted my blessings. I didn't have to work in the rain or hot sun, or with my hands, and I had more time for my own work than I did with any other kinds of job I'd had.

KB: Do you have any urge to write a novel?

RC: No. But I may have this time next year. Ask me then. I may write a novel and I may not. And if I don't that's okay too. I don't feel as if I have to write a novel.

KB: Anne Tyler wrote that the reason you write such good stories is because you're not saving the best things up for writing a novel.

RC: She said I was a 'spendthrift'. That's good. I think that a writer ought to spend himself on whatever he's doing, whether it's a poem or a story, because you have to feel like the well is not going to run dry; you have to feel that there's more where that came from. If a writer starts holding back, for any reason whatsoever, that can be a very bad thing. I've always squandered.

KB: I read that you've written screenplays.

RC: Yes, I did two. Tess Gallagher and I did them. One of them was published—it was on Dostoevsky. A part of it was published in the States. It's very long. And we did another screenplay. I think every writer wants to do that at least once, to be involved with

Hollywood, and all that sort of thing. I went through that time, I did it, and I'm not interested in doing it any more. But who knows—maybe in five years I'll be interested again. It was work for hire, and I didn't like that. I don't like to have a boss. 'My goal was always / to be shiftless'—to quote a line from a poem I like. I much prefer to write a poem than to do a piece of journalism.

KB: Has *Dostoevsky* been filmed?

RC: No.

KB: Have any of your stories been filmed?

RC: A story called 'Feathers' has just been made into a film. They did a very good job on it. And then some people in Hollywood made a film of 'A Small, Good Thing'. I think that they did a good job too.

KB: A few weeks ago I saw the film of John Cheever's 'The Swimmer'.

RC: Isn't that just a wonderful film? I saw it when it first came out, and I talked to John Cheever about it. We were teaching together in Iowa. He claimed he just took the money and never went to see the film. I loved the film, and told him so. That ending, in the story and in the movie—just extraordinary.

Fiction & America: Raymond Carver
David Applefield/1987

From *Frank: An International Journal of Contemporary Writing & Art* [Paris], no. 8/9 (Winter 1987-88), 6-15. Reprinted by permission of David Applefield. Conducted Summer 1987.

Raymond Carver speaks in a low voice, a voice that at first doesn't seem to match the narrative voice in his stories, but belongs more to one of his reticent, hauntingly real characters. He's an attentive listener. Careful not to cut you off, he yields at the start of another voice. He's polite. If obsessed with anything, Raymond Carver might insist on being a good person. There are hints of repentance and thankfulness in his manners. He speaks like a man who has gotten a second chance; he considers himself lucky. He marvels at simple things, puts his own small needs behind his interest in carefully and sensitively "bearing witness," in communicating with other humans properly, in being moved by what people say and do. He lets his omelette get cold as he slowly answers a question, making sure you've asked what you've wanted and are satisfied with the reply. He isn't difficult to follow; his sentences are straightforward, his philosophy nearly self-evident. And his slow, timid and almost-embarrassed way of talking about his life and work rings with a sense of surprise that anyone would want his opinion. He is honored.

Carver doesn't theorize; he rarely analyzes, he only blandly criticizes, and he never self-applauds. You wonder if this is really the man whose prose style is filled with amazingly crisp dialogues, carefully reduced descriptions, and gnawingly provocative and understated resolutions, if this is the intellect that has created these contemporary American gems that have so deeply influenced the direction of fiction-writing in the U.S. over the last decade. Yes, you suppose, your mind trying to collate the two images, to synthesize the work with the voice behind it. One thing is clear; Raymond Carver is not being coy; this is not a game of the ego. There is no hype to this personality; he is shooting from the hip. He has few affectations, no pretensions. He dresses like he talks: quietly, comfortably. He enjoys and relies on his morning coffee and his cigarettes. You push him to explain more, to reveal his techniques. His voice retreats to a whisper, "I'm just trying to do the best I can." You fear even the mike won't pick up his diminishing volume. He's calm. Gentle. Yet a big man with broad hands. You can picture walking with him across fields and not saying a word. He won't say what his style means or even allude to the self-consciousness of his craft. He does admit working hard, though, and you believe him. He insists his stories depict "real life," and that his style of fiction falls cleanly into the tradition of realism in that it attempts to render reality truthfully, honestly. No more.

The style, he implies, is innate, natural, sharpened and honed by ear. Carver has Bill Miller try on his neighbor's underwear in the story "Neighbors" because people really do these things. Honesty is Carver's driving force, his tablet of commandments. And maybe it's precisely this insistence on capturing real life honestly with all its quirkish banality, domesticity, and common perversity that causes the seeming contradiction between the simplicity of the man and the crafted, stylized and manipulated stories. Carver's reality cuts too close to the real thing for comfort. What we'd call style or technique he calls "just being honest." His details reverberate like symbols, cultural icons, large metaphors, but for Raymond Carver they're just well-observed objects and gestures from life.

Born in 1938 in the logging town of Clatskanie, Oregon, where he worked with his father filing saw blades in a mill, Raymond Carver now lives in Port Angeles, Washington, with writer and poet Tess Gallagher. Deeply influenced early on by John Gardner, who was his instructor at Chico State College, Carver later received his B.A. at Humboldt State University before attending the writing program at the University of Iowa and later teaching at Syracuse University. First published by Capra Press, his collections of stories include *Will You Please Be Quiet, Please?*, *Furious Seasons and Other Stories*, *What We Talk About When We Talk About Love* and *Cathedral*. His volumes of poetry include *Near Klamath*, *Winter Insomnia*, *At Night the Salmon Move*, *Where Water Comes Together with Other Water*, *Ultramarine*, and *In a Marine Light*. *Fires* is his book of prose, poetry, and essays. He has also edited *American Short Story Masterpieces*,

The Best American Short Stories 1986, and other anthologies.
Currently, Carver is writing full-time, supported by a five-year grant
from the American Academy of Arts. In Paris twice in the summer of
1987 to promote his latest collection of poems *In a Marine Light*
(Collins Harvill, 1987), Raymond Carver spoke to *Frank* editor David
Applefield. The interview then continued in a series of letters
between France and the United States. *Frank* attempts here to
explore Raymond Carver's visions and ideas as part of its continuing
dialogue on *Fiction & America.*

DA: Could you comment on Robert Coover's reply (*Frank* 6/7) to a
question on the two opposing movements in American writing,
metafiction and hyperrealism? Coover, although praising your work,
called you a "minimalist" and a godfather of a burgeoning school of
workshop storywriters, all of whom sound more and more like one
another.
  RC: I feel awkward being called a "godfather." I don't like being
called a minimalist writer, either. Nor do I like the appellation
"minimalism." It's useless. It was a French critic, in fact, in his review
of *What We Talk About When We Talk About Love* for the *Partisan
Review,* who called my work "minimalist." He meant it as a compliment, but certain critics and reviewers picked it up and used it to start
hammering on some writers. I think the sooner such labels go away
the better. Writers should be talked about in terms of what they write
and how they write, as individuals, instead of being lumped together
in groups. I thought John Barth's recent essay in *The New York
Times Book Review* was one of the best things that has been said on
the subject. He talked about Samuel Beckett being a minimalist
writer, if you want to stick labels on somebody, or Emily Dickinson
being a minimalist writer. Having said that, there are a certain number
of writers, perhaps myself included, who do on occasion write rather
sparely. True, there is a split between the so-called metafictionists or
post-modernists and writers who have begun to write "stories" again,
trying to create recognizable people and place them in life-like
circumstances. Some people have called it hyper-realism or super-
realism. So be it. To a large extent, people—not just writers, of
course, but readers—have gotten tired of fiction that's gotten too far

away from the real concerns. Poets, too, began writing only for themselves and lost their audience. Something very similar nearly happened to fiction. I think there has been a return to realism, yes. The work of many of the writers who came into prominence in the Sixties is not going to last. I think there's a very real and definite turning away from fabulism and metafiction. Literature is coming back to the things that count, the things that are close to the writer's heart, the things that move us.

DA: What are these things?

RC: Survival, for one thing. I think that any good piece of fiction has to feel authentic and true. Nothing can be trumped-up. How does one get along in this life? How should a man or woman act? How should we behave? My stories take place on a personal level as opposed to a larger political or social arena. But it has to begin with the personal. Chekhov said once that there are two poles in a story, "him" and "her," the North Pole and the South Pole. I like that because in most of my stories there is a "him" and a "her." Sometimes it works out for the "him" and the "her," and sometimes it doesn't. But my characters, my people, are survivors. They're not so downtrodden or whipped-out as one might think at first glance. What I want is a feeling of authenticity, and of things being "at stake" or "at risk." That's why I'm impatient with a lot of contemporary work, whether it's poetry or fiction. The writers seem to be just fooling around. And that's the stuff that's not going to last. The stuff that does last, whether it's Chekhov's stuff, or Tolstoy's, or Flaubert's, is work that's genuine, and is going to look a hundred years from now as genuine as when it was first written and published. If it was valid for that time, and if that time was captured accurately, then it might have a chance to be valid for all time.

DA: So, essentially people don't change even when their social and political environment does?

RC: No, they don't. Details do, of course. We ride in automobiles today instead of carriages. But we can still be moved by reading a story by Chekhov, or a novel by Tolstoy, or Flaubert, or whomever.

DA: But surely you're not just telling stories in a conventional late 19th-century realist mode. There is a deliberate style—a careful collection of details, sparse dialogue, a marked absence of extensive description, and understated conclusions—that would appear to the reader to correspond to and reveal significant aspects of contemporary American life and relationships.

RC: If I were to say yes, I'd feel a bit self-serving. I don't feel I should be making these very large and general statements. I cannot speak for the population as a whole. People, though, often do find it hard to communicate. And so there's always a mystery to every story. Something else is happening under the surface. The people I'm writing about often have difficulty communicating head-on. But, things *do* get done, things *do* get said in the stories. Sometimes, the meanings are a little askew, but things do transpire. I don't think there's ever any wasted dialogue, or anything else wasted, for that matter.

DA: So there's nothing more you'd want to say about the social implications of your writing style?

RC: No.

DA: What is striking when reading your stories, especially *What We Talk About When We Talk About Love,* is the importance given to the moments of silence. So much happens without words, between the lines.

RC: I like that, if that's the case. I don't know if I myself can talk about what is left out and I don't know if it's appropriate. But it is a conscious thing. I think people most often talk like this (*makes his fingers miss each other as he brings them together*), instead of like this (*makes his fingers meet each other*). Hemingway has been called a master of dialogue. And yet I don't think anyone has ever talked in Hemingwayese. It's part of his style.

DA: Some literary editors claim that nearly half of the short fiction they receive seems imitative of your style. How would you estimate the influence you have in terms of fiction writing in America today? Do you feel a sense of responsibility in that your work is so widely read and absorbed?

RC: I feel rather awkward talking about it. Still, I think a young writer could have a worse model than myself and I don't want to sound immodest when I say that. When I write a story, I try to be clear and accurate, try to write about things that matter. I suppose that a lot of young writers may find this appealing. The work is taught in colleges and universities, that's true. It's on reading lists; creative

writing teachers and literature teachers use it. In that regard, I
suppose the stories could be considered influential. But it's always
been the case that a young writer sees work by an author he admires
and thinks he can learn from it. My stories have a surface simplicity
about them. Still, I think it's not only a question of imitation; as I
already mentioned, there's a real turning away from the fabulists and
the metafictionists in general. Maybe five years from now everyone
will be writing like someone else. I remember when I was a graduate
student and everyone was trying to write like Donald Barthelme;
probably 40% of the stories coming to editors then were all like
Barthelme. I've come around to liking his stories a good deal. He's
wonderfully unique and he's created a whole world that is his own,
and if a writer can do that, my hat's off to him. In so far as sense of
responsibility is concerned, I don't think about that. My stories are
changing with each book. I get letters from people telling me how
much they like *What We Talk About When We Talk About Love* when
I'm no longer interested in that book. Those letters seem like com-
munications from another planet, about something that has very little
to do with me now. I think that perhaps some of the writers who are
writing like me—and I'm surely not criticizing them at all, in the
largest sense I'm flattered—don't have a similar sense of loss. I try to
write the best story I can without thinking about whom I'm
influencing or what sort of impression I'm making. However, I am
very conscious that my stories are changing.

    DA: How are they evolving? And what do you think is at the root
of this?

    RC: I'm not entirely sure, but I can tell you this—when a book of
stories is finished and put together and off in the hands of the
publisher, I tend not to write anything for awhile, for several months.
I'll write an essay or some poems. I don't know if it's a conscious
period of taking stock of what I'm going to do next, but there's a
period of just being quiet, of not writing any fiction. For instance, after
I wrote *What We Talk About When We Talk About Love,* for about six
months afterwards I didn't write any fiction at all. Then the first story
I wrote was "Cathedral" and I knew that was a departure for me
somehow; and all of the stories in that book came together very
quickly and were all somehow different. I mean different to the extent
that they weren't pared down as much as the earlier stories. They

were fuller, more generous. After the book publication of *Cathedral*, I
didn't write any fiction at all for two years. I wrote a couple of books
of poems. Poems and several essays. I had no desire to write stories. I
didn't start writing fiction again until about 18 months ago. Then I
realized I would be in a period of story-writing, and I signed a
contract for a book. But I didn't take a contract before that, because,
in part, I didn't even know if I'd write any more fiction! It's all a gift
and a blessing anyway. It's given to you, and I suppose it can be
taken away. When I finish a book, as far as I know it may be my last.
Since I started writing fiction again, the stories have come very
quickly. Now they deal not just with husband and wife domestic
relationships but with family relationships: son and mother, or father
and children; and they go into these relationships more extensively.
All these stories, with the exception of a Chekhov story in *The New
Yorker* in June, were written in the first person. And they're all longer,
more detailed and somehow more affirmative, I believe. And
although the relationships are more complex, I'm somehow dealing
with them in a more simplified or straightforward manner.

DA: The voices that you capture—where do you hear them,
where do they come from? Your imagination? Your past? Public
places?

RC: Every story I've written, with maybe one or two exceptions,
has had its starting point in the real world. The fiction I most admire
always has lines of reference back to the real world. Stories don't just
come out of thin air. At least the kind of stories I'm interested in. I
don't like to read about the experience of writing, the self-reflexive
thing of writing fiction about writing fiction and so forth. I have very
little patience with that. I don't have much time on this earth and I
don't want to waste any of it. Usually the first line in a story or poem
remains the same, everything else is subject to change. . . . I saw a
man, once, sitting next to me on a plane and just as we were flying
into the city, he took the wedding ring off his finger. And this little
thing stuck in my head. The story "Fat" in *Will You Please Be Quiet,
Please?* is about a waitress waiting on a fat man, a story told to me
by my first wife many years ago when she was a waitress. She came
home from work one night and said, "I waited on this strange
character tonight who spoke of himself in the plural. He called
himself 'we': 'We would like some more bread and butter'; 'We

would like some water'; 'We'll have beef tournedos.' " And I thought how unusual it was that a man would speak of himself in that way. But I didn't do anything with the story for years and then it came time to write the story and it was a question of how best to tell it, whose story it was. Then I made a conscious decision how to present the story, and I decided to tell it from the point of view of the woman, the waitress, and frame the story as if she were telling it to her girlfriend. She can't quite make sense out of the story herself, all of the feelings that she experienced, but she goes ahead and tells it anyway. I once had a conversation with a heart doctor in El Paso, Texas, that evolved into the idea for "What We Talk About When We Talk About Love." In the story, the main character drinks as heavily as I used to. In another story a character breaks a key off in the lock of a door. This happened to me once. There isn't a story in any of my books that hasn't really come from something I've either witnessed, lived through, or overheard.

DA: Although you are best known for your short stories, poetry seems to have continued to be extremely important to you.

RC: It's something very close to my heart. I can do things in the poems I can't in the stories. I feel more vulnerable in the poems, that's true. And I do things in them sometimes that I wouldn't allow myself to do in the stories. The period in which I wrote all these poems, truly, was one of the most extraordinary times in my life. I could have died happy then. It pleases me to no end that the poems are being well received. It pleased me immensely to write them.

DA: The poems are highly personal. You evoke your past, your family, your sense of place. What kind of upbringing did you have? And what traditions or sense of history do you maintain?

RC: I grew up in eastern Washington State. Nobody in the house had gone beyond the sixth grade. My parents could barely read and write. My dad was a laborer. My mother was a housewife. So, what can I say? My upbringing was culturally impoverished, that's the long and short of it. My parents and my relatives migrated to the West Coast from Arkansas. But I didn't grow up with any traditions; we didn't light candles for dinner or anything like that. I started out in blue-collar jobs, working with my hands. My early life made a very large impression on my later emotional life. I've taught off and on for 15 years and I don't think I've ever written anything at all having to do with academia. I like reading history books and I read a lot of history, maybe because I don't have much of a history of my own. I've just finished a biography of Voltaire, of all things.

DA: You're a particularly American writer in terms of your characters, themes, and language. I'd like to ask you how you interact with your own culture and society. It's generally agreed upon that sentiment in the U.S. continues to slip to the right, having become increasingly conservative, isolationist, and ethnocentric. How do you respond as a citizen and writer to these tendencies?

RC: I don't like any of what I'm seeing. It's a horrible situation. Every time one looks around, one sees another social program being cut and another arts program being cut. The private sector has to take up the slack. That's what we're told. And we're told that nobody's going to fall through the cracks! People *are* falling through the cracks. Of course I don't like this. Certain right-wing critics don't like my writing, in particular, people associated with Hilton Kramer's *The New Criterion*. They want me to put a happy face on America. They say that the stories of mine that are going out into the world are not showing America in the best light, and if there are people like this, the ones I depict, the dispossessed, well, they deserve what they get; and the implication is that I'm rather un-American for bringing these stories to public attention, including, and maybe especially, to foreigners.

DA: So, there's critical objection to your highlighting the lives of people, who, essentially, are disenfranchised by the current economic structure, by "Reaganomics" and all that accompanies it?

RC: That's it exactly.

DA: A close look at your characters might suggest that they are not only people who face difficult personal situations—sexual, emotional, social—but reflect certain classic psychological tendencies. Do you have any particular interest in psychiatry? Has Freud or Jung, for example, informed your understanding of the people you depict?

RC: I don't feel adequate saying anything about the subject of psychology or psychiatry. I wish I could! I haven't read any of the great ones you mention, nor the lesser lights, either. Maybe in the next life there will be time for this, and more. Time for everything. But it's this life, right now, that has me baffled, and hog-tied, sometimes. There aren't enough hours in the day to even begin to do

the things I want, like reading this and that, not to mention some of
the things I'd like to write. I'll die first, I'm quite sure of that; there
simply isn't enough time to go around.

DA: Earlier, you made a reference to Hemingway, who's clearly
had an influence on you. Who else would you add to this list? Who
do you read?

RC: Chekhov for sure. There's that story of mine that came out
recently, a tribute, an homage to Chekhov. It has something to do
with Chekhov's last days and his death. It's different from anything
I've ever done. I can always go back to his stories with great pleasure.
Hemingway's early stories, too. The cadences of his sentences I find
very exciting. They get into the blood. Tolstoy, certainly. I love his
short fiction, particularly, in addition to *Anna Karenina,* of course,
and the short novels. Frank O'Connor. And Isaac Babel. His short
stories mean a great deal. And the stories of writers like Richard Ford
and Tobias Wolff. Ford is coming out with a dynamite collection of
short stories this fall called *Rock Springs,* which I highly recommend.
There's also Andre Dubus. Many of his short novels are quite to my
liking. There are many, many good writers at work today. So many
it's hard to begin naming, obviously.

DA: To conclude, how would you characterize the state of
American fiction writing in the Eighties?

RC: On the whole we're in a very healthy and productive period.
There's been, on the part of many writers, a concentration on detail
and the moment. I think writers are trying to capture and hold on to
something. There is a gale wind blowing. And things are so uneasy or
so insecure in so many ways that I think it's important to try to
concentrate on detail and specificity, to try to nail down something
when the center's not holding. This is a period of great change in
American literature. There's no question about that. I don't know
what's going to come out of all the work that's presently being done,
especially in short stories. But, we're in an uncommonly healthy
moment in terms of the quantity and quality of serious fiction by
younger writers being published. It will get sorted out somewhere
down the line. And that's fine. You write the best you can, and you
take your chances.

After the Fire, into the Fire: An Interview with Raymond Carver

Michael Schumacher/1987

From *Reasons to Believe: New Voices in American Fiction* (New York: St. Martin's, 1988), 1-27. Copyright © 1988 by Michael Schumacher. Reprinted by permission of Michael Schumacher. Conducted Summer 1987.

Much has been written and said about the great interest publishers have been paying to fiction over the last decade. This is especially true of short fiction, with some observers calling the period a "Short Story Renaissance" in America, while others argue that readers have always been interested in quality fiction, that it is more visible today because publishers are marketing and promoting it more aggressively. Either way, there is certainly no shortage of fiction on bookstore shelves today, and more of it is being purchased than ever before.

One cannot begin to seriously study the trend without looking at the works of the writers who paved the way—people such as Barry Hannah, Richard Ford, Mary Robison, Ann Beattie, John Cheever, Andre Dubus, Tobias Wolff, and, of course, Raymond Carver. Without the steady persistence of these and other writers, much of today's fiction would not be receiving the attention and serious critical notice that it is.

For nearly two decades, Raymond Carver was one of the best-kept secrets in the literary world. His short stories and poems, generally published by literary magazines and small presses, were read with great enthusiasm by a solid cult-following interested in the wonderful kind of work which never seems to gain a lot of attention. A large national following was slow in coming, but his work won awards and prizes, and was considered almost a staple in anthologies and "best of" collections. He was at the cutting edge of a resurgence of interest in the short story, but he was hardly a literary presence caught up in either book-biz glitz or the halls of academia.

Today, Raymond Carver is both "bankable" and well-honored. Large, high-paying magazines solicit his work, while students, writers, and interviewers solicit his time and opinion. He is considered to be one of the best—if not *the* best—of the modern short story writers. He is in constant demand on the lecture, teaching, and writers conference circuits. His papers and manuscripts are gaining value with collectors and university libraries.

To escape the brouhaha and constant work interruptions, Carver and Tess Gallagher, the poet and short story writer who has been his companion, critic, and inspiration for the past decade, have moved from upstate New York to Port Angeles, Washington. But even there, they have to unplug the phone or hang out a hand-painted No VISITORS sign to elude the attention and get down to real work.

Carver admits that his past and present are two different lives, and his success has only sharpened his focus and perception of the past. He is lucky to be alive, he says, adding that his stories and poems "bear witness" to his past and, unfortunately, to all too many people's presents.

His life story, in fact, reads like one of his fictional works. Born in Clatskanie, Oregon, in 1938, Carver was the product of a father with a penchant for wandering and drinking—a sawmill worker who moved from paycheck to paycheck; Carver's mother supplemented the family's income by working as a waitress or clerk. Art and literature were the furthest things from discussion at the Carver dinner table.

Still, Junior (as Carver was called) wanted to be a writer, but it wasn't going to be easy: Carver married his high-school sweetheart and had two children before his twentieth birthday. Though he followed his father to the sawmills, Carver and his then-wife shared dreams of escaping their lives of blue-collar tedium.

Carver's writing career began when he moved his family to California and enrolled at Chico State College; there he took a creative writing class taught by John Gardner, the late novelist, essayist, and teacher who became a vital influence on Carver. From then on, Carver worked menial jobs to support his family, stealing time whenever he could to write. He published plenty of his work—much of it to great critical acclaim—but there was little or no money in it.

"We had great dreams, my wife and I," Carver wrote years later, remembering those hard times. "We thought we could bow our necks, work very hard, and do all that we had set our hearts to do. But we were mistaken."

Their marriage ended and Carver took to drinking. Not even the 1976 publication of his first collection of short stories, *Will You Please Be Quiet, Please?*, could reverse his slide. As his first life was reaching its end, Carver, like one of his fictional characters, was virtually powerless to alter his life's direction. Discussing this period with Mona Simpson in an interview for *The Paris Review,* Carver's assessment was brutal in its honesty: "You never start out in life with the intention of becoming a bankrupt or an alcoholic or a cheat or a thief. Or a liar."

Carver's survival is testament to the resilience of the human and creative spirits. His second collection of stories, *What We Talk About When We Talk About Love* (1981), was a sort of catharsis, a compilation of works stylistically stripped to the bone, an anthology of the pain and despair his life had become. At the core of the stories was Carver's modern version of Sisyphus—the working stiff, perched near the summit of the mountain, shoulder to the boulder, unable to push it to the top, too proud or stubborn to let it roll to the bottom, frozen in a seemingly endless test of strength and endurance. The book, like his first, was greeted with overwhelmingly favorable response, and Carver became recognized as one of the most powerful forces in short fiction since Hemingway.

Carver's second life fell into place two years later, with the publication of *Cathedral* and his receiving the prestigious Mildred and Harold Strauss Livings Award from the American Academy and Institute of Arts and Letters; the former allotted Carver still more critical acclaim—a nomination for a National Book Critics Circle Award—while the latter afforded him the opportunity to devote all his time to writing. With this newfound freedom, Carver left his creative writing teaching post at Syracuse and turned his writing skills to poetry, publishing *Where Water Comes Together with Other Water* in 1985 and *Ultramarine* a year later. Like his stories, Carver's poems are dynamic and compressed, with each word a carefully chosen tool used to stretch tension to near-breaking point.

In 1988, Carver published *Where I'm Calling From: New and Selected Stories.* There has been talk of a novel over the years, but Carver is clearly in no hurry to write it—*if* he ever writes it. He has written a screenplay—for director Michael Cimino—and he hints that he would like to write another. He was guest editor for the annual anthology *The Best American Short Stories* in 1986, and he and Tom Jenks collaborated in editing *American Short Story Masterpieces,* an ambitious collection of what they consider to be the best American short stories published between 1953 and 1986. He continues to write poetry.

Despite the demands placed on his time, Carver is a warm and cooperative man who doesn't seem caught up in all the hoopla surrounding his work and literary reputation. He is soft-spoken, even when he is talking about topics he cares passionately about. He is modest, yet confident in assessing his present status: "I feel that I *am* going to survive—I'll not only survive but I'll thrive. It hasn't been easy but, again, I'm sure other writers have had it as hard or harder. But this is my life and my experience."

Carver is rarely asked more than a few passing questions about his poetry—a situation I found peculiar, given the nature of his terse, exact writing style, which owes more than a nod of recognition to the craft of poetry. I began my questioning in this area, hoping it would fan out into a better understanding and discussion of his fiction. I was glad I did.

You've published more volumes of poetry than short fiction. How did your career as a poet evolve?

Back when I began to write and send things out, I gave an equal amount of time to short stories and poems. Then, in the early Sixties, I had a short story and a poem accepted on the same day. The letters of acceptance, from two different magazines, were there in the box on the same day. This was truly a red-letter day. I was writing both short fiction and poetry in a more or less hit-or-miss fashion, given the circumstances of my life. Finally I decided, consciously or otherwise, that I was going to have to make a decision as to where to put the energy and strength I had. And I came down on the side of the short story.

You continued to write poetry, though.

Yes. For many years, I was an occasional poet, but that, to me, was better than being no poet at all. I wrote a poem whenever I could, whenever I had the chance and wasn't writing stories. Those earlier books of poems were small-press publications that are now out of print. The best of those poems are preserved in the collection *Fires,* which *is* in print. There are, I think, about fifty poems that I wanted to keep from those earlier collections, and those poems went into *Fires.*

For the last couple of years, you've been more than an occasional poet. Your output of poems during this period has been prodigious. How did that come to be?

After the publication of *Cathedral* and the attendant hubbub, I couldn't seem to find any peace and quiet or a place to work. We were living in Syracuse. Tess was teaching and there was a lot of traffic in the house, the phone kept ringing, people were showing up at the door. And there was her school business, and some socializing. But there was little time to work. So I came out to Port Angeles, to find a quiet place to work. I came here to this little house with the intention of writing fiction. I had not written any poems in well over two years and, so far as I knew, I felt it was conceivable I might not ever write another poem. But after I'd gotten out here and had just sat still and was quiet for about six days, I picked up a magazine and read some poems, and they were poems I didn't care for. And I thought: Jesus, I could do better than this. (*laughs*) It may not have been a good motive to begin writing poems, but whatever the motive, I wrote a poem that night and the next morning I got up and wrote another poem. And this went on, sometimes two or even three poems a day, for sixty-five days. I've never had a period in my life that remotely resembles that time. I mean, I felt like it would have been all right, you know, simply to have died after those sixty-five days. I felt *on fire.*

So I wrote all those poems, many of which went into *Where Water Comes Together with Other Water,* and then I didn't do anything for a few months. We took a trip to Brazil and Argentina, to do some readings and lecture. In the meanwhile, the book of poems had been accepted for publication. When I came back from South America, I started writing poems again—and, again, I'm not sure if the motive was correct or not, but I thought: What if the book comes out and it gets a good pasting (*laughs*) and I'm told I should never write any more poems, that I should stick to my fiction? Whatever the reasons, I began writing poems again, and by the time *Where Water Comes Together* was published, I had a new book in the drawer. When I look back on this period of time, the period when I wrote those books of poems, I can't really account for it. This is the truth! All the poems seem now like a great gift—the whole period seems a gift. Right now, I'm back writing stories and in a way it's almost as if that time never happened. It did, of course, and I'm glad it did, and I don't want to make more of it than it is—but it *was* a wonderful time. It was a high time. I've written a few poems since the publication of *Ultramarine* last fall, but mainly now I'm concentrating on fiction. I hope that when I finish this collection of stories I'm working on I will go back to the poems because, for me, when I'm writing poems, I feel there's nothing in the world so important. You know, as far as I'm concerned, I'd be happy if they simply put "poet" on my tombstone. "Poet"—and in parentheses, "and short story writer." (*laughs*) And way down at the bottom someplace, "and occasional anthologist."

And "teacher."
And "teacher," yes. (*laughs*) Teacher would be at the bottom.

When I talked to Jay McInerney about having you as a teacher, he spoke of you much the same way you've talked about having John Gardner as your teacher. Did you enjoy teaching?
I did. See, my teaching career was unique for several reasons, one reason being the fact that never, in my wildest imaginings, could I have seen myself as a teacher. I was always the shyest kid in class—*any* class. I never said anything. So the idea of conducting a class or having anything to say or being able to help students was the furthest thing away from my mind. Coming, as I did, from a family where nobody had gone past sixth grade, the idea of being around the university in such a capacity, as a teacher, was important, I suppose, to my self-esteem. Most important was the fact that I had summers off, and I was earning a more or less decent living while I was doing it. I had done so many different kinds of jobs in my life; no work for wages that I had done before had ever paid me as much money and at the same time given me as much freedom to write. As you know, there are a lot of writers who teach and bad-mouth the schools and

the writers who teach, all of that, but I never got into that situation; I was glad to have a teaching job.

When I began teaching, I think I did a decent job with it. The real role model I had, of course, was John Gardner. But there was also another fiction writer, at Humboldt State University, named Richard Day, and a poet in Sacramento named Dennis Schmitz. I tried to teach a writers workshop class the way they did. I tried to give people a lot of personal attention and help them to the best of my ability. There was a literature class that Jay took from me in which I might have been, you might say, a little ill-prepared, so I'd always call on Jay to get the conversation going. (*laughs*) "So what do you think about this book, Jay?" And he'd take off and talk for ten minutes. (*laughs*)

Do you think it's a good idea for aspiring writers to attend these schools or workshops?

Yes, I do. Obviously, it's not for everybody, but I can't think of any writers or musicians who have just sprung full-blown without some kind of help. De Maupassant was helped by Flaubert, who went over all his stories and criticized them and gave him advice. Beethoven learned his business from Haydn. Michelangelo was an apprentice for a long while to someone else. Rilke showed his poems to someone early on. Same with Pasternak. Just about any writer you can think of. Everybody, whether it's a conductor or composer or micro-biologist or mathematician—they've all learned their business from older practitioners; the idea of the maestro-apprentice relationship is an old and distinguished relationship. Obviously, this is not going to guarantee that it's going to make a great—or even a *good*—writer out of anybody, but I don't think it's going to hurt the writer's chances, either. There's a lot of flap and controversy and discussion and analysis of what's happening with the writers workshop concept— "whither are we going?"—but I think it'll all get sorted out by and by; I don't think it has to be a harmful situation for a young writer.

If nothing else, the encouragement is important.

Yes, exactly so. I don't know, frankly, what would have happened to me had I not run into John Gardner when I did. A writer can see that he's not in this alone, that there are other young writers around who care passionately about the same things he cares about, and he can feel heartened. Once you're out there in the world, on your own, nobody cares. I think a writers workshop situation is a shared endeavor, and an immensely important endeavor. It can be abused by students or teachers, but for the best teachers and students, it's a good thing.

Do you encourage your students to read a lot? How important do you see reading being to the writer?

I think writers—especially young writers—should want to read all the books they can get their hands on. To this extent, that's where it's helpful to have some instruction as to what to read and who to read, from somebody who knows. But a young writer has to make a choice somewhere along the line whether he's going to be, finally, a writer or a reader. I've known good, bright, young, putative writers who felt they couldn't begin to write until they had read *everything* and, of course, you simply can't read everything. You can't read all the masterpieces, all the people that you hear people talking about— you just don't have the time. I mean, I wish there were two of me— one to read and one to write—because I love to read. I probably read more than many people, but I don't read as much as I'd like when I'm writing full-time. Then I read very little if anything. I'm just writing, and that's all. When I'm not actively writing, I tend to read anything—history books, poetry, novels, short stories, biographies.

What do you encourage your students to read?

Flaubert's letters—that's one book I'd recommend. Every writer should read those letters. And Chekhov's letters, and the life of Chekhov. I'll recommend a great book of letters between Lawrence Durrell and Henry Miller, which I read some years back. What a book! But writers should read other writers, yes, to see how it's done, for one thing, how the others are doing it; and there's also the sense of shared enterprise, the sense that we're all in this together. It's been my experience that poets, especially, are helped by reading books on natural history, biography, in addition to the usual reading they do in the area of poetry.

You write in the American idiom and pay close attention to what's called the minute particulars, which brings to mind William Carlos Williams and William Blake. Were they influences?

William Carlos Williams certainly. I didn't come to Blake until a good long while after I had started writing my own poetry. But Williams—very definitely. I read everything of Williams that I could get my hands on when I was nineteen or twenty years old. In fact, I started a little magazine when I was at Chico State College. It was a little magazine that ran for three issues, and it was called *Selection*. I published an original poem by Williams in the magazine. I wrote him a fan letter and said I was starting a little magazine (of course, I couldn't promise anything but contributors' copies) and he sent me this wonderful poem. He scrawled his signature across the bottom of it. It was one of the great thrills of my life, and it happened shortly before he died. It was called "The Gossips" and it was included in that posthumous volume of his, *Pictures from Brueghel.*

How about his short stories? There's quite a similarity in his and your styles in short fiction.

I like his stories a lot, but I can't say for sure how much of what he was doing—the *way* he was doing it—got into my own stories. They may have, you know, because at that time it seemed like I was influenced by almost everything. I was just nineteen or twenty years old, and John Gardner was my teacher. He hadn't published anything at the time, but he seemed to know everything. He was directing me to authors—people I *should* read, books I *had* to look at—so, consciously or otherwise, Williams's poetry influenced me, and maybe the stories did, too. It wasn't long, as a matter of fact, after reading Williams that I wrote this little story I called "The Father." But he was a more direct influence on my poetry. I suppose the influence on my fiction would be the early stories by Hemingway. I can still go back, every two or three years, and reread those early stories and become excited just by the cadences of his sentences—not just by what he's writing about, but the *way* he's writing. I haven't done that in two or three years, and I'm beginning to feel like it's time to go back and reread Hemingway.

When you're in one of those periods when you're writing a lot of poetry, do you find your mind working like a camera, where you see things like a snapshot—everything's taken in instantly and you see the importance of what's before you?

I think so, yes. A lot of my poems begin with a visual image of

some sort, like what you're talking about, a snapshot. These
snapshots happen often. Most writers have trained themselves to be
alert to these moments, but some of us, myself included, aren't
always as alert as we'd like to be. Still, when these moments do
happen—either at that moment or not too long afterwards—there
might be a few words or a line that attaches itself to the image and
brings this picture back again. That line often becomes that first line in
the poem. Nothing that I write is inviolable—I often change virtually
every word that's in a story or poem—but usually that first line, which
is the thing that set me off to write the poem or story in the first place,
that line remains unchanged. Everything else is up for grabs. But
usually that first line stays intact. But I like the idea of the picture
because there's a glimpse of something that stays fixed in your head.

*When you have that first line in your head, do you know right
away whether it's going to be in a poem or a short story?*
I'm not making a conscious decision to use a line in a poem or
story. When I'm writing poems, it's invariably, inevitably going to
become a poem; when I'm writing stories, it's going to become part
of a story. Some writers write poetry and fiction at the same time,
they can move easily from this to that, but I don't seem to be able to
work that way. When I'm writing fiction, I'm in a period of writing
fiction; when I'm writing poetry, everything I touch seems to turn to
poetry. So if that first line comes when I'm in a period of writing
poetry, it's going to become a poem.

*Some lines in your poetry have also appeared, almost verbatim, in
your fiction.*
I know. There's been a crossover like that in at least three or four
stories and poems. There's a poem of mine in *Fires* called "Distress
Sale," where the people haul all their gear out on the sidewalk and
somebody witnesses this, and then that's in my story "Why Don't
You Dance?" It's happened in a few other instances. There's a poem
called "Mother" that has some lines that come up in a story called
"Boxes." In every case, it was dealt with first in the poem. Then I
must have felt it making such a large claim on my emotional life that I
felt somehow it was unfinished business and went back to it and
dealt with it in a larger, fuller way.

The poem "Mother" works very well by itself, but that incident—

*the idea of the mother calling on Christmas and saying she's going to
kill herself if it doesn't stop snowing, that the only time she wants to
see that place again is from her coffin—was interesting when it was
part of "Boxes." It seemed to heighten the tension you established
earlier in the story. I don't know if this was conscious or not, but in
"Mother" the narrator's thinking of seeing a psychiatrist, while in
"Boxes" the narrator is thinking of having his mother see a psychiatrist.*

There's a different kind of spin to it, yes. Most of my stories and
poems have a starting point in real life, in reality, but I'm not writing
autobiography. It's all subject to change—everything is—in a story or
a poem. Whatever seems to suit the work best, that's the direction I'll
go in. The stories and poems may have, as their genesis, some lines
of reference to the real world but, as I've said, I'm not writing
autobiography by any account.

*Still, it appears that you're getting closer to the bone, more auto-
biographical, when you're writing poetry.*

I think so. The poetry gives me a chance to be intimate or open or
vulnerable—or even surreal sometimes—in a way that I don't often
engage in when I'm writing fiction. I'm more removed, more at a
distance when I'm writing fiction. I feel I'm much closer to the center,
the core, in the poetry.

*When you're writing a poem, does the content usually dictate the
form your poem is going to take? Do you automatically know how
you're going to write it?*

Sometimes I work considerably hard in making it attractive—
making it look "right" to the eye, and hoping it'll be right to the ear
as well. I'll work with it on the page well after it's been finished. But
other times, just the content alone will dictate how it looks on the
page.

*Let's turn to your work as a short story writer. Interest in the short
story seems to be resurging lately, with more and more story collections published every year. How do you account for this?*

I think it's the single most eventful literary phenomenon of our
time. I don't think there's ever been a time like it for the short story,
or for short story writers. Many short story writers today are not even

interested in writing novels. As you know, some short story writers can command advances that are every bit equal to some of the advances being paid for novels. The bottom line is always how many copies are being sold, and books of short stories are being sold these days like never before. It's a most remarkable thing. There was a time when, by and large, the commercial presses looked on publishing short stories as an enterprise that would be better left to the small presses and the university presses, but now that situation is completely turned around. Short story writers figure prominently on publishers' lists. Their books are reviewed prominently and supported in important ways by the publishing houses.

You, of course, have been mentioned as one of the main reasons for this trend.
Well, anything I can say to that sounds a little self-serving, and I feel a little awkward talking about this. I feel that there are a number of other good writers who began working more or less at the same time I was starting out writing stories; any success that might have come my way, or someone else's way, has helped all this along. But, sure, the good things that have happened to me have been good for every other short story writer as well. But don't forget that the publication of John Cheever's short stories in 1978 helped things considerably, too. I think maybe a lot of young writers saw what was happening and felt heartened: They felt it was all right to write short stories exclusively and not worry about writing novels. This gave license to lots of short story writers. There were a number of short story writers at work, and I feel I'm one of many.

Who, of the short story writers, do you like?
Oh, I like Toby Wolff—he's a wonderful writer. Joy Williams is another. Richard Ford. Charles Baxter has published a couple good collections. I like Ann Beattie's stories. Alice Munro, the Canadian writer, has to be one of the great story writers. Jayne Anne Phillips. Andre Dubus. Mark Helprin is first-rate as a story writer. Barry Hannah. I like many of John Updike's stories and Bobbie Ann Mason's stories. Joyce Carol Oates. We're talking about living writers now; there are the great dead writers, too, like Chekhov and Tolstoy, Hemingway and Frank O'Connor and Flannery O'Connor. Isaac Babel. And there are so many others.

*In addition to this interest in the short story itself, there has been a
growing interest, even on the part of literary elitists, in tales of
survivors, whether they're found in the stories by writers such as
yourself, Richard Ford, Barry Hannah, Charles Bukowski, Tobias
Wolff, and so forth, or in the music of Bruce Springsteen, John
Cougar Mellencamp, and Tom Waits. Why do you think that is?*

Well, in part, of course, it simply has to do with the fact that these
people are bearing witness to what they have experienced; they're
able to talk about it. There's a fascination with somebody who's been
there and come back—lived to talk about it, as it were. You know:
"I'll tell you what it's like. This is my song, this is my poem or short
story. Make of it what you will." I think there's a rock-hard honesty
about what many of these writers and musicians are offering up
which is of more than passing interest to the public, so the public is
paying attention.

*When you wrote about your father in "My Father's Life" for
Esquire, you mentioned the time you told him you wanted to be a
writer, and his advice was "write the stuff you know about." That's
great advice—which a lot of writing instructors have been giving out
over the years. Can you explain how your blue-collar background
helped you with your writing, both in terms of subject and approach?*

For certain I had a *subject*, something to write about, people and
events that I knew well. I never had to go around looking for
material. Also, I think that blue-collar life put a premium on directness
and being straightforward. In that life, there wasn't a whole lot of
room for, or patience with, the Henry Jamesian kind of indirection.

*I guess the reason I mention this is I've been to too many creative
writing classes and workshops where you have people with back-
grounds similar to your own, and they were writing about being
college professors or something.*

Yes, I know. They ought to be writing about what they know
about. There's a lot that they know about, other than the college
campus scene, and the professor-student situation. God knows, that's
a subject matter all right, and some people can make art out of it. But
a writer, young or old, can't fake it. He's got to write with authority,
and he'd do well to write about something he's acquainted with and
about the things that move him—not the things that *should* move

him, but the things that *do* move him. There are significant moments
in everyone's day that can make literature. You have to be alert to
them and pay attention to them. That's what you ought to write
about.

In Ultramarine, *there is a poem called "What You Need for
Painting," which really struck me. It's a list poem taken from a letter
by Renoir, but used in the context of writing, it seems like your advice
on the ingredients needed to write a good poem or short story.*
    Especially those last three lines.

*Which read: "Indifference to everything except your canvas. / The
ability to work like a locomotive. / An iron will." Those are great
instructions for the young writer.*
    In the beginning, when I was trying to write, I couldn't turn off the
outside world to the extent that I can now. When you're writing
fiction or poetry—or when you're painting or making music or composing music—it really comes down to this: indifference to everything
except what you're doing. Your canvas, as it were. Which, translated
to fiction or poetry, means indifference to everything except that
piece of paper in the typewriter. As for the ability to work like a
locomotive and an iron will—by God, that's what it takes. Anyone
who has written anything knows all of these things are necessary—
requirements. Of course, those lines that struck home are from the
Renoir letter, and so it was a *found* poem. But a young writer could
do worse than follow the advice given in those lines. I think all of
those things are necessary. If the car needs to have an all-important
service job but the Muse is with you, so to speak, you just have to get
to your typewriter and stay there and turn the rest of the world off
somehow, forget about everything else. I'm glad you remarked on
that poem and those lines because that is my philosophy of writing, if
I have one. You could put those words on my tombstone, too.
(laughs)

In discussing technique in your Introduction to The Best American
Short Stories 1986, *you listed the five elements you consider
important in the short story: choices, conflict, drama, consequence,
and narrative. Do you have these things mapped out in your head
before you start writing?*

No. I begin the story and it takes a natural course. Most often I'm not aware, when I start a poem or story, of where it's going until I get there. Not while I'm writing it. There's a passage from a Flannery O'Connor essay, "Writing Short Stories," where she says that when she began a story she never knew where the story was going until she got to the end. And I read a little essay by Hemingway called "Monologue to the Maestro," in which somebody asked him if he knew where he was going with a story, and Hemingway answered that he never knew, that he just wrote and the situation developed and unfolded. I don't have any kind of program in writing a story. The drama enters the story, and the consequences and choices present themselves. I guess I tried to separate them in the essay, but they're all connected together. They're not really separate.

You do have that opening line you were mentioning before.
Yes, I have that opening line, and then everything seems to radiate out from that line.

Very often, when reading one of your short stories, I get the impression that something very, very important has happened just before the story begins—or will happen after the story ends. Your stories, like Hemingway's, really deal with the tip of the iceberg. When it works, it's wonderful, but a lot of beginning writers have problems in this area: They assume that their readers know what's going on—occurrences that are never mentioned in their stories. What's the cutting edge to you? How do you teach that to your students?
Well, you can't keep necessary information from the reader. You can assume that the reader can put a face on some of these characters—you don't *have* to describe the color of their eyes, and so forth. Insofar as the stories are concerned, you have to presuppose some kind of knowledge on the part of the readers, that they're going to fill in some of the gaps. But you can't leave them drifting around without enough information to make them care about these people; you can't obfuscate what's going on. To this extent, I had problems with some of the postmodernist writers of the Sixties. You'd sometimes read the work and you never knew what the problem was—just that there *was* some kind of problem or difficulty. Everybody was out of sorts in the story, but the fiction was divorced from reality in every

way, shape, and form. I'm much more interested in stories and
poems that have some bearing on how we live and how we conduct
ourselves and how we work out the consequences of our actions.
Most of my stories start pretty near the end of the arc of the dramatic
conflict. I don't give a lot of detail about what went on before; I just
start it fairly near the end of the swing of the action.

Your stories begin at crisis point.
Yes, I think so. I don't have a lot of patience for the other, I guess.
But there *is* a fine line—the cutting edge, as you put it—where you
have to give the reader enough, but you don't want to give him *too*
much. I don't want to bore the reader, or bore myself.

*Kurt Vonnegut wrote that short story writers should just write their
stories and then toss out the first few pages when they were done.*
There's something to that. D. H. Lawrence made a remark to the
effect that you finish your story and when it's all finished, you go
back and shake the branches of the tree, prune it again.

*About revision: Some of your early stories have really been over-
hauled between the time they were originally published in little
magazines and their eventual publication in your collections. Sometimes the endings and even the titles were changed. In explaining
these revisions in your Afterword to* Fires, *you wrote that "maybe I
revise because it gradually takes me into the heart of what the story is
about. I keep trying to see if I can find that out. It's a process more
than a fixed position." Could you explain that a little further?*
There was a time when I revised everything, and they were often
quite extensive revisions. I don't know, maybe I didn't know what
was around the corner, if *anything* was around the corner, so I was
just more interested in messing around with the work I had on hand.
At that time, I didn't feel that the stories were in any kind of fixed
place, and I wanted to get them there—wherever that was. Now, I
don't feel this need to do all the revising that I once did. Maybe I'm
feeling more secure with the stories I'm writing, or more satisfied, or
more confident. Something has happened, at any rate. Now I tend to
write the stories and for the most part lose interest in them after
they're written. In some way, after they're published, they don't seem
to belong to me any longer. I don't mean to make more out of it than

there is, but I guess I feel now like there's everything to do and little enough time to do it in, so I tend not to be so keen on revising the stories. Now I do all the revisions when I'm writing the story. I'm just not coming back to them after they're published, as I once did.

Maybe that's the result of your maturation as a writer.

Maybe so. I didn't have the confidence then that I do now. I didn't know too much of what I was doing then—I wasn't satisfied. And now, for whatever reasons, I feel more assured and I'm seeing my way more clearly. A lot of things that work now were not working for me six or ten years ago. Whether that's growing as a writer, or maturing, as you say, I don't know, but I feel good about it.

When you're revising, what are you looking for? What do you tend to change?

I want to make the stories interesting on every level and that involves creating believable characters and situations, along with working on the language of the story until it is perfectly clear, but still a language capable of carrying complex ideas and sophisticated nuances.

In a number of your stories written in the first person, you've written from a woman's point of view. When you were writing them, did you feel that the stories' impact—their "rightness," so to speak— was strengthened by the woman's point of view? Was it difficult to write a story this way?

The first time I ever attempted to write a story from the point of view of a woman, I was nervous about it. It was a real challenge to me. When I brought it off, it was like a rush. I was excited. I like to be able to write with authority in either gender. Now when ideas for stories come to me they seem to present themselves to me with the point of view as nearly an inevitable thing. But, again, I think the choices are being made for me because of the nature of the material, and because of the way I'm approaching it. I just gear up and do it, and I like it.

Point of view is so important to a story. I've heard of people who have changed from first to third person in a story after it's been written.

Well, my friend Richard Ford changed the point of view of one of his novels. He worked on it for two years, and he felt it wasn't right, so he spent another year changing the entire point of view. That's dedication. And real seriousness in what you're doing. You want it right and you don't have that many chances at it. I don't know how many books a person's going to take to the grave with him, but you want to have it right, or else what's the point?

When you're writing steadily, what's your typical workday like?
I get up early, somewhere between six o'clock and six-thirty, and have coffee and a bowl of cereal or something like that. I'm always at my desk by eight o'clock. If it's a good day, I'll just stay at my desk until at least eleven or twelve o'clock, when I'll break for a late breakfast. On a good day, I can stay at my desk and do something all day, because I like to work, I like writing. When I'm working, I put the phone on the answering machine and unplug the phone upstairs, so if it rings downstairs, I can't hear it ring. I can check in the evening to see if there are any messages. I don't watch much TV—I watch the news usually—and I go to bed fairly early. It's a pretty quiet life, generally.

Do you prefer to write a story from beginning to end in one sitting?
Yes. I'm afraid of interruption and losing the story—whatever it was that made me want to write the story in the first place. I don't think I've ever spent longer than two days writing the first draft of a story. Usually only one day. I spend lots of time after that typing it up and reworking it, but I think it's good to try to get that story down before you lose sight of it. It might not look so good tomorrow. So on the first draft, you have to put your trust in whatever, just hope and assume that something's going to come of it, just barrel on through and try to get the first draft quickly before you lose it. Then it's subject to change and what-have-you. Then you can be slow and thoughtful with it.

I remember reading somewhere that, in the early days, you used to steal away and write in your car.
It's true. I wouldn't recommend it as a place to work (*laughs*), but it was necessary for me at that time of my life. I don't know if I got anything lasting out of it, but at least I was working on *something*. I was trying to do something and I had no place to go. I was young

and there was just no room in the house. I didn't want to have to go out in the car—it wasn't that I wanted to go for a quiet drive in the country and park next to the river and muse. No, I'd just go out and sit in the car in the parking lot, just to be away from my kids and the turmoil and confusion in the house. That was my office, as it were. (*laughs*)

Do you warn your students about how tough the writing life is?

Oh, I talk about it a little sometimes, but you can't tell them how hard it is. Not really. You can't truthfully tell a young poet or fiction writer they have to have not only the utmost seriousness in regard to their writing but that they're going to have to devote the rest of their lives to it if they intend to be any good at it. But you can't tell them what they're going to have to go through. You can sort of tell them, but they'll have to live through it themselves; they'll have to survive that themselves. You don't have to say much to the best of them. If they're smart, they have an idea of what it's like, and they know it won't come easy to them; if they're not smart and they're not hard on themselves, then they won't be writing very long after they graduate.

I've always been curious about the relationship between the hunger to publish and the hunger to create. What do you think that relationship is? Is the hunger to publish a good motivating factor?

I think it is. Even when I was teaching, I always felt it was too much of a hothouse and rarified atmosphere if there was never any talk about the young writers submitting work to magazines. And on occasion I'd take in some bound galleys, or show them page proofs I was working on, so they could actually see this stuff. They don't know the first thing about the process a book goes through from inception to manuscript, from letter of acceptance to copy-edited manuscripts and galley proofs. So I'd show them these things and talk about possible markets for their stories. I don't think it diminishes the work to talk about publishing that work. Quite the contrary: There's literary *creation* and there's literary *business*. Art and commerce do sometimes go hand in hand. When I first got something accepted, it gave my life a validation that it didn't otherwise have. It was very important to me. I think I got paid a dollar for the first poem

I ever published, but that didn't dampen my enthusiasm. No, I was thrilled with that one-dollar check.

There are, however, a lot of serious writers out there who have to try to balance art with budget: You want to write good, strong work, but you also have to feed your family. Sometimes you feel like you're playing "Beat the Clock": If you don't get something out, you don't pay the rent next month. Did you find that happening to you?

My situation was similar *and* different. I knew I was never going to get rich writing poems, not when I was getting paid a dollar or five dollars, or else being paid in contributors' copies. And, for years, I was writing short stories, of course, and if I got paid at all, it was twenty-five or fifty dollars. So, in truth, I never faced that same dilemma. The problems were similar, in that the kids were there, eating me alive, and I had to make all those monthly payments— some of which we didn't make—but the fact that I was writing stories and poems didn't make any great financial difference to us. The first story in *Esquire* brought me six hundred dollars; but then, I didn't publish in *Esquire* for a very long while after I started writing, so I knew I wasn't going to get rich writing stories, either. Had I been able to write them any faster and still take the time that was necessary for them, I would have done so, but I seemed to be teaching or working or raising a family and so forth, so I simply did the best I could, on what I could.

When you were thinking about becoming a writer, you were hoping just to be able to publish your work in the types of magazines you had around your home, publications like True *or* Argosy. *They were paying markets with reputations of their own, but they were hardly known in the literary community as being places where great literature was created. What made you decide to devote your work to the more serious markets?*

Until I met John Gardner, I had no concept of serious literature. I simply knew that I wanted to be a writer and, of course, nobody in my family did any reading so there was no guidance of any sort whatsoever. I just had to continually follow my nose, whether it led to a historical novel or an article in *True*. Everything was more or less of equal merit, or value, until I met Gardner. This is one of the most important things about our meeting: He'd say something like "I'm not only here to teach you how to write, but I'm also here to tell you who to read." That was immensely important to me. I began to read Joseph Conrad and Isak Dinesen, along with so many other important writers. For the first time in my life, I had some direction. I was introduced to the little magazines by Gardner, and I became interested in the stories and poems they were publishing, so that's what I set out to do: to write well and publish what I wrote. I don't want to seem snobbish about the other magazines—it wasn't that I turned up my nose at things like *Argosy* and *True* and so forth—I simply didn't have enough time in my day to read everything and write everything.

One of your big breaks was meeting Gordon Lish, your longtime friend and editor. How did that happen?
Our relationship goes back to the mid-1960s. He was working for a textbook publishing firm across the street from the textbook firm where I was working, in Palo Alto. That's how we became acquainted. Then he went off to become the fiction editor for *Esquire*. The next I heard from him, he was writing a letter on someone else's stationery. It was from *Esquire,* and he'd crossed off the older editor's name. In the note, he said, "I've taken over the fiction editor's desk from the above-named good gentleman. Send me whatever you have." I was still working at the publishing company, and I proceeded to dispatch all the stories I had in the house—four or five stories—and, by God, they all came back by return mail (*laughs*) with a message saying "Try me again, these are not right." I didn't know what to make of this. If my close friend becomes the fiction editor at *Esquire* and I still can't get a story in, what chance do I have? You're in *real* trouble then. (*laughs*) But I pulled up my socks, sat down and began writing more stories, and he finally took one. It was a story called "Neighbors," and that was one of the turning points in my life. And then he took another one, and so forth. Then he left *Esquire* and became an editor at Knopf. He gave me a contract there for a book of stories. So we go back a long way.
He was always a great advocate of my stories, at all times championing my work, even during the period when I was not writing,

when I was out in California devoting myself to drinking. Gordon read my work on radio and at writers conferences and so forth. I don't think I ever had a greater advocate for the work, when I needed it, than Gordon. He was like Gardner in the sense that he offered encouragement. He was also like Gardner to the extent that he would say that if you could say something in twenty words instead of fifty words, say it in twenty words. He was very important to me at a time when I needed to hear what he had to offer. He's still championing the work of young writers.

There seems to be a trend in the publishing business for greater writer-editor relationships. Have you noticed that?

Yes. I was talking about this with Tess the other night, as a matter of fact. We were talking about Robert Gottlieb and his move from Knopf to the editorship of *The New Yorker.* And as we talked, I realized that this is probably the first age in literary history where editors have become public personalities, in some cases even greater personalities, or figures, than many of the writers they are involved with. Gottlieb goes to *The New Yorker* and it's a front-page piece in *The New York Times* and news in papers and magazines all across the country. And the distinguished editor Gary Fisketjon: They've written an article about him in *Esquire,* and he's been profiled in other magazines. I know any number of writers who will go with their editors when they move from one house to another. Writers have established a close relationship with their editors, and they will go wherever their editors go. The first editor I ever heard of was Maxwell Perkins, and he had that relationship with Thomas Wolfe, Heming- way, and so many other writers. Editors are playing a larger role in a writer's life these days, and I don't know whether this is a good or bad thing. I don't know what conclusions to draw from it, but it's a fact that they have become public personalities in their own right, and this is quite remarkable, I think.

Your survival as a writer has been a source of inspiration to a lot of struggling writers. Somehow, you've been able not only to work your way past a number of imposing barriers, but you've been able to translate your experiences into universal stories. How do you feel about all this today?

I just feel like an instrument. . . . It *has* been a question of survival,

and had I been able to do something else . . . I don't know, maybe I
would have done something else. But I *had* to write. You know, the
flame went out: I think it was flat-out extinguished there toward the
end of my drinking days. But, yes, I did survive. In fact, after I got
sober and had quit drinking entirely, there was a period of time, for a
year or so, when I didn't write anything and it wasn't even important
for me to write anything. It was so important for me to have my
health back and not be brain-dead any longer that whether I wrote or
not didn't matter any longer. I just felt like I had a second chance at
my life again. But for about a year or so, I didn't write anything. And
then, when things were right, when I was well again, I taught for a
year in El Paso, and then, suddenly, I began to write again. And that
was just a great gift, and everything that has happened since then has
been a great gift. Every day is a bonus. Every day now is pure cream.

POSTSCRIPT:

Raymond Carver died on August 2, 1988.

*This interview took place shortly before Carver learned that he had
lung cancer. As is evident by the tone of the conversation, Carver was
cheerful and hopeful, confident that some of his best work was still
ahead of him. Despite joking about the words that would be chiseled
into his headstone, there was no sense of finality in either the man or
his words.*

*Nor would there ever be. Even after he grew ill and had much of
his left lung removed, Carver remained optimistic. The last time I
spoke to him, not long before the publication of* Where I'm Calling
From, *he offered no complaint of tiring radiation treatments or failing
health; instead, he looked ahead to the new book, as well as to a
return to writing poetry.*

*In his final months, he married Tess Gallagher, was inducted into
the American Academy and Institute of Arts and Letters, and finished
his collection of poems,* A New Path to the Waterfall. *Only hours
before he passed away, Tess Gallagher told* The New York Times,
*Carver mentioned how much pleasure he'd taken from the stories of
Anton Chekhov.*

*Raymond Carver was a man with his own personal and artistic
credo, much of which was stated in this interview, much of which is
inherent in the title of this book, chosen with Carver very much in*

mind. Rather than change the interview or its introduction to accommodate the remainder of events in Carver's life, I decided to leave it intact—a slight expansion of the way it originally appeared in print.

The way Ray liked it.

PW Interviews Raymond Carver

Penelope Moffet/1988

From *Publishers Weekly*, 27 May 1988, 42, 44. Published by the Bowker Magazine Group of Cahners Publishing Co., a division of Reed Publishing USA. Copyright © 1988 by Reed Publishing USA. Reprinted by permission of Penelope Moffet and Cahners Publishing Co. Conducted Spring 1988.

During Raymond Carver's 25-year writing career, he's been alternately honored and maligned for the careful, sparely written, usually bleak stories about working-class life with which he first came to national attention. Many of those stories were published in two books, *Will You Please Be Quiet, Please?* (McGraw-Hill, 1976) and *What We Talk About When We Talk About Love* (Knopf, 1981). In recent years, however, Carver's fiction has been swerving in new directions as the writer has added some glimmerings of hope to his steely-eyed examinations of contemporary angst, as in the stories of *Cathedral* (Knopf, 1983), his last collection of fiction. Since 1982, Carver has also returned to his first love, poetry. He's published two well-received collections of poems, *Where Water Comes Together with Other Water* and *Ultramarine,* in 1985, and 1986.

With *Where I'm Calling From: New and Selected Stories,* issued this month by Atlantic Monthly Press, most of what Carver hopes are his "most durable" stories from the first three collections are gathered under one cover. Seven newer, previously uncollected tales close out the book. The stories are selected, rather than collected, so he could leave out "some of the stories, which I just don't like and would never write again," Carver explains.

When *PW* visits Carver in his Port Angeles, Wash., living room, the writer seems alert yet relaxed. He's a bulky man who moves slowly and carefully, and the eyes behind his tinted glasses are serious, a little shy, but immensely kind. His breathing is somewhat labored, the legacy of an operation for cancer last October that took two-thirds of one lung, but he speaks clearly and is rarely at a loss for words. Occasionally he folds his hands in front of his mouth while considering a question—particularly if the question touches on how the

238

treatment he's undergoing for a new tumor is affecting his life and writing—but he doesn't hedge his answers. Spending half of each week in Seattle for radiation therapy has greatly disrupted his life, Carver admits, but, "God willing, when all this mess is over with, I'll have my mornings clear and be able to get back into the swing of things. Things are sort of up in the air right now. It's hard to get focused in this interregnum."

The first hardcover copies of *Where I'm Calling From* are expected from Atlantic Monthly Press any minute, but the books don't arrive, much to Carver's disappointment. Late in the day, when Gary Fisketjon, the Press's editorial director, calls to get his author's reaction to the books, Carver is able to air his feelings in a friendly yet definite manner. "He and I go back a long way," Carver says of Fisketjon. Fisketjon describes himself as a Carver fan since the mid-1970s, who while "working up the food chain" to a top editorial position at Random House was instrumental in arranging for the allied paperback house, Vintage Books, to reprint *What We Talk About, Cathedral* and *Fires*, a collection of Carver essays, poems and stories first issued by Capra Press. Random House also published Carver's two recent poetry collections in hardcover. When Fisketjon moved to Atlantic Monthly in 1986, Carver followed him.

Carver was born in Clatskanie, Oreg., 50 years ago and grew up in nearby Yakima, Wash. His father was an alcoholic sawmill worker, and his mother worked off and on as a waitress and a clerk. Carver married, had two children and began to hold a series of low-paying jobs before he was 20 years old.

He started writing poetry and fiction at 17 or 18, and "I got serious about it in my very early 20s," he says, although he never made a conscious decision to become a writer. The decision "was sort of made for me. I liked to read, and I simply wanted to make my own stories," he says. Eventually he attended Chico State College in California, where he studied fiction with John Gardner, the late novelist, essayist and teacher, before going on to earn a degree at Humboldt State College. He won a Stegner Fellowship to Stanford to study fiction, and later attended the Iowa Writers' Workshop for one year.

Poverty cut short his stay at Iowa. But soon Carver began publishing his stories and poems in both small magazines and larger

publications such as *Esquire*. He began teaching writing at universities around the country, and finally became a literature and creative
writing professor at Syracuse University.

"I never figured I'd make a living writing short stories," Carver
says. "How far in this world are you going to get writing short stories?
I never had stars in my eyes, I never had the big-score mentality." He
was "very startled" when he became well-known, Carver says, and
fame "never ceases to amaze me. And that's not false modesty,
either. I'm pleased and happy with the way things have turned out.
But I was surprised."

One big surprise came in 1983, when Carver was given a Mildred
and Harold Strauss Livings Award by the American Academy and
Institute of Arts and Letters, which gave him $35,000 a year for five
years. With the Strauss fellowship, Carver said goodbye to his
Syracuse teaching job and moved to Port Angeles, where his current
mate and fellow writer Tess Gallagher has deep roots. While on the
fellowship, Carver wrote many poems, some essays and a few new
stories. He edited *Best American Short Stories 1986* (Houghton
Mifflin) and he co-edited *American Short Story Masterpieces*
(Delacorte, 1987) with Tom Jenks.

Recently the Strauss fellowship ended, and Carver has been asked
back by Syracuse, but "with any luck I won't have to teach," he says.
"The books have been translated into a lot of languages, so there is
income that comes in from Japan and Holland and England and
other places. I'm also counting on income from the books I'm going
to write. I recently signed a three-book contract with Atlantic Monthly
Press for a book of poems, a book of stories, and the third book will
be either a novel or a memoir. Maybe I'll write the memoir. Tell all,"
he says, laughing quietly.

"I've never made a commitment like this before now. I've been
offered contracts before for books of stories or novels, but when I
wasn't writing stories and had no intentions of writing a novel, I shied
away from signing a contract or taking money. Now I want to
become more organized, and I can see my way clear," Carver says.
"I know I'm going to continue to write. It gives me a good feeling, it
gives me a sense of security, that I kind of know what I'll be doing the
next few years."

Much of the new poetry book is already written, Carver says, and

"I can feel the stirring now of wanting to write stories, but I'm going to finish the poems first. Poems seem like a great blessing, a mystery to me; I can't account for where they come from. When I'm writing poems, I don't know if I'll ever write a short story again, I feel incapable of it, because the poetry is so much with me." His agent of the last seven years, Amanda Urban of International Creative Management, "won't say much, but she'd much prefer I'd be writing fiction. But she knows it keeps me happy to write poetry," says Carver, who adds that Urban is "aces, she's the best. She's well-respected, and she's a straight-shooter, and I like her a lot person-ally."

Carver's poetry often draws on the real events of his life, on memories of his father, on fishing and hunting trips, and on his rela-tionships with Gallagher, his two children and others. He says that "I'm much more vulnerable in the poems than in the stories. I can be much more intimate in the poems than in the stories." Yet, as fond as he is of writing verse, if he had to choose between writing in one genre or the other, "it would be hard, but I guess I would come down on the side of the stories," Carver says. "I just don't think I could give up the fiction."

Carver's stories also draw on his life, but while real incidents or people may spark the tales, much more is invented than in the poetry. For instance, in one of the newer tales, "Boxes," a man tries to balance his own needs, those of a mother who's losing touch with reality and those of a new lover. The mother character, Carver says, is "not really my mother, but there are certain characteristics I guess the character shares with my mother. I'm not writing autobiography, but there are certain reference points, real lines and real ropes that are going out from the story to the real world."

While many of Carver's earlier stories drew on his memories of his impoverished boyhood and difficult early adult life and first marriage, "that doesn't happen so much anymore," he says. "Most of these stories now, they're taking place right now. The stories are changing. They've experienced a real sea change, for which I'm grateful." One of the new stories, "Errand," is an imaginative recreation of events that took place around the death of Chekhov, one of Carver's literary idols.

Carver's decade-long relationship with Gallagher, a well-known

poet, fiction writer and essayist, has influenced some of the changes
in his fiction, Carver says. Gallagher's example also helped him
return to poetry and begin writing essays. The relationship has made
Carver happier. "It's healthy, it's a good thing, I can't imagine living
with somebody who's not a writer," he says. "You share a set of
common goals and assumptions, you understand each other's need
for privacy and solitude." Carver and Gallagher read and critique all
of each other's work. Gallagher is a "very tough" critic, Carver says.
"She cuts me no slack at all, and that's the best way." Gallagher has
her own house, a few minutes away from Carver's, so the writers can
separate for work and get together for company.

While he initially settled in Port Angeles (where Gallagher was
born) because his partner is happiest there, Carver says he's become
fond of the town. Yet, he adds, because Port Angeles is out of the
mainstream, "if I didn't have the writing, I couldn't live here. I'm just
not hung up on a pretty place to live, the mountains and water. I'd be
gone in a flash if I didn't have any writing." Several times a year he
does leave Port Angeles, to spend time in New York or travel
overseas.

Often called a "minimalist" writer in the past, Carver has never
been fond of that term, which he says "seems to be going away. I
think there's enough different kinds of stories so I won't be hammered with that hammer again. I've been hammered by the right-
wing critics because they say I'm 'putting America in a bad light.
Foreigners are getting a false impression of America.' But how can
you say that about a story like 'Boxes'? There's nothing political
about that story, [the protagonist] losing his mother to madness. Or a
story like 'Errand.' Chekhov said you don't have to solve a problem
in a story, you just have to present a problem accurately."

If a label is going to be put on him, Carver adds, he'd prefer that of
writer. "I can't think of anything else I'd rather be called than a writer,
unless it's a poet. Short-story writer, poet, occasional essayist."

Raymond Carver: Darkness Dominates
His Books, Not His Life
Gail Caldwell/1988

From *The Boston Globe*, 1 June 1988, 25, 27. Reprinted
courtesy of The Boston Globe. Conducted Spring 1988.

Raymond Carver is a large, bearish man with penetrating blue eyes,
but the first thing you notice is how kind he seems—someone you'd
pick for a little league coach, say, or a small-town pediatrician. His
laughter is infectious, his curiosity compassionate, his talk thoughtful
and forthcoming. He is so down to earth about his work and the life
behind it that it's easy to overlook the critical reputation he's attained
in the past decade. As America's foremost practitioner of the contemporary short story, Carver is noted for the dark, often ominous
complexities he conveys in such a tight, demanding form—a world
where ringing phones or footsteps on the porch are far more likely to
signal bad news than good.

It is not entirely a world of the imagination. Carver, who just turned
50, has inside knowledge of the grittier side of fate. By 20, he was
married and the father of two; working nights at a series of blue-collar
jobs, he attended writing classes during the day, sending out stories
and poems for years before receiving the recognition he was due. A
recovering alcoholic, he stopped drinking 11 years ago, with the help
of AA, when his drinking threatened to kill him. Last fall, he was
diagnosed with lung cancer and underwent surgery; a former chain
smoker, he "took an immediate drop from 60 cigarettes a day to
none." He has just finished seven weeks of radiation therapy in
Seattle, near his home in Port Angeles, where he lives with the poet
Tess Gallagher. The doctors assure him his prognosis is good. He tires
easily, but he seems weak rather than fragile, much like a redwood
fighting to keep its place in the sun. "Everything is OK," he says now,
"for which I am grateful."

Certainly the life—the bad time from which Carver draws so much
of his fiction—has turned toward the light in the last several years. He
gave up a professorship in English at Syracuse University to accept

the Strauss Livings Award in 1983, which provided an annual stipend
of $35,000 for five years. In February, he was elected into the
American Academy and Institute of Arts and Letters. He has made
this trip to the East Coast for his induction into the academy and to
receive an honorary doctorate of letters from the University of
Hartford. Atlantic Monthly Press has just published a retrospective
collection of stories, *Where I'm Calling From,* which illuminates the
best of Carver's work from the past three decades.

A feathery touch

Most of Carver's characters are ordinary people rescued from the
bin of anonymity; they wage a Sisyphean struggle against dead end
lives, or, worse, give up before the fight is over. They are not so much
victims as innocent bystanders, peripheral people in a world too
mean and too random to provide the bare essentials. Much of this
grimness is evoked by a tensile delicacy of tone—by the whisper of
not only what has already gone wrong, but of the accident around
the next curve. The splendid truth of Carver's stories lies in what
hasn't happened yet, and he invokes this sense of dread with a touch
so feathery that it only underscores the trouble his people know.

"You must remember, I'm a poet," says Carver about the con-
straints of the short story. "I suppose I put my stories together in a
similar fashion to how I put my poems together: They're narrative, I
think, with a beginning, a middle and an end. I'm interested in stories
that do go someplace, that do have some kind of movement.

"I started writing poetry before I started writing fiction. You know,
one day after I had sent some things off, I had two letters in the mail:
one from a magazine in Arizona, one from Utah, and one was
accepting a poem, the other a story. It was a red-letter day! I had
never had a day like it." He laughs. "It was quite wonderful. So I was
hooked.

"But oftentimes I just have to feel my way to a story I go near. I
begin a story with an urge to write the story, but I don't know quite
where it's going. Usually I'll find out what I want to say in the act of
saying it. And I always write more than enough; I always overwrite,
and I have to go back and cut. Especially in the early days, when a
10-page story might have represented a 30-page original one—I'd go

through 20 drafts. It's not quite that way anymore; the new stories in *Where I'm Calling From* I didn't rewrite so much. And I tend now not to turn around and look over my shoulder."

There's always a crystalline denouement in Carver's stories, whether epiphany or gentle turn on the horizon. It can be as uneventful as a porch light going off across the street, as thudding as the realization that "dreams, you know, are what you wake up from." "Sometimes those moments have to be found," says Carver. "Imagined.

"I don't know—it would be nice to have a scheme, or schema, writing stories, but mostly in my writing I'm just flying blind—flying by the seat of my pants!" He laughs at the image, shakes his head. "I'll tell you all my secrets."

If two of Carver's earlier collections of stories, *Will You Please Be Quiet, Please?* and *What We Talk About When We Talk About Love*, suggested a vision of despair, his 1983 *Cathedral* extended that viewpoint to include a range of possibility, even grace. Read chronologically, the stories in *Where I'm Calling From* take on a gentler terrain in recent years, but the world they depict is still one to be embraced warily, if at all.

"I think my stories are more companionable, if that's the right word," says Carver. "I think they're more affirmative than they used to be. I can't change all my spots overnight. The germ of a story comes from something that really happened, with all my stories."

A changing vision

But then critics often grab onto a darkness of vision as a way of talking about the work, while a writer may embellish a perspective as a fictional device. Given the profound change his life has undergone, I ask Carver if he still finds the world as bleak a place as his stories suggest.

"I don't, I don't," he says. "I mean, I used to hold to that much more rigidly and steadily than I do now. And it's not just because my own circumstances have changed, which they have. I still think it's a bitter—a grim scene out there. But I feel a little more affirmative, a little more cheerful. Some of that's been effected in the stories, some of it hasn't.

"All my stories are a little bit dark, though, aren't they? But there's humor in them, too, often. I think 'Elephant' is funny. I read it aloud once, and it was hard to get through the story because of the laughter."

"Elephant" is a funny story, as Carver stories go, even though its protagonist is a weary man trying to care for his deadbeat family. He wakes up in the middle of the night to this memory: "In the second dream, somebody had offered me some whiskey, and I drank it. Drinking that whiskey was the thing that scared me. That was the worst thing that could have happened. That was rock bottom. Compared to that, everything else was a picnic. I lay there for a minute longer, trying to calm down. Then I got up."

The early years

Raymond Carver was born in 1938 in Clatskanie, Ore., and grew up in Yakima, Wash. He married at 19 and moved to Paradise, Calif., where he studied writing under John Gardner, an early mentor to whom he pays homage in the foreword to Gardner's *On Becoming a Novelist*. "I did learn from him," he says now. "I was like a sponge, an overwhelmed sponge that had washed up on the beach some-place. I didn't know anything, but I *knew* I didn't know anything.

"So he would tell me writers I should read, mostly writers I'd never heard of. He would humanize it somehow, make it seem like it was possible to do this. I can't tell you how important he was.

"Some of it was just a question of following my nose and reading people I liked, or didn't like. Seems like even then, time was short. I'd read two or three stories and move on to someone else. It was a time of education—that's what I was doing, educating myself.

"And then I lost Gardner as a teacher, because I moved from Chico, where he was, over to Eureka, Calif., and began a different part of life over there. I was workng nights in a sawmill, going to school days. And my wife was working at the telephone company days, and looking after the kids at night, and packing lunch for me, and so forth. And I was trying to learn to write. So there was sort of the feeling I was doing it alone: I no longer had anyone like John Gardner."

Among the writers Carver learned to revere were Hemingway and

Chekhov. He pays homage to Chekhov in the last story of *Where I'm Calling From,* and says he still re-reads Hemingway's early stories every two or three years. "I'm interested in the cadences of the sentences," he says now, "the way the words fall on the page."

It's a typical Carver image, as though the words were tossed there by serendipity, or the wind. He seems equally humble about his own writing, which threatened to disintegrate altogether during the drinking years. "I wasn't doing any writing; I was incapable of writing," he says. "I would sober up for three or four days and write a story, but that was nothing, you know. . . . There was no question of writing better, or differently, or sobering up and beginning again. I wasn't thinking that far ahead."

Carver talks about that period of his life with an equanimity punctuated by pauses; he describes his stopping drinking as "certainly the most profound thing that ever happened to me.

"You know, these troubles I've got now, these health problems—in those days when I was drinking, I had a terminal disease. I couldn't stop drinking; I just had no choice in the matter. I was going out with it.

"My life was a mess domestically, my health was a shambles—this, in a way, is like a picnic, compared to that. Things are much better. Things could never be so bad, you know, as they were then."

Carver took those years—"write about what you know," he says—and incorporated them into his work. Certainly there's no more intimate construction of an alcoholic world in contemporary fiction: Carver's drinkers inhabit a boozy, interior space invaded only by the shrill persistence of the telephone or the need for more liquor. But the real region his fiction inhabits, whiskey-sick or otherwise, is a territory of the heart. There are familiar landmarks all over the place in Carver Country, its borders as stringently defined by random cruelties, by the haunting voice that suffers them, as by any external parameters.

"People talk about the stories having a specific locale in the Northwest," says Carver, "yet I don't see them having such a specific place. Most of the stories, it seems to me, could take place anywhere. So I suppose it's an emotional landscape I'm most interested in. These four people in 'What We Talk About When We Talk About Love' could be sitting around a table in Albuquerque, or El Paso—

but they could just as easily be in Wichita or Syracuse. Tuscaloosa!"
Carver smiles. "Most of my stories take place indoors, anyway."

Carver is both quick and generous with his praise for other writers,
speaking of his own circumstances as though they were the usual
hurdles of life. Remembering John Gardner (who died in 1982), he
says, "He kept the faith—was indefatigable." I comment that the
same could be said of Carver. He shrugs; smiles. "Most of the time I
did, tried to.

"I am happy," says Carver. "I feel—I think I'm one of the luckiest
men around."

"I've Got a Book to Finish, I'm a Lucky Man"

Gianni Riotta/1988

From *Corriere della sera* [Milan], 7 August 1988, 12. Reprinted
by permission of *Corriere della sera.* Conducted Spring 1988.
Translated by Susanna Peters Coy.

An interview with coughs and sighs. For months we'd been trying to
meet with Raymond Carver, the American writer who died a few
days ago, and each time he had to apologize: "I can't do it, I'm not
well, I have to go to Seattle for radiation," the treatment he was
undergoing for his lung cancer.

He never showed annoyance but rather a kind of concern: "I *am*
interested. I'm living on the royalties from Italy, from Holland, from
England. The critics are great." Coughing. The half-joke was for his
prickly countrymen who accuse him of "giving a bad idea of America
with stories about poor, desperate, hopeless folk."

"But this is my world." Carver coughed and sighed, explaining
why he had to put off once again the appointment on the other side
of the continent, in Port Angeles, Washington, where he lived with his
companion, the poet Tess Gallagher. "I'm a full-time member of the
working poor. I was one as a child, and I've been one as an adult."
To gain time, I explained that I wanted to know how he felt about the
label "minimalist," this writer who tells of the darkness of middle
America while Leavitt and McInerney buzz around the lights of
Manhattan. He grumbled, "I've gone beyond, gone beyond minimalism. There's more than that in my stories, there's more, don't you
think? The rest is just labels."

And the definitions surely must have weighed heavily on him, as
heavily as the lung surgery ("What a scare!"), on this man who had
made an art of "cutting." "Make one cut in my stories and they
disappear," he loved to say.

From the few words that he let filter through, either in person or on
the page, there never emerges the bitterness that seemed to grip the
great Salinger. "No, I feel good in my own skin. Sure, the radiation is
tough, but it will be okay. I have faith. I'm calm. I feel I'm in a state of
grace." He has been described as a black poet, an explorer of the

dark side of life. He explained (and he would do so at greater length in the interview, he promised) that this was true especially of the hard years when he was underemployed, rootless, with a wife and two children, writing poetry and stories at night.

There followed different seasons, writing with Tess, trips to New York when he needed a bit of city rhythm to recharge himself, sitting by the big window looking out on the sea, while Tess was writing in the other side of the house, by the big window looking out on the mountain.

In the end it was better to ask him, "How do you feel?"

"Good, you know? I find it hard to write but I think I'll bounce back soon. I've got a book to finish, memoirs (can you believe it?) to put together, poems to publish. I'm a lucky man." Dry in death as in literature, Carver ended coughing and it seems to me that in the course of his polite postponements, he had found a way to say everything.

Index

251